Good Faith in Long-Term Relational Supply Contracts in the Context of Hardship from A Comparative Perspective

Peng Guo

Good Faith in Long-Term Relational Supply Contracts in the Context of Hardship from A Comparative Perspective

Springer

Peng Guo
Graduate School of Business and Law
RMIT University
Melbourne, VIC, Australia

ISBN 978-981-16-5512-8 ISBN 978-981-16-5513-5 (eBook)
https://doi.org/10.1007/978-981-16-5513-5

This Springer imprint is published by the registered company Springer Nature Singapore Pte Ltd.
The registered company address is: 152 Beach Road, #21-01/04 Gateway East, Singapore 189721, Singapore

To Shu and Emily

Foreword

Our life is undoubtedly and significantly affected by the unexpected and unforeseen COVID-19 pandemic. So are international commercial transactions. Very often hardship is discussed in this context, and the first respective cases are already pending in arbitration. Dating back to Roman law, pacta sunt servanda and clausula rebus sic stantibus have been applied to tackle issues of the same nature as the COVID-19 pandemic. In modern national jurisdictions, various doctrines based on the Roman doctrines have been designed, such as *imprévision* in French law, *Störung der Geschäftsgrundlage* in German law and frustration in English law. At the international level, Article 79 of the CISG and the hardship doctrine of the UNIDROIT Principles are of particular importance and relevance. However, these rules vary in one way or another, and no uniform solution has been formed.

A vast amount of literature exists in the research area. Recently, the CISG Advisory Council has published an opinion on 'Hardship under the CISG'.[1] Dr Guo, however, does not follow the traditional approach to comparing and analysing the historical background, theoretical foundations, and similarities and differences of these doctrines. Dr Guo chooses to discuss the hardship issues from a narrower and practical perspective, by embedding it in long-term relational supply contracts and by basing it on good faith in general, and by analysing the hardship rules in the UNIDROIT Principles in particular. This book innovatively combines three important and closed-intertwined elements, hardship, long-term relational contracts and good faith.

The 2016 edition of the UNIDROIT Principles adds provisions on long-term contracts, arguably long-term relational contracts, the special characteristics of which are rarely addressed by national legal systems and solutions to hardship issues relating to them are seldomly provided. Dr Guo argues that the UNIDROIT Principles, for the first time, provide a 'better' solution, which is most recently adopted by the Chinese Civil Code 2021, to hardship issues affecting long-term (relational) contracts by adopting the so-called 'better law' approach.

[1]CISG Advisory Council Opinion No. 20, Rapporteur: Prof Dr Edgardo Munoz, 2020, www.cisgac.org.

Despite the advantages of the hardship rules under the UNIDROIT Principles, Dr Guo correctly identified potential gaps or shortcomings in those rules. The boundary of the duty to renegotiate is rather vague. The courts' or arbitral tribunals' power to adapt or terminate a contract is too discretionary. Dr Guo, in his book, takes a bold, possibly brave, step to fill the gaps or overcome the shortcomings. Dr Guo imposes a 'compelling reason' boundary on the duty to renegotiate, proposes a 'double construction' approach to determining whether parties have behaved in good faith in renegotiations before the courts or tribunals adapt the contract, and sets a 'complete breakdown' requirement to temper the unfettered power to terminate the contract.

Scholars, practitioners or alike may or may not be persuaded by Dr Guo's proposals. But it is undeniable that this book is a meaningful attempt to perfect a uniform solution to hardship issues in the post-pandemic age, from the 'better approach' to the 'best approach', which is a significant and challenging task that we may eventually need to complete one day, if not sooner.

Dr Guo has now embarked on his academic journey as a young scholar with unfading enthusiasm on uniform law, particularly the CISG and the UNIDROIT Principles. My best wishes accompany him and his future endeavours.

Müllheim, Germany
28 September 2021

Ingeborg Schwenzer

Acknowledgements

This book is an updated version of my doctoral thesis. Neither this book nor the completion of my doctoral thesis would have been possible without the guidance, support and assistance of many scholars to whom I am deeply indebted. I wish to express my appreciation to all of them. My deepest appreciation goes to my PhD supervisors, Professor Leon Trakman and Professor Luke Nottage. They played a crucial role in my success in completing my PhD. Without their supervision and encouragement, I would never have completed my thesis. I also owe special gratitude to many scholars, including but not limited to, Professor Hugh Beale, Dr Simone Benvenuti, Dr João Ribeiro-Bidaoui, Professor Michael Bonell, Professor Michael Bridge, Professor David Campbell, Professor John Carter, Professor Hugh Collins, Mr José Angelo Estrella Faria, The Honourable Paul Finn, Professor Martijn Hesselink, Professor Hans Schulte-Nölke, Professor Ulrich Schroeter, Professor Ingeborg Schwenzer, Professor Wenhua Shan, Professor Jingxia Shi, Dr Lisa Spagnolo, Dr Marco Urban, Professor Anna Veneziano, Professor Pilar Perales Viscasillas, Professor Stefan Vogenauer, Professor Therese Wilson, Professor Bruno Zeller, Professor Reinhard Zimmermann and Professor Haicong Zuo. They all helped me with my research in one way or another.

I also owe an enormous debt of gratitude to a number of institutions and organisations, which have offered significant help to my PhD research. My appreciation first goes to the Faculty of Law at the University of New South Wales for providing me with the wonderful opportunity and for awarding me a scholarship to complete my PhD. I also would like to thank the Max Planck Institute for Comparative and International Private Law, the International Institute for the Unification of Private Law, and the Swiss Institute of Comparative Law for granting me scholarship to carry out research in their libraries, and the School of Law at the University of Warwick, the Centre for the Study of European Contract Law at the University of Amsterdam, the European Legal Studies Institute at the University of Osnabrück, and the University of Sydney Law School for allowing me to use their research facilities. I am profoundly grateful for all the help provided by staff members working at these institutions.

In addition, I would like to thank many friends who have helped me during my study: Dr Won Jae Hwang, Ms Shelby Long and Ms Wiebke Naber for their support in Germany; Mr Ewan O'Connor, Dr Xue Bai, Dr Jie Huang, Dr Xiaochuan Weng and Dr Weihuan Zhou for their help in Sydney; and Dr Megan McElhone and Dr Armin Alimardani for being such good 'neighbours' . Special thanks go to Ms Jenny Jarrett for her wholeheartedly and strong support during my entire PhD period in the Faculty of Law at the University of New South Wales.

Finally, I express my gratitude towards my family members, especially to my father, Heli, who has always believed unconditionally in me; to my mother, Sujuan, who gave me love and strength; and to my wife, Shu, for her unwavering love and support.

Overview

A change in circumstances is of particular commercial and legal interest to businesses engaging in international trade. The consequences of the change of circumstances may be more significant in longer transactions or relationships. The greater the consequences of the change of circumstances, the more crucial it becomes for the parties to find a satisfactory solution.

In international trade practice, a change of circumstances frequently occurs in long-term contracts. Therefore, it is vital to have a set of rules that assists international businesses in achieving a satisfactory and equitable result when dealing with issues that arise from a change of circumstances.

There are at least three aspects related to the change of circumstances issue. Firstly, a change of circumstances threatens the certainty and stability of the contract and the contractual relationship. A change of circumstances is of particular relevance to long-term contracts as such contracts are more easily and dramatically affected. The second aspect is the unpredictability of change and the flexibility required to enact solutions. The third aspect is the need for satisfactory solutions and involves justice, fairness, good faith and/or equity. One or more of these concepts form the foundation for a satisfactory and equitable solution. The combination and interaction of the three aspects renders the change of circumstances issue complicated and controversial.

Rules and mechanisms have been developed to deal with issues relating to a change of circumstances. However, these vary greatly across regions both nationally and internationally. For example, several normative solutions have been proposed in different legal instruments, such as United Nations Convention on Contracts for the International Sale of Goods (hereinafter: the CISG) and the UNIDROIT Principles of International Commercial Contracts (hereinafter: the UNIDROIT Principles). It is difficult and time consuming to study all the existing rules, mechanisms or solutions. Currently, it is not feasible to find a solution that suits every jurisdiction's requirements.

The core research question of this book concerns hardship in long-term relational supply contracts and what actions the parties, courts and arbitral tribunals should take in good faith to address the consequences of the hardship. Hardship, long-term relational supply contracts and good faith are the three dimensions of the core research question.

Given the complexity and the controversy associated with a change of circumstances and the variety and diversity of the rules, this book will examine this topic in a narrower and more concrete context. Long-term relational supply contracts experience a change in circumstances more often. Hardship is a common type of change of circumstances and is a challenging issue in international trade. The term 'hardship' is defined in at least two ways. Firstly, the doctrine or rules related to hardship. Secondly, it can refer to a hardship event or events that trigger the invocation of the hardship doctrine or rules. This book adopts the second understanding and hardship serves as a background of the book.[1] Good faith offers a framework of co-operation between the parties and forms the foundation of the solutions proposed in this book.

This book addresses the core research question by analysing three dimensions of the question from two perspectives – the perspective of the parties involved and that of the courts or arbitral tribunals. The parties should renegotiate different contract terms to deal with hardship issues. On the other hand, the courts or arbitral tribunals, depending on the circumstances of the individual case, adapt the contract in order to restore its equilibrium and to maintain an ongoing relationship between the parties or terminate the contract as the last remedy. It is worth noting that the duty to renegotiate and the power to adapt the contract are not unrestrained. The parties can be discharged from the duty to renegotiate if there is a compelling reason that will cause a complete breakdown of the ongoing relationship between the parties. Similarly, judges or arbitrators can adapt a contract only to the extent that they do not rewrite the contract for the parties, that there is no complete breakdown of the ongoing contract relationship between the parties, and that the proposed amendment will not cause one.[2]

Therefore, to address the research question, the proposed key solution is that in the context of hardship, the parties to a long-term relational supply contract should have a duty to renegotiate the contract unless there is a 'compelling reason' not to do so. If the renegotiation fails, the judges or arbitrators have the power to adapt the contract on the basis of good faith and the relational nature and characteristics of the contract. Where there is a complete breakdown of the ongoing contract relationship, or where an adaptation will cause such a complete breakdown or rewrite the contract, the judges and arbitrators have the power to terminate the contract. Put another way, the duty to renegotiate and the power to adapt and terminate are the concrete manifestations of good faith. This takes into account the ongoing relationship between the parties to a long-term relational supply contract upon the occurrence of

[1] Wherever the term 'hardship' is used in the first meaning, hardship rules or the hardship doctrine will be used to mark the distinction. It is worth noting that the similarities and differences among rules on hardship, frustration and impossibility in different legal systems are beyond the scope of this book.

[2] In this sense, the adaptation itself becomes a compelling reason which will cause a complete breakdown of the ongoing relationship between the parties.

hardship. This solution is original, because it sets a 'compelling reason' boundary to the duty to renegotiate[3] unlike other solutions to hardship issues adopted by domestic legal systems or international instruments. It also proposes a boundary on the power to adapt a contract based on a 'complete breakdown of the parties' relationship' being that stage at which continuing with the contract is manifestly unreasonable for the parties to maintain it.[4] The originality of this book also lies in the proposition that judges or arbitrators wield the power to adapt or terminate the contract with a 'double-construction' approach. This approach proposes that both the contract itself and the parties to the contract determine the rights and duties of the parties.[5]

[3] More details on the 'compelling reason' boundary, see Chap. 5, section "Compelling reasons as a boundary on the duty to renegotiate".

[4] More details on the 'complete breakdown' boundary and the test, see Chap. 5, section "Boundaries on adaptation".

[5] More details on the double construction approach, see Chap. 5, Sect. 5.4.1.

Contents

Chapter 1
Introduction

This chapter introduces the book and summarises the contents of each section. Section 1.1 states a hypothesis that a new principle of *pacta sunt servanda bona fide,* based on relational contract theory, is emerging in international trade, where hardship issues arise in performing long-term relational supply contracts. The main proposition is that in the context of hardship, the parties to a long-term relational supply contract have a duty to renegotiate the contract unless there is a 'compelling reason' not to do so. Additionally, the judges or arbitrators have the power to adapt the contract based on good faith, the relational nature, and the characteristics of the contract. Where there is a complete breakdown of the ongoing contract relationship or the adaptation will cause one or the adaptation will rewrite the contract, the judges or arbitrators have the power to terminate it. Section 1.2 explores the general background of the topic. It explains why research on long-term contracts and, in particular, long-term relational supply contracts, is necessary and important in the context of hardship. Section 1.3 explains the aim and the importance of the book. Section 1.4 presents the scope of the book. It identifies the issues and jurisdictions that are covered by this book. It also deals with the comparative methodology adopted for this book. Section 1.5 outlines the structure of the book.

1.1 Hypothesis

Hardship often occurs during the discharging of an international long-term relational supply contract. However, domestic laws and international instruments have different approaches to hardship issues, and the mechanisms designed to solve the problems arising from a hardship event vary.[1] To date, there are no uniform and

[1] For a more detailed discussion, see Chap. 3.

P. Guo, *Good Faith in Long-Term Relational Supply Contracts in the Context of Hardship from A Comparative Perspective*,
https://doi.org/10.1007/978-981-16-5513-5_1

accurate rules which both the parties and the judges or arbitrators can refer to when facing a hardship issue. The diversity of existing mechanisms for regulating hardship issues may result in inadequate or harsh consequences for the parties.

Against this backdrop, this book proposes that a new principle of *pacta sunt servanda bona fide,* developed based on relational contract theory, is emerging in relation to hardship issues arising in long-term relational supply contracts in international trade relationships. According to this principle, good faith and the relational nature of long-term relational contracts impose on the parties a duty to renegotiate in the event of hardship. It also grants the judges or arbitrators the power to adapt or terminate the contracts where parties cannot reach an agreement via renegotiations.

The main proposition of this book is that in the context of hardship, the parties to a long-term relational supply contract have a duty to renegotiate the contract unless there is a 'compelling reason' not to do so. Where renegotiations fail, the judges or arbitrators have the power to adapt the contract on the basis of good faith and the relational nature and characteristics of the contract. If there is a complete breakdown of the ongoing contract relationship, an adaptation to the contract will cause one or the adaptation will rewrite the contract, the judges or arbitrators have the power to terminate it. The book argues that the parties' duty to renegotiate the contract and the power of courts or arbitral tribunals to adapt and terminate the contract should be limited to international long-term relational contracts, and in particular, in international long-term relational supply contracts.[2]

The main proposition is partially based on relational contract theory and on the relational understanding of a contract relationship. It also adopts a controversial concept: good faith as it relates to the issue of hardship. In addition, it identifies new considerations on how to determine whether the parties have acted in good faith and in determining the substantial and procedural requirements of the duty to renegotiate. Therefore, to better articulate the main proposition and to assist in understanding it, several other propositions that relate to the main proposition have been developed.

First, based on the description of a long-term contract in the UNIDROIT Principles,[3] this book proposes a definition of a long-term relational contract. A long-term relational contract is intended to endure, includes a course of future dealings between the same parties and is sufficiently long for the parties to reasonably establish or maintain an ongoing relationship of mutual trust and confidence based on their exchanges and interactions. This definition reflects and combines the nature and characteristics of both a long-term contract and a relational contract. Together, these constitute one of the foundations of the main proposition.[4]

Secondly, this book proposes that, from a contextual perspective, the application of good faith has many facets and various levels. Good faith can mean different

[2] See Chap. 5.

[3] See Chap. 2, Sect. 2.3.

[4] See Chap. 2, Sect. 2.4.

things in different contexts. Based on the circumstances of an individual case, good faith can impose concrete duties that encourage the parties to honour their contracts in a fair and just manner. For example, when parties are negotiating a contract, good faith can become a duty to not break off negotiation in bad faith. In the performance of a contract a duty to co-operate can derive from good faith. In the context of hardship, good faith may become a flexible and useful tool that the judges or arbitrators can use to reallocate the emerging risks and re-establish the equilibrium between the parties in order to achieve fairness and justice, and to reach an equitable solution by adaptation or termination of a contract. These different facets and various levels of good faith provide the second foundation underlying the main proposition.[5]

Thirdly, taking into account the gaps and vagueness of the hardship rules in the UNIDROIT Principles, this book makes several suggestions on how to improve those rules. It proposes that there should be a boundary that limits the scope and application of the duty to renegotiate. The existence of a compelling reason can serve as the boundary on this duty.[6] If either party can raise and prove a compelling reason for terminating the contract based on that party's economic or other circumstances, then the party can be discharged from the duty to renegotiate. Moreover, the power of the courts or the arbitral tribunals to adapt a contract should be limited. In cases where there is a complete breakdown of the ongoing relationship between the parties, it would not be ideal for the courts or the arbitral tribunals to adapt the contract.[7] Similarly, the judges or arbitrators should not adapt a contract to the extent of rewriting it or causing a complete breakdown of the relationship between the parties.

Fourthly, in the course of determining whether the parties have acted in good faith and deciding whether to adapt or terminate a contract, this book proposes that the courts or the arbitral tribunals should adopt a double-construction approach and take into account a list of factors. The double-construction approach proposes that both the contract itself and the contractual relationship viewed horizontally or vertically, determine the rights and duties of the parties to exercise good faith in their long-term relational supply contract.[8] The relationships between the parties are viewed as horizontal, while the relationships between parties and industries or governments are considered as vertical.[9]

Finally, this book will emphasise the significance and necessity of good faith, understanding of hardship rules, and will predict the future trends in the development of rules regulating hardship. This book proposes that good faith may assist in the resolution of the conflict and strikes a balance between the certainty and

[5] See Chap. 4, Sect. 4.4.

[6] The concept of a compelling reason was proposed to be used as a separate ground for termination of contracts to be included in the 2016 edition of the UNIDROIT Principles of International Commercial Contracts; however, it was too controversial for the UNIDROIT to accept it. This concept may be of great value in a narrower context as a boundary on the duty to renegotiate in the event of hardship. See Chap. 5, Sect. 5.3.2.

[7] See Chap. 5, Sect. 5.3.2.2.

[8] See Chap. 5, Sect. 5.4.1.

[9] Ibid.

flexibility required by long-term relational contracts in the context of hardship. A new principle of *pacta sunt servanda bona fide* is emerging in international commercial law.

1.2 Background to the Problem

A change in circumstances is an issue that businesses engaging in international trade frequently have to confront. The consequences of a change of circumstances could have a significant impact on the parties, their businesses and relationships. In international contract practice, the most important principles relating to a change of circumstances are the principle of *pacta sunt servanda* and the principle of *clausula rebus sic stantibus.*

The principle of *pacta sunt servanda*, dealing with the binding force of a contract, is a widely recognised and accepted principle in international commerce and investment.[10] It means that agreements must be kept,[11] or that the contract has to be respected.[12] In another definition, the parties agree on their contractual rights and obligations in their original contract, or in the adapted contract that follows.[13] This principle causes dilemmas in international trade. If judges or arbitrators can adapt a contract in the absence of an expressed contract term, this fundamental principle of *pacta sunt servanda* is threatened and may give rise to uncertainty and unpredictability. Conversely, it is not always desirable to strictly apply the principle and not allow adaptation, as it may lead to unsatisfactory or even inequitable consequences to unforeseen circumstances.[14] It may also not be aligned with the interests of the parties that intend to preserve the contractual relationship.[15]

The principle of *clausula rebus sic stantibus* is an exception to the principle of *pacta sunt servanda*, which means that 'a contract is binding only while matters remain the same as at the time of conclusion of the contract'.[16] It is regarded as the

[10] Norbert Horn, 'The Concepts of Adaptation and Renegotiation in the Law of Transnational Commercial Contracts' in Norbert Horn (ed), *Adaptation and Renegotiation of Contracts in International Trade and Finance* (Kluwer Law International, 1985) 3, 6.

[11] Joseph M Perillo, 'Force Majeure and Hardship under the UNIDROIT Principles of International Commercial Contracts' (1997) 5 *Tulane Journal of International and Comparative law* 5, 7.

[12] Hans van Houtte, 'Changed Circumstances and Pacta Sunt Servanda' in Emmanuel Gaillard (ed), *Transnational Rules in International Commercial Arbitration* (ICC Publishing, 1993) 105, 107.

[13] Joachim G Frick, *Arbitration and Complex International Contracts* (Kluwer Law International, 2001) 146.

[14] Philip Ridder and Marc-Philippe Weller, 'Unforeseen Circumstances, Hardship, Impossibility and Force Majeure under German Contract Law' (2014) 3 *European Review of Private Law* 371, 371–2.

[15] Frick, above n 13, 146–7.

[16] Reinhard Zimmermann, *The Law of Obligations: Roman Foundations of the Civilian Tradition* (Oxford University Press, 1996) 579.

most interesting and dangerous challenge to the otherwise pervasive principle of *pacta sunt servanda*.[17] It is designed to deal with issues relating to the application of the principle of *pacta sunt servanda*.

The conflict between the principle of *pacta sunt servanda* and the principle of *clausula rebus sic stantibus* has never been adequately resolved and is particularly challenging in addressing situations of hardship. Firstly, hardship is a controversial issue at both national and international levels.[18] Secondly, hardship rules are designed to maintain the contractual relationship, which is different from the all-or-nothing approach in which the relationship is either preserved as is or terminated.[19] In responding to these issues, the hardship rules reflect the spirit of the principle of *clausula rebus sic stantibus*.[20]

It is also important to recognise that a long-term contract is more likely to be affected by hardship than a short-term one.[21] In long-term contracts, it is almost impossible to anticipate all contingencies and regulate all future possibilities at the time of entering into a relationship, particularly when they extend over a lengthy period of time and are concluded between international parties with different backgrounds.[22] Also, it is very difficult for such parties to detail in advance all their rights and duties that might arise over the duration of the long-term contract.[23] Moreover, although the allocation of risks is of great importance in negotiations and the drafting of certain long-term contracts, the parties often do not pay sufficient attention to it.[24] Therefore, a conclusive, comprehensive and everlasting contract is neither possible nor pragmatic.[25] This is particularly true if the parties to a long-term contract have mutual trust and confidence and intend to maintain an ongoing relationship, thereby adding the relational characteristics to a long-term contract.[26]

Hardship situations may also make the fulfilment of a long-term relational contract in particular, excessively onerous and this may alter the fundamental economic equilibrium between the parties. These problems occur more often in long-term

---

[17] Ibid.

[18] See, Chap. 3.

[19] See, Chap. 3, Sect. 3.2.

[20] Ibid.

[21] Ottoarndt Glossner, 'Contract Adaptation through Third Party Intervener; the Referee Arbitral' in Norbert Horn (ed), *Adaptation and Renegotiation of Contracts in International Trade and Finance* (Kluwer Law International, 1985) 191, 191.

[22] Michael F Hoellering, 'Emerging Techniques of Private Dispute Resolution in Long-Term Contracts' in Fritz Nicklisch (ed), *The Complex Long-Term Contract: Structures and International Arbitration* (C F Müller Juristisch Verlag, 1987) 523, 523.

[23] Victor P Goldberg, 'Discretion in Long-Term Open Quantity Contracts: Reining in Good Faith' (2002) 35 *University of California Davis Law Review* 319, 321.

[24] Marvin O Young, 'Construction and Enforcement of Long-Term Coal Supply Agreements-Coping with Conditions Arising from Foreseeable and Unforeseeable Events-Force Majeure and Gross Inequities Clauses' (1981) 27 *Annual Rocky Mountain Mineral Law Institute* 127, 127.

[25] Nagla Nassar, *Sanctity of Contracts Revisited: A Study in the Theory and Practice of Long-Term International Commercial Transactions* (Martinus Nijhoff Publishers, 1995) 171.

[26] See Chap. 2, Sects.2.2 and 2.4.

contracts due to the fact that each party may not be familiar with the other's political, economic and legal systems or the fact that international business relations and commercial contracts are not always established in stable political, economic or legal environments.[27] To solve these problems, it would be ideal for parties to take reasonable measures that are not included in long-term contracts.

Additionally, it is important for the parties to long-term contracts to ensure the continuance of their relationship, while maintaining the flexibility to both adapt their contracts to hardship situations and guard against opportunistic behaviour.[28] They often need the freedom to adapt their contracts to hardship situations in order to maintain their ongoing relationship, and to protect their mutual interests.[29] Moreover, at the heart of long-term relational contracts is the parties' interest in maintaining the ongoing relationship and future co-operation which supports a more flexible approach in dealing with hardship issues.[30] Therefore, the principle of *pacta sunt servande* is not desirable for long-term contracts insofar as it renders co-operation between the parties and other flexible mechanisms impossible for them to utilise.[31]

National legal systems, although they have different mechanisms and rules for dealing with hardship situations, cannot adequately or satisfactorily meet the parties' needs, especially where an international long-term relational supply contract is involved. Therefore, given the complexity of the hardship issue it is vital to seek a more appropriate and satisfactory solution both domestically and at an international level.

Against the aforementioned backdrop, the research focus of this book is how to deal more effectively with hardship in international long-term relational supply contracts. Two important instruments, the CISG and the UNIDROIT Principles, will be analysed in detail.

---

[27] Karl-Heinz Böckstiegel, 'Hardship, *Force* Majeure and Special Risks Clauses in International Contracts' in Norbert Horn (ed), *Adaptation and Renegotiation of Contracts in International Trade and Finance* (Kluwer Law International, 1985) 159, 159–160.

[28] In long-term supply contracts for petroleum coke or coal, the parties often insert a price adjustment clause to provide flexibility to adapt their contracts to changing market situations. Victor P Goldberg and John R Erickson, 'Quantity and Price Adjustment in Long-Term Contracts: A Case Study of Petroleum Coke' (1987) 30 *The Journal of Law and Economics* 369, 375; Paul L Joskow, 'Price Adjustment in Long-Term Contracts: The Case of Coal' (1998) 31 *The Journal of Law and Economics* 47, 51, 59–60.

[29] Frick, above n 13, 152–3. It should be noted that although businessmen from many countries, one of which is Japan, would agree to renegotiate and adapt a long-term contract in the event of hardship, there are still certain countries such as New Zealand the laws of which do not allow renegotiation and adaptation of a contract. See Luke Nottage, 'Planning and Renegotiating Long-Term Contracts in New Zealand and Japan: An Interim Report on an Empirical Research Project' (1997) *New Zealand Law Review* 482, 489–528. See also Luke R Nottage, 'Economic Dislocation and Contract Renegotiation in New Zealand and Japan: A Preliminary Empirical Study' (1997) 27 *Victoria University Wellington Law Review* 59, 59–97.

[30] Ibid, 153.

[31] Soili Nystén-Haarala, *The Long-Term Contract: Contract Law and Contracting* (Kauppakaari OYJ, 1998) 200.

The CISG was drafted and proposed by the United Nations Commission on International Trade Law (hereinafter: the UNCITRAL).[32] The CISG is regarded as the most successful text prepared by the UNCITRAL[33] and it represents a landmark[34] or milestone[35] in the course of the unification of international trade law. No other conventions relating to contract law have an impact as profound as the CISG does.[36] The goal of the CISG is to remove legal barriers to international trade and to promote its further development.[37] Considering the success of the CISG, it would be ideal for it to provide sustainable solutions to hardship issues. The CISG's approach to hardship issues is controversial. It is unclear and debatable whether the CISG covers the hardship issue at all.

The UNIDROIT Principles are a non-legislative codification of the general law of international commercial contracts, prepared by a group of scholars and experts invited by the International Institute for the Unification of Private Law (hereinafter: the UNIDROIT).[38] The UNIDROIT Principles first appeared in 1994, followed by revised editions in 2004 and 2010.[39]A fourth edition, the 2016 edition, of the UNIDROIT Principles was published online.[40] The 2016 edition is not an entire update of the 2010 edition. It includes new black letter rules dealing with issues that are of particular relevance and importance to long-term contracts and makes necessary changes to relevant comments in other black letter rules. The UNIDROIT Principles have not only generated academic discussions and much literature, but have also influenced the reform of national laws and the development of international contract practice.[41] Also, they have become an essential tool for the

[32] *United Nations Convention on Contracts for the International Sale of Goods*, opened for signature 11 April 1980, 1489 UNTS 3 (entered into force 1 January 1988) ('The CISG').

[33] Steven D Walt, 'The Modest Role of Good Faith in Uniform Sales Law' (2015) 33 *Boston University International Law Journal* 37, 41.

[34] Michael Joachim Bonell, 'The UNIDROIT Principles of International Commercial Contracts and CISG – Alternatives or Complementary Instruments?' (1996) 1 *Uniform Law Review* 26, 26.

[35] Gyula Eörsi, 'A Propos the 1980 Vienna Convention on Contracts for the International Sale of Goods' (1983) 31 *The American Journal of Comparative Law* 333, 334.

[36] Reinhard Zimmermann, 'European Contract Law: General Report' (2007) 15 *Europäische Zeitschrift für Wirtschaftsrecht* 455, 457.

[37] Preamble of the CISG.

[38] Michael Joachim Bonell, 'Towards a legislative Codification of the UNIDROIT Principles?' (2007) 12 *Uniform Law Review* 233, 233.

[39] For a general introduction to the development of the UNIDROIT Principles, see Stefan Vogenauer, 'The UNIDROI Principles of International Commercial Contracts at twenty: experiences to date, the 2010 edition, and future prospects' (2014) 19 *Uniform Law Review* 481, 481–513.

[40] Unless otherwise indicated, the UNIDROIT Principles referred to in this book are the UNIDROIT Principles 2016 edition. UNIDROIT, *UNIDROIT Principles of International Commercial Contracts* (International Institute for the Unification of Private Law, 2016 ed, 2016) available at https://www.unidroit.org/instruments/commercial-contracts/unidroit-principles-2016.

[41] Marcel Fontaine, 'The International 'Rayonnement' of the UNIDROIT Principles' (2017) 22 *Uniform Law Review* 202, 205–9; Reinhard Zimmermann, 'The UNIDROIT Principles of International Commercial Contracts 2004 in Comparative Perspective' (2006) 21 *Tulane European and Civil Law Forum* 1, 4.

development of international commercial law,[42] and have made 'a significant contribution to the development of a veritable world contract law'.[43] They are considered to be more than a reflection of international contract practice, but as a code consisting of a complete set of rules governing international commercial contracts.[44] In effect, the UNIDROIT Principles represent the highest level of achievement in the international restatement of the general principles of international commercial contracts and reflect the trend toward harmonising the general contract laws relating to international commercial transactions and practices.

The UNCITRAL officially endorsed the UNIDROIT Principles and recommended that these Principles be invoked to complement the CISG.[45] The UNIDROIT Principles include black letter rules especially designed to deal with hardship issues and identify solutions that best suit the particular needs of international trade. Even though they do not reflect the majority view in domestic laws, such as rules on hardship,[46] these rules may offer a better solution to both overcome the difficulties that jeopardise the certainty of relational contracts, and to provide flexibility to the parties to control their contractual relationships.[47]

1.3 Aim and Importance of the Book

The aim of this book is to provide a more satisfactory and acceptable solution to hardship issues in long-term relational supply contracts. This book proposes an approach that strikes a balance between the traditional approach underlying classical contract law which emphasises the almost absolute prevalence of the principle of *pacta sunt servanda* and a flexible approach that is based on the principle of

[42] Fabio Bortolotti, 'Reference to the UNIDROIT Principles in Contract Practice and Model Contracts' in the International Chamber of Commerce (ed), *UNIDROIT Principles: New Developments and Applications, ICC International Court of Arbitration Bulletin, 2005 Special Supplement* (ICC Publishing, 2005) 57, 57.

[43] Michael Joachim Bonell, 'The CISG, European Contract Law and the Development of a World Contract Law' (2008) 56 *American Journal of Comparative Law* 1, 18.

[44] Marcel Fontaine, 'The UNIDROIT Principles: An Expression of Current Contract Practice' in the International Chamber of Commerce and the UNIDROIT (eds), *UNIDROIT Principles of International Commercial Contracts: Reflections on their Use in International Arbitration, ICC International Court of Arbitration Bulletin, 2002 Special Supplement* (ICC Publishing, 2002) 95, 98.

[45] *Report of the United Nations Commission on International Trade Law* (UNCITRAL 45th sess.) UN GAOR, 67th sess, Supp No 17, UN Doc A/67/17 (25 June–6 July 2012) para. 140 (endorsing the UNIDROIT Principles 2010 edition); *Report of the United Nations Commission on International Trade Law*, (UNCITRAL 40th sess.) UN GAOR, 62nd sess, Supp No 17, UN Doc A/62/17(Part I) (25 June-12 July 2007) para. 213 (endorsing the UNIDROIT Principles 2004 edition).

[46] Bonell, 'Towards a Legislative Codification of the UNIDROIT Principles', above n 38, 234.

[47] It should be noted that there is also an argument that although the rules relating to hardship provided by the UNIDROIT Principles can be considered as better rules, they do not necessarily correspond to current international contract practice. Fabio Bortolotti, 'The UNIDROIT Principles and the Arbitral Tribunals' (2000) 1 *Uniform Law Review* 141, 144–5.

clausula rebus sic stantibus. The book argues for an emerging principle of *pacta sunt servanda bona fide* on the basis of the relational contract theory. A further aim is to demonstrate how good faith can serve as a foundation for imposing a duty to renegotiate on the parties. It is also directed at granting courts and arbitral tribunals the power to adapt long-term relational supply contracts to restore the equilibrium of rights and obligations between the parties and to terminate their contracts when adaptation is not appropriate.[48]

Nevertheless, it should be noted that this book does not intend to promote a single overarching theory, given the existing competition among the various theories relating to sustaining long-term contractual relationships. It is not intended to 'take apart the magnificent doctrinal Crystal Palace';[49] nor will this book 'try to build a new contract law on the ruins of the old, a law that would be more solidly founded on the empirical regularities observed in the decided cases, and that would make articulate their hitherto unstated but implicit bases in ethics, policy, and social function.'[50]

The purpose of this book is rather to propose how relational contract theory can be applied to the analysis of specific legal rules in general. It also aims to demonstrate how the duty to renegotiate and the power to adapt a contract can be further developed upon the occurrence of hardship, based on good faith and the relational nature and characteristics of a long-term relational supply contract. The reason to do this is that the existing research on relational contract theory concentrates primarily on its application in domestic contract laws, particularly in the regulation of long-term contracts in American contract law. Considering that rules relating to long-term contracts have emerged at the international level, significantly due to the wide adoption of the UNIDROIT Principles,[51] it is useful and important to examine whether relational contract theory suits the rules of the UNIDROIT Principles. And further, whether the theory can be used as a theoretical basis for the solutions reached by the contractual parties themselves, or by courts or arbitral tribunals addressing hardship issues. When a shortcoming of the existing rules is identified, the book proposes solutions to amend it, such as by placing suitable boundaries around the duty to renegotiate or on the procedural preference between adaptation and termination.[52]

---

[48] See Chap. 5.

[49] Robert W Gordon, 'Macaulay, Macneil, and the Discovery of Solidarity and Power in Contract Law' (1985) *Wisconsin Law Review* 565, 566.

[50] Ibid.

[51] The 2016 edition of the UNIDROIT Principles has new black letter rules and comments relating to long-term contracts. These rules are specifically designed for long-term contracts given their broad usage and importance in international trade. Also, it is the first time that rules particularly targeting long-term contracts have been included in a non-legislative instrument for the harmonisation of international or regional general laws of contract. These rules have the potential to become successful. Therefore, it is valuable and urgent to examine these rules, particularly those that could frequently be invoked by the parties, such as the hardship rules. The UNIDROIT Principles are undoubtedly an ideal and excellent starting point.

[52] See Chap. 5, Sect. 5.3.2.

The main contribution of this research is to improve understanding of the research subject and enrich the legal literature in that regard. The research aims to provide a more feasible and satisfactory approach for courts or arbitral tribunals to undertake when facing hardship issues in international contract disputes. It seeks also to pave the way for the broader international acceptance of the black letter rules provided by the UNIDROIT Principles by proposing certain clarifications and revisions. The results outlined in this book aim to present a strong argument for a transnational law that accommodates domestic legal solutions, but also provides common ground in reconciling inconsistencies in how different domestic legal systems treat hardship issues in long-term supply relationships. It can assist, too, in guiding countries in reforming their domestic laws relating to hardship in contracting.

1.4 Scope of the Book

Long-term contracts are often drafted and utilised in the trade of natural resources and other industries. There are many types of long-term contracts that may be affected by hardship events during the lifetime of the contracts. These include long-term investment contracts, long-term construction contracts, long-term joint-venture contracts, long-term service contracts, long-term patent licenses contracts, long-term transport contracts, long-term know-how contracts, long-term loan contracts, long-term supply contracts and so on. Different types of long-term contracts encounter different problems, such as hardship events or force majeure events. However, it is impossible to sufficiently cover all these types of long-term contracts in a single book. As a result, this book will concentrate on long-term relational supply contracts in international rather than domestic transactions.

Similarly, the issues relating to long-term relational supply contracts are various, from formation to performance, and from non-performance to dispute resolution and enforcement. As this book cannot cover every problem relating to long-term relational supply contracts from establishment to termination, it focuses on solutions to hardship issues relating to long-term relational supply contracts.

This book stresses that hardship events may render the fulfilment of long-term relational supply contracts excessively onerous. The result is that hardship can lead to a failure or suspension of performance. This, in turn, may have a significant impact on the obligations and expectations of both parties. To solve these problems, this book stresses how good faith can assist parties to long-term relational supply contracts to reasonably renegotiate contract terms in order to continue their performance. In cases where renegotiations fail, the courts or arbitral tribunals can adapt or terminate the contract.[53]

A brief overview of good faith in domestic laws is provided below to assist in contextualising disparate conceptions and receptivity towards good faith in national

[53] See Chap. 5.

legal systems. Both common law and civil law jurisdictions are discussed. At least two common law and two civil law legal systems are discussed to demonstrate the different treatments of good faith even within each legal family. In common law jurisdictions, this book will examine American law, English law and Australian law, while German law and French law will be analysed in civil law jurisdictions.

The book will also investigate rules on good faith embodied in two important international instruments for international trade: the CISG and the UNIDROIT Principles. It will demonstrate that good faith is not well reflected in the CISG, whereas the UNIDROIT Principles are generally recognised and widely applied. Where relevant, this book will also cover the Principles of European Contract Law (hereinafter: the PECL),[54] the Draft Common Frame of Reference (hereinafter: the DCFR),[55] the Common European Sales Law (hereinafter: the CESL),[56] and the TransLex-Principles of transnational commercial law (hereinafter: the TransLex-Principles).[57]

This book will use the black letter rules relating to hardship in the UNIDROIT Principles as a framework to propose a suitable solution to deal with hardship issues. It will identify the potential advantages and disadvantages of such black letter rules and suggest how to better tackle problems relating to hardship under the *Lex Mercatoria*[58] and the development of a uniform international commercial contract law. This book will not only analyse good faith as a foundation of black letter rules

---

[54] The Principles of European Contract Law were prepared by the Commission on European Contract Law, published in 1995, and revised in 1999 and 2003, separately.

[55] The Draft Common Frame of Reference was prepared by the Study Group on a European Civil Code and the Research Group on EC Private Law (Acquis Group). An Interim Outline Edition was published in 2008 and a Full Edition was published in 2009.

[56] The Common European Sales Law was prepared by a group of scholars organised by the European Commission with a view to drafting a proposal for the European Parliament and the Council that could be used to harmonise different domestic contract laws of the member states of the European Union.

[57] The TransLex-Principles are a systematic collection of principles and rules of international commercial law and they are being used by arbitrators, contract drafters, academics and other stakeholders in international commercial arbitration and relevant research all around the world. They are prepared and published online by Professor Klaus Peter Berger and the TransLex Research Team. See https://www.trans-lex.org/principles.

[58] There is no unified definition of the Lex Mercatoria. Lord Justice Mustill has gathered some typical definitions. The Lex Mercatoria can mean:

> A set of general principles, and customary rules spontaneously referred to or elaborated in the framework of international trade, without reference to a particular national system of law.

A single autonomous body of law created by the international business community.

This phenomenon of uniform rules serving uniform needs of international business and economic co-operation is today commonly labelled *lex mercatoria*.

The customs of the business community may combine all general principles of law to create a system of commercial self-determination.

… un droit "transnational", réceptacle des principes communs aux droits nationaux, mais creuset aussi des règles spécifiques qu'appelle le commerce international.

concerning hardship. It will also examine the manifestations of good faith in the context of hardship, including the parties' duty to renegotiate and the possibility of judicial intervention to deal with potential issues arising from the failure of the parties to renegotiate their contracts in response to intervening hardship.

1.5 Methodology

This research is doctrinal and theoretical. It intends to promote a normative solution to hardship issues. Its methodology is comparative and functional.

This book will make a comparative survey of hardship rules and good faith in several common law and civil law systems including English Law, American Law, Australian Law, German Law and French Law. These various laws sometimes view an issue from different perspectives and hence adopt different approaches in dealing with it. In addition to national jurisdictions, the book will also investigate international documents, namely the CISG and the UNIDROIT Principles.[59]

For the civil law system, the French law and the German law are chosen to represent the civil law jurisdictions in this book. First of all, the laws in countries within the civil law tradition often have a French or Roman origin.[60] The French law is on the basis of Code Napoléon, while the German law is one of the most important successors of the Roman law. Using them as examples, to a large extent, represents the civil law system.

In addition, the French Civil Code and the German Civil Code have directly influenced civil codes and civil laws in various countries. For example, the French Civil Code has influenced the Mexican Civil Code, the Bolivian Civil Code and the Peruvian Civil Code;[61] the German Civil Code has influenced the Dutch Civil Code and the Japanese Civil Code.[62] For example, German law empowers the judges or arbitrators to adapt contracts in the context of hardship, as do the Dutch law and

Lord Justice Mustill, 'The New Lex Mercatoria: The First Twenty-five Years' in Maarten Bos (ed), Liber Amicorum for the Rt. Hon. Lord Wilberforce (Oxford University Press, 1987) 86, 87–88 (citations omitted).

[59] The kind of selective comparison is also conducted by other scholars and leads to fruitful results. See, eg, Luke Nottage, 'Changing Contract Lenses: Unexpected Supervening Events in English, New Zealand, US, Japanese, and International Sales Law and Practice' (2008) 14 *Indiana Journal of Global Legal Studies* 385. In this article domestic laws of US, England, New Zealand and Japan, as well as international instruments such as the CISG and the UNIDROIT Principles are compared.

[60] Bruno Zeller, 'The UNIDROIT Principles of Hardship and the Application of Article 79 CISG: Are They Compatible?' in Ingeborg Schwenzer and Lisa Spagnolo (eds) State of Play the 3rd Annual MAA Schlechtriem CISG Conference (Eleven International Publishing, 2012) 113, 116

[61] Edgardo Munoz, *Modern Law of Contracts and Sales in Latin America, Spain and Portugal* (Eleven International Publishing, 2011) 16–7.

[62] van Houtte, above n 12, 122.

Japanese law.[63] This approach is followed by Spanish Law, Argentinian law and Brazilian law, as well as others.[64] Again, the French Civil Code and the German Civil Code have also indirect impacts on civil codes or civil laws in some countries. For example, the Indonesian Civil Code is based on the French Civil Code, and the old Dutch Civil Code is based on German Civil Code.[65] That means some parts of the Indonesian Civil Code are directly influenced by French law, while others are indirectly influenced by German law. Also, most civil codes in Eastern European and Central Asian have been influenced by French law or German law in one way or another, such as that of Bulgaria's and Hungary's.[66] For example, after the dissolution of the Soviet Union, some of these countries directly adopted the German model, such as Georgia and Turkmenistan, or indirectly, such as Estonia's code of obligations which followed the Swiss and Dutch Models.[67]

The French law and the German law are chosen on account of their reforms in the Twenty-First Century. The recent reform of the French contract law in 2016 may have a significant impact on the legal systems which have inherited French legal tradition. Before the reform, hardship was neither recognised by nor stipulated in the French Civil Code. French courts have a dual approach to hardship. On the one hand, in commercial contracts, not including the government, courts have focused on the principle of *pacta sunt servanda* and the absence of fault by the obligor and have applied only the doctrine of force majeure. Meaning that, if the parties did not insert a contract term on hardship into their contract, the court could not imply one.[68] On the other hand, in administrative contracts, including the government, courts have recognised the principle of *clausula rebus sic stantibus* (changed circumstances), and developed the doctrine of *imprévision*.[69] In the German law, a new article 313 dealing with interference with the basis of the contract was introduced into the German Civil Code.[70] According to this new article, in the case of hardship

---

[63] Ibid. It should be noted that the 2017 reforms to the Japanese Civil Code did not codify lower court judgments adapting contract in extreme situations nor did they adopt the hardship provisions in the UNIDROIT Principles, although these were urged by a semi-official study group earlier. See Takashi Uchida, 'Contract Law Reform in Japan and the UNIDROIT Principles' (2011) 16 Uniform Law Review 705, 710.

[64] Munoz, above n 61, 452–3.

[65] Gary F. Bell, 'New Challenges for the Unification of laws: How the CISG is Challenged by "Asian Values" and Islamic Law' in Ingeborg Schwenzer and Lisa Spagnolo (eds), Towards Uniformity the 2nd Annual MAA Schlechtriem CISG Conference (ELEVEN International Publishing, 2011) 11, 18–9

[66] Natia Lapiashvili, *Modern Law of Contracts and Sales in Eastern Europe and Central Asia* (Eleven International Publishing, 2011) 22–33.

[67] Ibid, 20.

[68] Zeller, 'The UNIDROIT Principles of Hardship and the Application of Article 79 CISG: Are They Compatible?' above n 60.

[69] David W. Rivkin, 'Lex Mercatoria and Force Majeure' in Emmanuel Gaillard (ed), *Transnational Rules in International Commercial Arbitration* (ICC Publishing, 1993) 161, 173–4.

[70] Christoph Brunner, *Force Majeure and Hardship under General Contract Principles: Exemption for Non-performance in International Arbitration* (Kluwer Law International, 2008) 405.

the aggrieved party may claim that the contract should be adapted. If that adaptation is not feasible, a court might grant termination in the last resort.[71] The change in the French law or German law is in line with the rules provided by the UNIDROIT Principles. They may have influences in which the law is based on either the French law or the German law in one way or another; they may entrench the UNIDROIT Principles' approach to hardship; and they may eventually lead the development of a unified solution to hardship issues in the context of international trade.

In the common law world, the English law, the American law and the Australian law are selected to provide an outline of the laws on hardship. In the English law, hardship issues are dealt with by the doctrine of frustration. It rejects any notion of relief for any change in circumstances that do not amount to impossibility.[72] Most common law jurisdictions follow the English approach.[73] Australia is one of those jurisdictions. Despite the similarities on hardship issues in English law and Australian law, the latter is chosen due to divergence between attitudes to good faith between the two jurisdictions. Unlike the English law and the Australian law, the American law recognised a doctrine of commercial impracticability and an express duty of good faith in contract performance. The inclusion of the American law in the comparison of domestic laws may offer a new 'blended' or 'harmonised' approach to the understanding and development of rules dealing with hardship at the international level.

It is argued that the 'national law is often ill adapted to deal with problems arising out of international contracts'.[74] Also, the aim of this book is to provide a feasible and more satisfactory solution to hardship issues. Taking into account these issues, in addition to divergences across national jurisdictions over the legal significance of hardship. The research also examines the CISG, the UNIDROIT Principles and the other international instruments mentioned above.

This research cannot cover more jurisdictions for certain practical reasons. It would be impossible and impractical to study good faith and hardship rules in depth in each jurisdiction.

Apart from the comparative method, this book will also adopt a functional method advocated by Rabel and further developed by Zweigert and Kötz. This method proposes that there is a presumption that different national legal systems may provide similar practical solutions to a certain legal problem.[75] It also argues

[71] Ibid.

[72] Brunner, above n 70, 408.

[73] Ingeborg Schwenzer, Pascal Hachem and Christopher Kee, *Global Sales and Contract Law* (Oxford University Press, 2012) 651

[74] Klaus Peter Berger and Olivia Johanna Erdelyi, 'Force Majeure in International Contract Law: A Comment on National Oil Corporation v Sun Oil' in Patrick Wautelet, Thalia Kruger and Govern Coppens (eds), *The Practice of Arbitration: Essays in Honour of Hans van Houtte* (Hart Publishing, 2012) 61, 62.

[75] Gerhard Dannemann, 'Comparative Law: Study of Similarities or Differences?' in Mathias Reimann and Reinhard Zimmermann (eds), The Oxford Handbook of Comparative Law (Oxford University Press, 2006) 383, 386–9.

that identifying the similarities may promote the unification or harmonisation of different legal rules in various legal systems,[76] and may 'serve as a yardstick to determine the "better law"' on the basis of the majority solution in case of the existence of differences among practical solutions provided by national legal systems.[77]

Despite different understanding of functionalism[78]and certain criticisms of the abovementioned functional method focusing on similarities, it is argued that 'it is easily overlooked that the presumption of similarity as proposed by Zweigert and Kötz has a much more limited field of application'.[79] Zweigert and Kötz's approach 'applies only to those areas of (a) substantive (b) private law which (c) are not culturally or politically sensitive, thus excluding all of public law, criminal law, procedural law, and even family and inheritance law'[80] and 'applies to only one aspect in the process of comparison, namely the results, that is, practical outcomes, which legal systems deliver in response to specific situations'.[81]

Zweigert and Kötz's functional methodology is chosen due to the pragmatic nature of the main research question which falls in the limited scope of application of the adopted functional methodology approach. First, the book will concentrate on how parties can and should respond to situations where external changes disturb the contractual equilibrium and then result in hardship to one party, but not how a legal doctrine relevant to hardship is developed and addressed.

Also, it is very difficult to construe legal concepts definitively, as one legal concept used in one legal system in one legal language does not always correspond to another legal concept used in another legal system and in another legal language.[82] Illustrating these differences is the concept of imprévision in the French law and frustration in the English law. The term hardship in this book encompasses imprévision, commercial impracticability and *Wegfall der Geschäftsgrundlage*.[83] Hardship is not a term recognised by domestic laws and is only used at the international level, such as in the UNIDROIT Principles and the ICC Hardship Clauses.[84] Therefore, the book will not examine the similarities and differences between these legal terms in different national contexts, but will concentrate on how these doctrines deal with the same issues and on the results that these doctrines provide. More precisely,

---

[76] Ralf Michaels, 'The Functional Method of Comparative Law' in Mathias Reimann and Reinhard Zimmermann (eds), The Oxford Handbook of Comparative Law (Oxford University Press, 2006) 339, 376–8; see also Dannemann, above n 75, 402–3.

[77] Ibid, 373–6.

[78] Ibid, 343–363.

[79] Dannemann, above n 75, 395.

[80] Ibid.

[81] Ibid.

[82] Eric Bergsten, 'Methodological Problems in the Drafting of the CISG' in André Janssen and Olaf Meyer (eds), CISG Methodology (Sellier European Law Publishers, 2009) 5, 18.

[83] Hardship is often used to cover different domestic doctrines dealing with similar hardship situations. See, eg, Schwenzer, Hachem and Kee, above n 73, 651–2, 666.

[84] Ibid, 666.

whether the parties are under a duty to renegotiate the contract or must they perform the contract on agreed terms in the context of hardship?

Moreover, considering different results provided by the chosen domestic laws and the regional and international instruments, the book will argue that the current situation in this field is so disparate that a better and more satisfactory solution should be provided as the 'better law'. The English law and the Australian law may be too harsh on the party facing hardship situations; whereas the German law and the French law may be too lenient in dealing with the hardship issue. The American law offers a blended approach recognising commercial impracticability and good faith performance but limits its application. This approach seems more reasonable and practical. At the international level, the UNIDROIT Principles take a similar harmonised approach. Despite certain gaps in the provisions on hardship under the UNIDROIT Principles, a principle of *pacta sunt servanda bona fide* can be derived from those provisions and can serve as a basis of the harmonisation on rules relating to hardship in international commerce and in the context of lex mercatoria.

Finally, hardship issues are dealt with by contract laws in domestic legal systems and in relevant regional and international instruments. This is an area which relates to substantive private law and is mostly not culturally or politically sensitive.

Chapter 2
Long-Term Contracts and Relational Contracts

2.1 Introduction

Long-term contracts are widely used in international trade and investment. The global economic environment is intricate and full of uncertainty, and therefore it is challenging, if not impossible, to predict accurately how economic circumstances in general or the situation of the parties in particular, will change during the period of a long-term contract.[1] Given all the possible contingencies, it is extremely difficult for the parties to a long-term contract to foresee all the issues that may arise in the future and to provide corresponding mechanisms to deal with them at the time of the conclusion of their contracts. It is, therefore, necessary to carefully examine what a long-term contract is and whether there are specially designed rules or adopted doctrines to tackle issues relating to it.

Relational contract theory asserts that a contract should be viewed in terms of the relations that it involves. The examination of a contract itself and the rights and obligations of the parties should start from the relations and end with the relations. This theory argues that a contract can be better understood through the relations based on which co-operation, fairness, and mutual trust and confidence evolve and develop between the parties and accordingly affect their behaviour under the contract. Therefore, both contracts and contract law should be considered and perceived from a broader perspective, and should include the social, political, cultural and economic factors surrounding them.

For contracts which endure over a long period of time, it is common that a special relationship between the parties can be gradually established, continuously developed, and effectively maintained in one way or another for their common

[1] Peter Bobeff, 'Long-Term Contracts for the Sale of Mineral Commodities' [1991] *Australian Mining and Petroleum Law Association (AMPLA) Yearbook* 335, 337.

P. Guo, *Good Faith in Long-Term Relational Supply Contracts in the Context of Hardship from A Comparative Perspective*,
https://doi.org/10.1007/978-981-16-5513-5_2

interests and mutual benefits in the long run. These contracts could then be considered as long-term relational contracts during the life of which the relationship of the parties plays a crucially vital role in their performance and dispute resolution.

This chapter examines both long-term contracts and relational contracts. Section 2.2 will examine the notion of a long-term contract and that of a relational contract in general. The differences and connections between them will be analysed as well. Also, this section will explain why the relational contract theory would be more appropriate as a means of understanding and regulating a long-term contract. Section 2.3 will explore the concept of the long-term contract under the UNIDROIT Principles which deal with long-term contracts extensively. The inclusion, in the 2016 edition, of provisions relating to long-term contracts is the most significant update. Section 2.4 will analyse the notion of a long-term relational contract which is one of the focuses of this book. A possible definition of a long-term relational contract will be proposed, and its important elements will be investigated. Section 2.5 concludes the chapter and explains why long-term relational supply contracts as a typical kind of long-term relational contract were chosen for this study.

2.2 Long-Term Contracts and Relational Contracts in General

2.2.1 Long-Term Contract

2.2.1.1 What Is a Long-Term Contract?

A long-term contract is a sociological rather than a legal concept which, regardless of its nature, gives rise to legal issues.[2] This view is accepted by other scholars.[3] Also, there is no accurate definition of a long-term contract.[4] Its definition varies according to the circumstances of the relevant transaction.[5] It is argued that 'a long-term contract is actually a contract to govern continuous long-lasting co-operational contractual relationship'.[6] It is also argued that 'a long-term natural resource

[2] John Bell, 'The Effect of Changes in Circumstances on Long-Term Contracts: English Report' in Donald Harris and Denis Tallon (eds), *Contract Law Today: Anglo-French Comparisons* (Clarendon Press, 1989) 195, 195.

[3] See, eg, Ewan McKendrick, 'The Regulation of Long-term Contracts in English Law' in Jack Beatson and Daniel Friedmann (eds), *Good Faith and Fault in Contract Law* (Clarendon Press, 1995) 305, 305.

[4] Fritz Nicklisch, 'Advantages of a Doctrine of Long-Term Contracts' in Fritz Nicklisch (ed), *The Complex Long-Term Contract: Structures and International Arbitration* (C F Müller Juristisch Verlag, 1987) 17, 24.

[5] Clayton P Gillette, 'Commercial Rationality and the Duty to Adjust Long-Term Contracts' (1985) 69 *Minnesota Law Review* 521, 521.

[6] Nystén-Haarala, above n 31 (Chap. 1), 6.

contract is an institutional agreement that specifies rules, and incentives, to encourage those associated with resource development to conform to a particular sequence of depletion, and to provide limited opportunity for adjustments to be made to the structure of an economic relationship over time'.[7] Moreover, there is no precise stipulation regarding how long a contract should be in order for it to be considered as a long-term contract. Normally, long-term contracts span a period of more than five years.[8] In the coal industry, a coal sales contract would be regarded as a long-term contract if it lasts from 5 to 15 years or more.[9] Many coal supply contracts last up to 35 years.[10] It has been suggested that you will know that it is a long-term contract when you see one.[11] One thing which is certain is that parties to long-term contracts, at first glance, are required to commit for an enduring period.[12] In addition, it is worth noting that '[a] long-term relationship may exist between the parties either as a matter of deliberate creation from the outset, or as a result of interaction between the parties over a period of time'.[13]

Long-term contracts may have different forms: 1. long-term contracts with a finite length, 2. long-term contracts with an indefinite length, and 3. long-term contracts constituted by a series of short-term or spot contracts.[14] The short-term or spot contracts could be either renewable or non-renewable, and the renewable ones are more likely to be considered as long-term contracts.[15]

Contracts falling within categories 1 and 2 could be regarded as direct long-term contracts because their long duration is straightforward, while it would be more suitable to consider contracts in category 3 as indirect long-term contracts because they consist of a series of short-term contracts which, taken together, make the

---

[7] B M H Sharp and B Simon, 'Long-Term Natural Resource Contracts' (1992) 26 *New Zealand Economic Papers* 27, 28.

[8] Chuanlong Tang, 'Structure and Price Adjustments in Long-Term Contracts: the Case of Coking Coal Trade in the Asian-Pacific Market' (1993) *September Energy Policy* 944, 945.

[9] David Barnett, 'Commentary on Long-Term Contracts' [1991] *Australian Mining and Petroleum Law Association (AMPLA) Yearbook* 351, 352.

[10] Paul L Joskow, 'Vertical Integration and Long-Term Contracts: The Case of Coal-Burning Electric Generating Plants' (1985) 1 *Journal of Law, Economics, and Organization* 33, 66.

[11] Carmel McLure, 'Long Term Contracts: Principles for Determining Content' in Kanaga Dharmananda SC and Leon Firios (eds), *Long Term Contracts* (Federation Press, 2013) 115, 116.

[12] Kanaga Dharmananda SC and Leon Firios, 'Introduction' in Kanaga Dharmananda SC and Leon Firios (eds), *Long Term Contracts* (Federation Press, 2013) 4, 4.

[13] Bell, above n 2.

[14] Hugh Collins, 'Competing Norms of Contractual Behaviour' in David Campbell and Peter Vincent-Jones (eds), *Contract and Economic Organization: Social-Legal Initiatives* (Dartmouth, 1996) 67, 87–92.

[15] These short-term or spot contracts may be considered as 'repeated dealing'. The boundary between 'repeated dealing' and long-term contracts becomes blurred; however, it is argued that there are several distinctive factors that differentiate them. For example, either party to 'repeated dealing' is free to terminate it. John Owen Haley, *The Spirit of Japanese Law* (University of Georgia Press, 1998) 147–9.

indirect long-term contracts last over a long period of time. This difference may be of assistance when determining the characteristics of a long-term contract.

The duration of a long-term contract will often overlap with the length of the commercial transactions in the case where the long-term contract is indefinite or with a fixed duration. In cases where the long-term contract is, in fact, constituted by a series of short-term contracts, the duration of a short-term contract could be very short, but the length of the commercial transactions between the parties may not be short at all. It starts from the beginning of the first short-term contract in a number of short-term contracts which constitute the long-term contract and ends with the completion of the last short-term contract of that series. Therefore, it seems that the length of the commercial transactions rather than the duration of the long-term contract is the significant factor that determines whether a contract or a series of contracts constitutes a long-term contract.

It is worth noting that due to the differences in form, long-term contracts may not be treated in the same way in different jurisdictions or even in the same jurisdiction, thereby making various kinds of remedies available to the parties.[16]

2.2.1.2 Characteristics of a Long-Term Contract

A long-term contract has the following characteristics in general:

1. Terms regarding duration
2. Flexibility in performance
3. Discretions (often coupled with good faith and reasonableness obligations)
4. Non-linear pricing structures
5. Terms governing the disclosure of information
6. Dispute resolution mechanisms
7. Rights governing termination and remedies (for example, liquidated damages)[17]

The characteristics of long-term supply contracts are:

1. An assumption that *ex ante* planning will be inadequate;
2. Reliance upon continuing ex post bargaining over price, quantity, delivery, and related terms;
3. The mutual interdependence of the parties;
4. The occurrence of transaction costs when a relationship is terminated;
5. The interest of dependent third parties and consumers in the continuity of the long-term relationship; and
6. The continuing risk of government intrusions into the private domain.[18]

---

[16] Reinhard Zimmermann et al., 'Long-term business relationships I' and 'Long-term business relationships II' in Reinhard Zimmermann and Simon Whittaker (eds), *Good Faith in European Contract Law* (Cambridge University Press, 2000) 532, 532–556.

[17] David Goddard, 'Long-Term Contracts: A Law and Economics Perspective' [1997] *New Zealand Law Review* 423, 444.

[18] Leon E Trakman, 'Winner Take Some: Loss Sharing and Commercial Impracticability' (1985) 69 *Minnesota Law Review* 471, 487–8.

These features are normally reflected in various clauses within a long-term contract, such as the term and quantity clauses,[19] the price clauses,[20] take or pay clauses,[21] arbitration clauses,[22] hardship clauses,[23] and force majeure clauses.[24]

Another important factor regarding long-term contracts is that the commercial realities will prevail almost all the time, meaning that even if a party's action is in breach of the express terms of a long-term supply contract, the other party may be forced to make concessions in order to maintain the long-term relationship.[25] This fact may seem sad, unfair or unjust to the aggrieved party. However, this is the reality, or was so back in the 1970s and 1980s.[26] Accordingly, parties with a desire to maintain the long-term relationship would be willing to adapt their contracts regardless of the specific contract terms in order to enjoy the perceived benefits that they expect to obtain from the long-term relationship,[27] particularly when the parties intend to extend their relationship beyond the current contract.[28]

2.2.1.3 Why Long-Term Contracts?

Although the parties may encounter various difficulties, such as complexity, uncertainty and unpredictability relating to a long-term contract, they still choose to conclude one for their business and projects. One possible explanation is that this may be more optimal and more attractive than other options.[29]

The parties commit themselves to a long-term contract of different types for various reasons. Firstly, the buyer can obtain a continuous and secure supply of whatever he or she purchases with a consistent quality and at a stable price, and the seller can secure a stable and guaranteed market for whatever he or she is selling.[30] Secondly, a long-term contract may provide a flexible framework for the parties to

---

[19] Bobeff, above n 1, 339–341.

[20] Ibid.

[21] J Harold Mulherin, 'Complexity in Long-Term Contracts: An Analysis of Natural Gas Contractual Provisions' (1986) 2 *Journal of Law, Economics, and Organization* 105, 108–111.

[22] John Garvey, 'Commentary on Long-Term Contracts' [1991] *Australian Mining and Petroleum Law Association (AMPLA) Yearbook* 362, 364–6.

[23] Barnett, above n 9, 358–9.

[24] Ibid, 359.

[25] Bobeff, above n 1.

[26] Ibid.

[27] Ibid, 349.

[28] Ibid, 338.

[29] Charles J Goetz and Robert E Scott, 'Principles of Relational Contracts' (1981) 67 *Virginia Law Review* 1089, 1095.

[30] Jeffrey M Petrash, 'Long-Term Natural Gas Contracts: Dead, Dying, or Merely Resting?' (2006) 27 *Energy Law Journal* 545, 569–571.

develop a relationship that could yield mutual benefits,[31] and that could develop and improve with time.[32] For example, parties prefer a long-term contract regarding farming because of their intention to establish and develop a stable and continuous relationship taking into account the necessity for the producer to invest in the contract for the long run.[33] Thirdly, the long term contract could provide a sound financial basis or robust economic support for raising capital.[34] Such contracts enable the parties to make specialised investments for the performance of the contracts,[35] and the investments can be better protected.[36] At the same time, long-term contracts can ensure a sufficient cash flow over a sustained period of time.[37] Fourthly, such contracts would generally contain agreed procedures relating to the administration of delivery, pricing and payment and other matters to smooth the performance.[38] Fifthly, they may be used to reduce costs and to better allocate risks efficiently over its duration.[39] Finally, long-term contracts may have positive impacts on social welfare.[40] A long-term energy supply contract may limit double marginalization, prevent abuse of dominance, promote market building and contribute to long-term generation adequacy and stability.[41]

2.2.1.4 Issues Relating to Long-Term Contracts

To some extent, it is inevitable that circumstances may change over the duration of long-term contracts and situations may arise that were not foreseen by the parties when entering into the contracts.[42] Therefore, it may be impossible for the parties to adequately and accurately predict or take into account the possible influences of the external market, government policy and other circumstances, which could make the

---

[31] Bobeff, above n 1, 349–350.

[32] Barnett, above n 9, 353.

[33] UNIDROIT/FAO/IFAD, *Legal Guide on Contract Farming* (the International Institute for the Unification of Private law (UNIDROIT), the Food and Agriculture Organization of the United Nations (FAO) and the International Fund for Agricultural Development (IFAD), 2015) 194.

[34] M E Wright, 'Effect of Changed Circumstances on Mineral and Petroleum Sales Contracts' [1984] *Australian Mining and Petroleum Law Association (AMPLA) Yearbook* 331, 332.

[35] Dharmananda and Firios, 'Introduction', above n 12, 5.

[36] Goddard, above n 17, 426–9.

[37] Oluseye Arowolo, 'Abolition of Long-Term Contracts: The Implications and Options for Bankability in Energy Project Financing' (2006) 24 *Journal of Energy and Natural Resources Law* 16, 19–20.

[38] Garvey, above n 22, 368.

[39] Goddard, above n 17, 424–6.

[40] Adrien de Hauteclocque and Jean-Michel Glachant, 'Long-Term Energy Supply Contracts in Europe Competition Policy: Fuzzy not Crazy' (2009) 37 *Energy Policy* 5399, 5401.

[41] Ibid.

[42] Wright, above n 34, 331.

fulfilment of a commercially sensible contract extremely and radically onerous as a result of the changes in economic, political, social or technological circumstances.[43] Hence, the parties face a huge challenge as it is very difficult for them to 'make an adequate judgment about what is going to be a rational course of action several years hence-what will be their requirement, how will their business operate, or what kind of alternative opportunities will be available.'[44] Many long-term contracts, due to incompetent negotiations, do not adequately provide for the unpredictability of the future or the establishment of appropriate mechanisms for tackling uncertainty.[45]

A long-term contract, therefore, may give rise to various problems which normally do not arise from a one-shot or short-term contract.[46] These issues are summarised by Collins as, but are not limited to the problem of:

(i) specifying in advance the details of the expected contractual performance;
(ii) coping with unexpected changes in circumstances, such as market conditions, during the period of performance of the contract;
(iii) monitoring whether satisfactory contractual performance has in fact been provided;
(iv) guarding against opportunistic behaviour in the form of attempts to renegotiate terms of the contract.[47]

Bonell has identified more issues with long-term contracts, such as arising from open or evolving terms within such contracts, agreements to negotiate in good faith, co-operation between the parties, restitution after termination, implementation relating to a group of linked contracts, and post-contractual obligations.[48]

2.2.2 *Relational Contracts*

The concept of a relational contract is of particular relevance to a long-term contract, the concentration of which is moving from emphasis on formality on contract formation or performance to the dynamic balance of the duties and the relationship between the parties.[49]

---

[43] Bell, above n 2, 198.

[44] Ibid.

[45] Selwyn D'Souza, 'Commercial Perspectives on Long Term Contracting' in Kanaga Dharmananda SC and Leon Firios (eds), *Long Term Contracts* (Federation Press, 2013) 9, 9.

[46] Bell, above n 2, 198.

[47] Collins, 'Competing Norms of Contractual Behaviour', above n 14, 72.

[48] Michael Joachim Bonell, 'The UNIDROIT Principles of International Commercial Contract and Long-Term Contracts', Principles of International Commercial Contracts Working Group on Long-Term Contracts, First Session, UNIDROIT 2014, Study L – Doc. 126, 1-14.

[49] Charles E F Rickett, 'Some Reflections on Open-Textured Commercial Contracting' [2001] *Australian Mining and Petroleum Law Association (AMPLA) Yearbook* 374, 377.

2.2.2.1 Meaning of a Relational Contract

The relational contract is a concept created by Ian Macneil and Stewart Macaulay.[50] Macneil developed and articulated a relational contract theory based on this concept.[51] This theory has, to a great extent, fundamentally changed how contractual relationship and contract law should be understood. The establishment of the relational contract theory has been regarded as highly significant in the formation of modern contract law.[52] It claims that '[w]e are all relationalists now… [a]ll contracts are relational, complex and subjective.'[53]

It has been argued that it is impossible to find a definition that separates relational contracts from non-relational contracts from a legal perspective.[54] It may not be fair to state that it is impossible to define a relational contract, although it could be challenging. Goetz and Scott once proposed that '[a] contract is relational to the extent that the parties are incapable of reducing important terms of the arrangement to well-defined obligations'.[55] The relational characteristic of contracts seems to depend on whether the parties can identify uncertain future contingencies or to characterise complex adaptations taking into account the foreseeable contingencies.[56] This definition has attracted criticism on the grounds of its inadequacy and inaccuracy as it is never possible for the parties to reduce all significant terms of the arrangement to well-defined obligations.[57] Another definition is: 'a relational contract is a contract that involves not merely an exchange but also a relationship, between the contracting parties'.[58] The definition is acceptable to the extent that it emphasises the core role of the relationship between the parties. The ongoing nature of the relationship is emphasised by another definition whereby 'a relational contract may be defined as an agreement of an ongoing nature between two or more

[50] It is argued that the relational aspect of a contract develops from Stewart Macaulay's empirical work and that the term 'relational contract' is conceptualised by Ian Macneil. See Morten Hviid, 'Long-Term Contracts and Relational Contracts' in Boudewijn Bouckaert and Gerrit De Geest (eds), *Encyclopaedia of Law and Economics: The Regulation of Contracts* (Edward Elgar, 2000) vol 3, 46, 53.

[51] Ian R Macneil, *The New Social Contract: An Inquiry into Modern Contractual Relations* (Yale University Press, 1980) 71–117; Macneil has relabelled his relational contract theory as essential contract theory in order to differentiate his theory to other relational contract theories. See, eg, Ian R Macneil, 'Contracting Worlds and Essential Contract Theory' (2000) 9 *Social and Legal Studies* 431, 431–7.

[52] Melvin A Eisenberg, 'Why There is no Law of Relational Contracts' (2000) 94 *Northwestern University Law Review* 805, 821.

[53] Robert E Scott, 'The Case for Formalism in Relational Contract' (2000) 94 *Northwestern University Law Review* 847, 852.

[54] Melvin A Eisenberg, 'Relational Contracts' in Jack Beatson and Daniel Friedmann (eds), *Good Faith and Fault in Contract Law* (Clarendon Press, 1995) 291, 291.

[55] Goetz and Scott, 'Principles of Relational Contracts', above n 29, 1091.

[56] Ibid.

[57] Eisenberg, 'Relational Contracts', above n 54, 294–6.

[58] Ibid.

parties that is typically adapted to changing circumstances and unique situations as they arise.'[59] This definition is supported by the view that 'relational contracts involve ongoing dealings between parties including the impact of periodic changes in their contractual relationships, such as arise from modifications over time and space in the nature of the goods and the quantity, price, and terms of delivery'.[60] Yet another statement focuses on the behaviour and interaction of the parties based on the ongoing relationship arguing that 'the parties are not strangers; much of their interaction takes place "off the contract", mediated not by visible terms enforceable by a court, but by a particular balance of co-operation and coercion, communication and strategy'.[61] Although no comprehensive and universally-accepted definition has been offered, the various definitions suggested to date do refer to or focus on one or more aspects of a relational contract.

Given these different definitions, it should be borne in mind that a relational contract cannot be understood in isolation. Instead, a relational contract should be perceived from a comparative perspective. The word 'comparative' here is better understood in a narrow sense, encompassing the opposite to an ongoing relational contract, namely, a discrete contract encompassing discrete transactions.[62] To better illustrate this point, Macneil stated that all contracts could be arranged along a contract spectrum with the discrete contract at one end, and the relational contract at the other.[63] In his later work, Macneil twice changed this view. In the first instance, he changed the terminology used for the relational pole and called it 'intertwined'; therefore, the discrete contract was at one end of the spectrum and the intertwined contract was at the other.[64] During this period Macneil placed greater emphasis on the combination of discrete and relational aspects of a contract. Later, he recognised the 'highly relational character of all contracts in real life'.[65] He then concluded that 'all contract is relational'.[66] Accordingly, he changed the two ends of the contract spectrum, to the as-if-discrete contract at one end and the relational contract at the other.[67] This change may reflect that, at that stage, Macneil was paying more heed

---

[59] Donald J Smythe, 'Bounded Rationality, the Doctrine of Impracticability, and the Governance of Relational Contracts' (2004) 13 *Southern California Interdisciplinary Law Journal* 227, 230.

[60] Leon Trakman, 'Pluralism in Contract Law' (2010) 58 *Buffalo Law Review* 1031, 1063.

[61] Gillian K Hadfield, 'Problematic Relations: Franchising and the Law of Incomplete Contracts' (1990) 42 *Stanford Law Review* 927, 928.

[62] Ian R Macneil, *Contracts: exchange, transactions and relations cases and materials* (Foundation Press, 2nd ed, 1978) 12–3.

[63] Ibid.

[64] Ian R Macneil, 'Relational Contract Theory as Sociology: A Reply to Professors Lindenberg and de Vos' (1987) 143 *Journal of Institutional and Theoretical Economics (JITE)/ Zeitschrift für die gesamte Staatswissenschaft* 272, 276.

[65] Ian R Macneil, 'Values in Contract: Internal and External' (1984) 78 *Northwestern University Law Review* 340, 344.

[66] Ian R Macneil, 'Relational Contract: What We Do and Do Not Know' (1985) *Wisconsin Law Review* 483, 497.

[67] Ian R Macneil, 'Relational Contract Theory: Challenges and Queries' (2000) 94 *Northwestern University Law Review* 877, 897.

to the relational aspect of a contract. These two changes indicate the evolution of Macneil's relational contract theory. The spectrum now shows the extent to which a contract is relational. Since the extreme relational end does not reflect most modern contract relations,[68] most contracts would be intertwined, floating between the as-if-discrete and relational ends.

A relational contract can be differentiated from a discrete contract in many respects, including relation type, measurability and actual measurement of exchange. It is also distinguishable in including other factors, such as basic sources of social-economic support, duration, commencement and termination, planning, future co-operation required in post-commencement planning and actual performance, incidence of benefits and burdens, obligations undertaken, transferability, number of participants and participant views of transaction or relation.[69]

> Discrete transactions are contracts of short duration, involving limited personal interactions, and with precise party measurements of easily measured objects of exchange, for example, money and grain. They require a minimum of future cooperative behaviour between the parties and no sharing of benefits or burdens. They bind both sides tightly and precisely. The parties view such transactions as deals free of entangling strings, and they certainly expect no altruism. The parties see virtually everything connected with such transactions as clearly defined and presented.[70]

It could be said that relational contracts exist in cases where the contractual relationship between the parties is closer and tighter, and the parties are in a sense 'married' to each other.[71] The most significant distinction lies in the fact that discrete contracts are reflected in 'rational utility-maximising' behaviour, whereas relational contracts require more cooperative behaviour.[72]

2.2.2.2 Characteristics of a Relational Contract

Relational contracts frequently face 'the problem of irreducible uncertainty about future conditions and behaviour.'[73] It is, therefore, vital to understand the features of relational contracts in order to better deal with the uncertainty issue.

It has been said that 'two features largely define what lawyers mean by a relational contract: incompleteness and longevity'.[74] Also, the parties to a relational

---

[68] Macneil, 'Relational Contract Theory as Sociology', above n 64, 280.

[69] Macneil, *Contracts: Exchange, Transactions and Relations Cases and Materials*, above n 62, 14–6.

[70] Ibid, 12.

[71] Nicklisch, 'Advantages of a Doctrine of Long-Term Contracts', above n 4, 25.

[72] Collins, 'Competing Norms of Contractual Behaviour', above n 14, 69.

[73] Christian Joerges, 'Relational Contract Theory in a Comparative Perspective: Tensions between Contract and Antitrust Law Principles in the Assessment of Contract Relations between Automobile Manufacturers and Their Dealers in Germany' (1985) *Wisconsin Law Review* 581, 605.

[74] Alan Schwarts, 'Relational Contracts in the Courts: An Analysis of Incomplete Agreements and Judicial Strategies' (1992) 21 *Journal of Legal Studies* 271, 271.

contract 'rely on each other to behave in a cooperative manner for the duration of the contract, rather than exploiting any opportunity which may come along'.[75] Moreover, the relational contract and the relationship between the parties evolve over time rather than remain unchanged, which makes a relational contract much more fluid and flexible.[76]

Macneil has summarised the typical characteristics of a relational contract:

> The relations are of significant duration (for example, franchising). Close whole person relations form an integral part of the relation (employment). The object of exchange typically includes both easily measured quantities (wages) and quantities not easily measured (the projection of personality by an airline stewardess). Many individuals with individual and collective poles of interest are involved in the relation (industrial relations). Future cooperative behaviour is anticipated (the players and management of the New York Yankees). The benefits and burdens of the relation are to be shared rather than entirely divided and allocated (a law partnership). The entangling strings of friendship, reputation, interdependence, morality, and altruistic desires are integral parts of the relation (a theatrical agent and his clients, a corporate management team). Trouble is expected as a matter of course (A collective bargaining agreement). Finally, the participants never intend or expect to see the whole future of the relation as presentiated at any single time, but view the relation as an ongoing integration of behaviour to grow and vary with events in a largely unforeseeable future (a marriage; a family business).[77]

Speidel has listed distinguishing characteristics of a relational contract:

> A. Extended Duration… B. Open Terms and Reserved Discretion… C. Future Cooperative Behavior is Expected and, Perhaps, Facilitated by Agreed Governance Mechanisms… D. Many Benefits and Burdens of the Relationship Are to Be Shared Rather than Divided and Allocated… E. There May Be 'Transaction-Specific' Investments… F. Close, Whole Personal Relations May Form an Integral Aspect of the Relationship…[78]

Gordon stated that:

> Parties treat their contracts more like marriages than like one-night stands. Obligations grow out of the commitment that they have made to one another, and the conventions that the trading community establishes for such commitments; they are not frozen at the initial moment of commitment, but change as circumstances change; the object of contracting is not primarily to allocate risks, but to signify a commitment to cooperate. In bad times parties are expected to lend one another mutual support, rather than standing on their rights; each will treat the other's insistence on literal performance as wilful obstructionism; if unexpected contingencies occur resulting in severe losses, the parties are to search for equitable ways of dividing the losses; and the sanction for egregiously bad behaviour, is always, of course, refusal to deal again.[79]

---

[75] Hviid, above n 50, 54.

[76] Carl J Circo, 'The Evolving Role of Relational Contract in Construction Law' (2012) 32 *The Construction Lawyer* 16, 16–8.

[77] Macneil, *Contracts: Exchange, Transactions and Relations Cases and Materials,* above n 62, 13.

[78] Richard E Speidel, 'The Characteristics and Challenges of Relational Contracts' (2000) 94 *Northwestern University Law Review* 823, 827–831.

[79] Gordon, above n 49 (Chap. 1), 569.

Relational contracts may include distribution contracts, joint ventures contracts, franchise contracts and employment contracts.[80] They can, in one way or another, reflect the characteristics discussed above.

It is of significant importance of bear the characteristics of a relational contract in mind as they provide a solid foundation for the argument that good faith plays a vital in a long-term relational contract.

2.2.2.3 The Relationship Between Long-Term Contracts and Relational Contracts

A long-term contract is normally contrasted to a short-term contract. Although the duration of the long-term contract seems to be the distinct characteristic which differentiates it from a short-term contract, it may not be its defining characteristic.[81] However, it is the duration that makes a long-term contract, to a large degree, a synonym for a relational contract.[82]

A relational contract is often equated with a long-term contract.[83] A relational contract is usually connected with long-term agreements consisting of open and flexible terms and those agreements always display a high degree of reliance on mutual trust and ongoing co-operation in performance.[84] A natural gas supply contract could be a combination of long-term and the relational factors that a contract contains simultaneously, as this type of contract is expected to be able to deal with both realistic uncertainties of gas production over a long duration of time and to handle various variations in the market and in the relationship between the parties.[85]

A counter argument is that, although a long-term contract and a relational contract are closely related, neither is a subset of the other.[86] The long duration of a contract is not the determining factor which makes it a relational one.[87] Although relational contracts are normally involved in continuing relations[88] and, in most cases, would be long-term contracts, they are not necessarily so.[89] In other words, a relational contract displaying a high degree of reliance might not necessarily be

[80] Goetz and Scott, 'Principles of Relational Contracts', above n 29, 1091.

[81] Ibid.

[82] Eisenberg, 'Relational Contracts', above n 54, 293.

[83] Goetz and Scott, 'Principles of Relational Contracts', above n 29, 1091.

[84] Catherine Mitchell, *Contract Law and Contract Practice: Bridging the Gap between Legal Reasoning and Commercial Expectation* (Hart Publishing, 2013) 175–6.

[85] Terence C Daintith, 'Contract Design and Practice in the Natural Resources Sector' in Fritz Nicklisch (ed), *The Complex Long-Term Contract: Structures and International Arbitration* (C F Müller Juristisch Verlag, 1987) 151, 152.

[86] Hviid, above n 50, 46.

[87] Goetz and Scott, 'Principles of Relational Contracts', above n 29, 1091.

[88] Schwarts, above n 74.

[89] Goetz and Scott, 'Principles of Relational Contracts', above n 29, 1089–1091.

long term, and a long-term contract might not be relational.[90] Also, a short-term contract could be highly relational, and a long-term contract could show many discrete features.[91] Therefore, long duration is not by any means closely linked to a relational contract, and short duration is not connected to a concrete contract.[92] Examples to illustrate this point have been provided by Eisenberg:

> A long-term fixed-rent lease in which the tenant is responsible for maintenance, insurance, and taxes may involve little if any relationship between landlord and tenant. Similarly, a long-term lease of capital equipment, like aircraft, may require almost no contact between the parties, so long as periodic payments are made. In contrast, a four-week contract to remodel a room may be highly relational, as may be a one-day contract between a photographer and a portrait sitter.[93]

2.2.2.4 Why Is the Relational Contract Theory More Appropriate?

A relational contract theory is underpinned by four key propositions:

> First, every transaction is embedded in complex relations. Second, understanding any transaction requires understanding all essential elements of its enveloping relations. Third, effective analysis of any transaction requires recognition and consideration of all essential elements of its enveloping relations that might affect the transaction significantly. Fourth, combined contextual analysis of relations and transactions is more efficient and produces a more complete and sure final analytical product than does commencing with non-contextual analysis of transactions.[94]

Classical and neoclassical contract law can deal well with issues relating to discrete contracts; however, when they are applied to problems arising from relational contracts, they are unable to tackle them adequately and effectively and often yield unfair results.[95] These propositions offer a framework for the relational contract theory and render it more attractive and ideal for the parties to a long-term relational contract.

Firstly, in a changing world, the parties need a contract law which has 'a *Grundnorm* recognising the embeddedness of all exchange in relations.'[96] The relational contract theory analyses, not only the exchange between the parties, but further the relations, including social norms and institutions, in which the exchange occurs.[97] It pays heed to 'the interdependence of individuals in social and economic

---

[90] Mitchell, above n 84, 175.

[91] Ibid.

[92] Eisenberg, 'Relational Contracts', above n 54, 294.

[93] Ibid, 293–4.

[94] Macneil, 'Relational Contract Theory', above n 67, 881.

[95] Paul J Gudel, 'Relational Contract Theory and the Concept of Exchange' (1998) 46 *Buffalo Law Review* 763, 766.

[96] Ian R Macneil, 'Reflections on Relational Contract' (1985) 141 *Zeitschrift für die gesamte Stattswissenschaft/ Journal of Institutional and Theoretical Economics* 541, 542.

[97] Ibid.

relationships'.[98] These relationships may create and focus on other-than-legal rules and sanctions, and parties who do not act according to acceptable practices may lose a relationship or position within a group including other current or potential business partners.[99] It is, therefore, significant for academics, lawyers, judges, arbitrators and other stakeholders to take the relationship between the parties seriously. This is because in contract practice, the 'paper deal' often does not capture the real deal and there is an implicit text between the explicit words.[100] It is important to look beyond the contract terms 'because parties who have, or anticipate, strong relational ties with their contracting opposites are not particularly worried about initial terms of agreement'.[101]

2.2.2.5 Relational Contract Theory in Hardship Cases

In the case of hardship, it is the parties' interdependence, rather than the design of the contract itself and its provisions, that ensures the long-term survival of the relational supply contracts and the continuation of the relationship.[102] This is particularly so in the case of long-term gas, uranium and iron ore supply contracts.[103] It is the real deal rather than the paper deal that determines the normative framework that governs the parties' contract.[104] Much long-term business operates on the basis of the mutual trust and co-operation between the parties and less upon the strict application of legal doctrines that confine that relationship.[105]

Secondly, the long duration of a contract may create complexity and uncertainty. Traditionally well-established contract doctrines may not be able to adequately deal with issues arising from long-term relational contracts due to their uncertain nature and disparate functions.[106] That is to say, those issues may not be effectively tackled by classical and neoclassical contract laws based on the analysis of discrete contracts as a model. For example, classical contract law is not well-adapted to cases where it is necessary and important to maintain a relationship on an ongoing basis.[107] However, those issues may be appropriately addressed by taking into account the

[98] Jay M Feinman, 'Relational Contract Theory in Context' (2000) 94 *Northwestern University Law Review* 737, 748.

[99] Stewart Macaulay et al., *Contracts: Law in Action, the Introductory Course* (Carolina Academic Press, 4th ed, 2016) vol 1, 464.

[100] Stewart Macaulay, 'The Real and the Paper Deal: Empirical Pictures of Relationships, Complexity and the Urge for Transparent Simple Rules' (2003) 66 *Modern Law Review* 44, 44–7.

[101] Thomas M Palay, 'A Contract Does Not a Contract Make' (1985) *Wisconsin Law Review* 561, 562.

[102] Daintith, above n 85, 165.

[103] Ibid, 162–7.

[104] Mitchell, above n 84, 186.

[105] Jonathan Morgan, *Contract Law Minimalism: A Formalist Restatement of Commercial Contract Law* (Cambridge University Press, 2013) 69.

[106] Goetz and Scott, 'Principles of Relational Contracts', above n 29, 1091.

[107] Sharp and Simon, above n 7, 29.

relational aspect of the long-term contract. Because 'the idea of relational contract has the virtue and comfort of being closer to the truth of reality than is the alternative distorted half-truth of the discrete contract idea',[108] and the relational contract law concentrates on 'the necessity and desirability of trust, mutual responsibility, and connection'.[109] The relational contract theory could therefore serve as a more feasible and effective alternative to classical contract law, mainly on the basis of its comprehensiveness in being able to accommodate all contractual issues, including those issues which classical contract theory treats as exceptions.[110]

Thirdly, the relational contract theory may help to bridge the gap between the law and the parties' commercial expectations considering the nature and long duration of the parties' contract. It can offer a combination of stability and flexibility to deal with changing circumstances and unforeseen contingencies.[111]

These advantages of relational contract theory prompt a different understanding of contracts and contract law. Contracts and contract law should be considered from a broader perspective that includes social, political, cultural and economic factors. Macneil defines relational contract law as the law 'which takes into significant account the fact that it is treating contracts towards the relational end of the relational/as-if-discrete spectrum'.[112] Goetz and Scott argue that there should be 'more specialized pre-formulated rules for particular varieties of relational contracts'.[113] There is, however, a view that there is no special relational contract law and all issues with regards to relational contracts should be and can be dealt with adequately using the general principles of contract law.[114] Also, the relational contract theory considers the reality of business and contract practice from a wider social, contextual and relational perspective. Therefore, it is argued that this theory cannot provide any overarching value,[115] and that it cannot offer proper models of contracting behaviour and yield reasonable results.[116]

---

[108] Ian R Macneil, 'Barriers to the Idea of Relational Contracts' in Fritz Nicklisch (ed), *The Complex Long-Term Contract: Structures and International Arbitration* (C F Müller Juristisch Verlag, 1987) 31, 44. To understand why the discrete contract idea reflects only half-truth of the reality, it is necessary and inevitable to bear in mind that the barrier to completely understand the core ideas of the relational contract lies in the conflict between the fact that each person is a selfish atom as Hobbes claimed and the fact that each of us is also a social animal living in various extremely intricate and interwoven relations.

[109] Feinman, 'Relational Contract Theory in Context', above n 98, 748.

[110] David Campbell, 'The Relational Constitution of the Discrete Contract' in David Campbell and Peter Vincent-Jones (eds), *Contract and Economic Organization: Social-Legal Initiatives* (Dartmouth, 1996) 40, 43.

[111] Gudel, above n 95, 765.

[112] Macneil, 'Relational Contract Theory', above n 67.

[113] Charles J Goetz and Robert E Scott, 'The Mitigation Principle: Toward a General Theory of Contractual Obligation' (1983) 69 *Virginia Law Review* 967, 1024.

[114] Eisenberg, 'Why There is No Law of Relational Contracts', above n 52.

[115] Mitchell, above n 84, 181.

[116] Stewart Macaulay, 'Relational Contracts Floating on A Sea of Custom? Thoughts about the Ideas of Ian Macneil and Lisa Bernstein' (2000) 94 *Northwestern University Law Review* 775, 783.

Determining whether there is an independent relational contract law is beyond the scope of the book. However, it appears to be not only necessary but also vital to recognise or develop general principles or rules for long-term relational contracts, taking into account their specific characteristics and potential issues that may arise from them.[117] Special rules proposed to deal with relational contract issues are summarised below.

> (1) Rules that, in the case of relational contracts, would soften or reverse the bite of the rigid offer-and-acceptance format of classical contract law, and the corresponding intolerance of classical contract law for indefiniteness, agreements to agree, and agreements to negotiate in good faith. (2) Rules that would impose upon parties to a relational contract a broad obligation to perform in good faith. (3) Rules that would broaden the kinds of changed circumstances (impossibility, impracticability, and frustration) that constitute an excuse for non-performance of a relational contract. (4) Rules that would give content to particular kinds of contractual provisions that may be found in relational contracts, such as best-efforts clauses or unilateral rights to terminate at will. (5) Rules that would treat relational contracts like partnerships, in the sense that such contracts involve a mutual enterprise and should be construed in that light. (6) Rules that would keep a relational contract together. (7) Rules that would impose upon parties to a relational contract a duty to bargain in good faith to make equitable price adjustments when changed circumstances occur, and would perhaps even impose upon the advantaged party a duty to accept an equitable adjustment proposed in good faith by the disadvantaged party. (8) Rules that would permit the courts to adapt or revise the terms of ongoing relational contracts in such a way that an unexpected loss that would otherwise fall on one party will be shared by reducing the other party's profits.[118]

Also, Feinman proposed a list of open-ended relational standards which he found more useful in resolving contractual issues by taking a relational approach:

> Role, status, and position - the idea that a party should conform to the essential attributes of a role, status, or position that has been defined in a relation; Reciprocity - the idea of mutuality, of a balance between benefits and burdens; Planning and flexibility - the idea of balancing party planning against maintaining flexibility as relations develop; Trust and cooperation - the idea of promoting trust and encouraging cooperation; External social policies and values - the whole range of social policies and values other than those that grow out of the relationship. This standard is differently focused than the others, the notion of internal and external implicated here is useful, but it can be misleading if not used with caution.[119]

Since there is no widely accepted conception of relational contract law, and none seems to be forthcoming in the foreseeable future, the better approach to applying the relational contract theory is to implement a relational understanding of classical and neoclassical contract law. Existing and dominant contract doctrines and rules based on 'one-shot', 'arm's length' and 'low-trust' transactions have been proven

---

[117] Nicklisch, 'Advantages of a Doctrine of Long-Term Contracts', above n 4, 27; See also, Fritz Nicklisch, 'Taking Account of Project Duration and Project Disturbances in Complex Long-Term Contracts' in Fritz Nicklisch (ed), *The Complex Long-Term Contract: Structures and International Arbitration* (C F Müller Juristisch Verlag, 1987) 365, 374.

[118] Eisenberg, 'Why There is No Law of Relational Contracts', above n 52, 817–8.

[119] Jay M Feinman, 'Relational Contract and Default Rules' (1994) 3 *Southern California Interdisciplinary Law Journal* 43, 56.

unable to adequately and effectively deal with issues relating to long-term contracts, especially long-term relational contracts; therefore, deviations from current contract law or creating special rules targeting long-term relational contracts are in high demand.[120] The combination of the theoretical framework and the specially designed rules intended for long-term relational contracts would better protect the parties' interests by reducing, if not eliminating, the uncertainties.

2.3 Long-Term Contracts in the UNIDROIT Principles

The most significant update of the UNIDRPIT Principles 2016 edition, as opposed to the 2010 edition, is the inclusion of articles specifically dealing with long-term contracts. There are no fundamental changes in the new edition. Altogether, there are 210 articles in the 2016 edition, the same number as in the 2010 edition. Of the 210 articles, changes have been made to 13 of them. For five articles,[121] both the black letter rules and their comments have been amended, while for the remaining eight articles,[122] only the comments have been revised. Twelve of the 13 articles deal with issues relating to long-term contracts in one way or another.[123]

2.3.1 'Definition' of a Long-Term Contract

It has been emphasised on various occasions that the UNIDROIT Principles do not offer a 'definition' of a long-term contract, but only a mere 'description' of it. However, the 'description' of a long-term contract does appear in Article 1.11 which is titled 'Definitions'. For this book, the differences between a definition and a description will be ignored and the terminology 'definition' will be used to avoid further confusion.

Article 1.11 states that in the UNIDROIT Principles, a long-term contract means 'a contract which is to be performed over a period of time and which normally involves, to a varying degree, complexity of the transaction and an ongoing relationship between the parties'.[124] A long-term contract is used in the sense that it is 'distinguished from ordinary exchange contracts such as sales contracts to be performed at one time'.[125] This is, to a certain extent, similar to the approach taken by Macneil.

[120] Roberto Unger, 'The Critical Legal Studies Movement' (1983) 96 *Harvard Law Review* 561, 617.

[121] Articles 1.11, 2.1.14, 5.1.7, 5.1.8 and 7.3.7 UNIDROIT Principles 2016.

[122] Articles 2.1.15, 4.3, 4.8, 5.1.3, 5.1.4, 7.1.7, 7.3.5 and 7.3.6 UNIDROIT Principles 2016.

[123] Articles 1.11, 2.1.14, 2.1.15, 4.3, 4.8, 5.1.3, 5.1.4, 5.1.8, 7.1.7, 7.3.5, 7.3.6 and 7.3.7 UNIDROIT Principles 2016.

[124] Article 1.11 UNIDROIT Principles 2016.

[125] Comment 3 of Article 1.11 UNIDROIT Principles 2016.

A long-term contract is defined as being the opposite of a discrete contract or a spot contract.

A long-term contract has three distinct elements: 'duration of the contract', 'an ongoing relationship between the parties', and 'complexity of the transaction'.[126] Of the three elements, the duration of the contract is the defining characteristic for a long-term contract; the second and third elements are not necessarily required.[127] As the duration factor is the most necessary element of a long-term contract under the UNIDROIT Principles, it seems that a series of short-term or spot contracts does not fit the definition provided by the UNDIROIT Principles. That is to say, only a contract which lasts over a significant period of time is considered as a long-term contract. Also, there is no indication as to how long a period of time should be in order for a contract to be considered as a long-term one.[128] Would three years be long enough? How about five years, or ten years? It is hard to know.[129]

2.3.2 *Scope of Application*

The ongoing relationship and complexity become more relevant and crucial when the application of an article in the UNIDROIT Principles presupposes an ongoing relationship and a transaction that is complex.[130] When the ongoing relationship between the parties is involved, the long-term contract between the parties evolves into a long-term relational contract. Therefore, the relevant articles would apply as default rules to long-term relational contracts. It seems reasonable to conclude that the black letter rules in the UNIDROIT Principles would be applicable not only to long-term contracts but also, to a certain extent, to long-term relational contracts. It could be argued that this view is directly and partially supported by several examples of long-term contracts such as distributorship contracts, supply contracts, operation and maintenance agreements, industrial co-operation contracts and

[126] Ibid.

[127] Ibid.

[128] That is probably one of the aspects which reflects what the UNIDROIT Principles mean that they offer only a description of a long-term contract rather than a definition.

[129] In another UNIDROIT document, the UNIDROIT/FAO/IFAD Legal Guide on Contract Farming provides neither a definition nor a description of a long-term contract. It just mentions that an agricultural production contract may be designed as a long-term contract, 'either by specifying a longer period of several years or simply by not specifying an ending term.' It seems that for a contract to be considered as a long-term contract under the Guide its minimum duration would be at least for several years, up till an indefinite period. On the one hand it is certain that a one-year contract is not a long-term contract, such as the annual contract for short-term corps; on the other hand, however, it is still unclear whether several years mean 3, 5 or 10 years. It is impossible to obtain a precise time spot for the determination of a long-term contract. In this regard, this Guide offers no further assistance to understand the 'definition' of a long-term contract in the UNIDROIT Principles. UNIDROIT/FAO/IFAD, *Legal Guide on Contract Farming*, above n 33.

[130] Comment 3 of Article 1.11 UNIDROIT Principles 2016.

construction contracts.[131] Take construction contracts for example: they normally extend over a long period of time and typically are of great complexity, and the relationship between the parties is continuous throughout the construction project.[132] Therefore, construction contracts are long-term relational contracts on the basis that they have all the three elements stated in Article 1.11, and the black letter rules apply to them.

In reality, many types of international, complex long-term contracts are widely used in infrastructure and technology projects, such as the Public-Private Partnership contracts, turnkey construction contracts, operation and maintenance agreements, off-take sales agreements and joint-venture agreements.[133] These contracts share similar characteristics:

complex long-term contracts derive from complex long-term projects,
regulate multi-party relationships through multiple contracts,
throughout a long period subject to changing circumstances,
on different hierarchical levels,
subject to sophisticated risk allocation and mitigation mechanisms,
forming a self-contained rules system,
with a self-enforcing structure,
often based on income stream derived from a market,
normally subject to international arbitration.[134]

Based on these characteristics, they could be regarded as long-term relational contracts; therefore, all fall within the scope of the definition of a long-term contract according to the UNIDROIT Principles. If the UNIDROIT Principles are chosen as the governing law or are to be applied in other ways, their rules could govern these contracts. Because default rules particularly aimed at complex long-term contracts are rarely provided,[135] the application of the UNIDROIT Principles may fill the vacuum.

2.3.3 Rules Relating to Long-Term Contracts

Various issues may arise from a long-term contract, such as open terms, hardship and termination. To better resolve these issues, the UNIDROIT Principles not only provide default rules and mechanisms, but also impose certain duties on the parties to facilitate the performance of the contract and to maintain the relationship between the parties. Regarding default rules and mechanisms, there are, for example, Article 2.1.14 on open terms, Article 4.8 on omitted terms, Article 5.1.7 on price

[131] Ibid.

[132] Herfried Wöss et al., *Damages in International Arbitration under Complex Long-Term Contracts* (Oxford University Press, 1st ed, 2014) 31.

[133] Ibid, 50–61.

[134] Ibid, 39.

[135] Ibid, 35.

determination and Articles 6.2.1 to 6.2.3 on hardship. As to specific duties, there are, for example, duty to co-operate in Article 5.1.3, duty to achieve a specific result and duty of best effort in Article 5.1.4. Apart from these specific treatments relating to long-term contracts, there is also the general principle of good faith in Article 1.7 which may have a vital role in long-term contracts. All these articles together form a comprehensive system consisting, not only of general principles but also specific rules to regulate long-term contracts. This would be of huge value and of great assistance in resolving issues in relation to long-term contracts. It would serve as a basis for the further harmonisation of various existing rules on different types of long-term contracts, and would eventually pave the way for the establishment of a general legal framework with regard to long-term contracts.

2.4 Long-Term Relational Supply Contracts

The differences and connections between long-term contracts and relational contracts have been discussed. Before engaging further, it is necessary to give my own definition of a long-term relational contract. In general, a long-term relational contract would consist of all the three elements that are mentioned in the UNIDROIT Principles.

However, what does a long-term relational contract mean exactly? A long-term relational contract is a contract that is intended to endure and include a course of future dealings between the same parties and is long enough for parties to reasonably establish or maintain an ongoing relationship of mutual trust and confidence based on their exchanges and interactions. Firstly, the contract should endure over a period of time. Regarding how long is enough, the duration should be adequately long for the parties to establish or maintain a close relationship. Without this kind of relationship, the contract would become a long-term contract which is not necessarily relational. Secondly, there must be interactions and exchanges between the parties which could be reflected by their course of future dealings. Time is not the only factor that determines whether they could develop an ongoing relationship: their exchanges and interactions also provide the physical basis for that relationship. Thirdly, the kind of ongoing relationship that is established and maintained between the parties should be based on mutual trust and confidence. If not, both the duration of the contract and the maintenance of the relationship would be adversely affected. Without mutual trust and confidence, a long-term relational contract would be neither long-term nor relational. Finally, the definition of a long-term relational contract is subject to an objective test. It is not the parties who determine whether or not their contract is a long-term relational one. It should be determined from the perspective of a reasonable person.

A minor difference between the requirements of my definition and the elements of the definition in the UNIDROIT Principles lies in the complexity of the dealings between the parties. In most cases, the dealings between the parties to a long-term relational contract are complex, but not necessarily so. It could be a long-term relational contract for sales which require simple exchanges, such as supply and acceptance of goods or services. Merely simple exchange without complex dealing does not affect the long-term relational nature of the contract, although this kind of situation is relatively rare in reality.

Also, it is worth noting that a long-term relational contract could be understood as an evolutionary process, based on which long-term relational contracts may be categorised into two groups. The first group consists of contracts that already have a relational basis at the moment of their conclusion. That is to say, before the parties conclude their long-term contracts, they have already established a relationship based on mutual trust and confidence. That relationship may rest upon their previous business dealings, friendship over a long period of time, or other interactions that have existed before they entered into their contracts. Long-term relational contracts of this type can be considered as 'straightforward' long-term relational contracts. When such a contract is made, the parties are aware of the relationship and the duration of this contract. More probably, because the relationship already exists, the parties decide to enter into the new contract more comfortably and easily.

Contracts in the second group are those that do not have a pre-existing relationship before they are concluded. They are designed as long-term contracts and in time become relational contracts because of the establishment and the evolution of a mutual understanding and a co-operative relationship between the parties. There is a point in time when this transformation occurs. Before reaching that point, those contracts would be as-if-discrete contracts as argued by Macneil. They are relational from a broad perspective but not typically relational as mutual trust and confidence is still being established. After passing that point, they become 'fully' relational and fall under my definition of a long-term relational contract. These types of long-term relational contracts can be regarded as 'evolving' long-term relational contracts.

Furthermore, although there are many types of long-term relational contracts due to different methods of categorisation, it is beyond the scope of the book to investigate all of them in detail. This book, therefore, will concentrate on long-term relational supply contracts. Only occasionally will other kinds of long-term relational contracts be used as ancillary examples to support propositions in this book. Long-term relational supply contracts could be either straightforward or evolving. This does not affect the nature of those contracts being both long-term and relational. They are designed for a long period of time. A liquefied natural gas supply contract can easily last over 25 years.[136] In addition, it could involve complex transactions, frequent interactions, varying commercial and legal circumstances. A long-term crude oil supply contract may include various issues regarding FOB or CIF, finance and so on.[137] Also, the commercial and legal circumstances may vary with time and

[136] Shane B McCarthy, 'Change and Stability in LNG Sales Contract Terms' [1985] *Australian Mining and Petroleum Law Association Yearbook (AMPLA Yearbook)* 210, 216.

[137] Richard M Wiseman, 'Current Problems in International Crude Oil and Petroleum Product Sales' [1985] *Australian Mining and Petroleum Law Association Yearbook (AMPLA Yearbook)* 225, 226–235.

performance continues.[138] Furthermore, such contracts are supported by an ongoing relationship based on the mutual trust and confidence of the parties. For example, long-term supply contracts relating to liquefied natural gas between foreign sellers and Japanese buyers often rest upon a deep and enduring relationship normally regarded as being very special analogous to a marriage and almost impossible for them to get a divorce.[139] This kind of relationship and its maintenance are, by and large, recognised by the parties as essential in order for the dispute resolution mechanisms in their contracts to function effectively.[140] Moreover, in certain long-term relational supply contracts, such as those relating to specialised commodities and services, the investments necessary for the performance of such contracts may be costly and may not be transferable to other contracts or may not be realizable in other ways.[141] For example, the moulds for the production of highly specialised precision tools may not be usable and suitable for other purposes.[142] Again, in contract farming cases, an installed underground water supply system might not be able to be transferred to other projects, or only at the cost of high economic waste. Accordingly, the parties to such contracts may have strong incentives and act in their own best interests to preserve their long-term contractual relationship.[143]

The last point to be made is that there is merit in exploring the distinction on the nature of the parties in the context of long-term relational supply contracts where one party is a state entity in contrast to where both parties are non-state parties, but it is beyond the scope of the book, given that it would require comparison of public law in each jurisdiction as this can have impact on state entities in the conclusion and implementation of contracts, as well as investment treaties in which the state entity may enter into a cross-border investment contract with investor including supply contract elements. Also, although the French law used to recognise hardship only in administrative contracts, it ultimately abolished this approach and recognised hardship in all types of contracts. The French law does not distinguish imprévision depending on whether or not the party is a state entity. This expansion in the scope of hardship may lead a new trend in other countries whose legal systems are based on developments in the French law. Considering this trend, the book considers administrative contracts and commercial contracts alike when examining the parties' duty to renegotiate and the courts or arbitral tribunal's powers to adapt or terminate a contract in the context of hardship. The book also concentrates on the

[138] K M Hayne, 'Problems with Long-Term Contracts: Conflict of Laws' [1986] *Australian Mining and Petroleum Law Association Yearbook (AMPLA Yearbook)* 467, 467–473; I J Hardingham, 'Problems with Long-Term Contracts: Change of Circumstance' [1986] *Australian Mining and Petroleum Law Association Yearbook (AMPLA Yearbook)* 474, 474–5.

[139] McCarthy, above n 136, 210–2.

[140] R M B Reynolds, 'Problems with Long Term Contracts: Alternative Methods of Resolving Disputes' [1986] *Australian Mining and Petroleum Law Association Yearbook (AMPLA Yearbook)* 451, 461–2.

[141] Bell, above n 2, 199.

[142] Ibid.

[143] Ibid.

influence of the nature and characteristics of long-term relational supply contracts and the relationships between the parties instead of focusing on the status of the parties on the parties' duties in the context of hardship.

2.5 Conclusion

Although it is difficult to define a long-term contract and a relational contract, their characteristics are distinguishable but also potentially complementary. These characteristics are important when determining whether a contract is a long-term contract or a relational contract, or a long-term relational contract. It should be borne in mind that a long-term contract is not necessarily a relational one and vice versa. The differences and similarities between the characteristics of a long-term contract and a relational contract renders the relational contract theory important and provoking. The relational contract theory highlights the great significance of the relationship between the parties and suggests that long-term relational contracts should be regulated by special rules. The UNIDROIT Principles, for the first time, put forward a description, if not a 'definition', of a long-term (relational) contract in the context of international commercial contract law. It is based on the description of a long-term contract in the UNIDROIT Principles and the relational contract theory that the book proposes a new definition of a long-term relational contract. In the definition, the ongoing relational and mutual trust and confidence between the parties are emphasised. It is believed that such a definition can help develop special rules for long-term relational contracts and long-term relational supply contracts in particular.

Chapter 3
Hardship Rules in Domestic Laws and International Instruments

3.1 Introduction

The current rules for hardship issues in international commerce are based on a fundamental principle of Roman law called the 'principle of contractual equilibrium'.[1] This principle has two parts dealing with disequilibrium at different stages of a contract. At the negotiation stage, this principle emphasises that there should be no initial disequilibrium in a contract between the parties, while at the performance stage it focuses on the measures that can be taken to tackle the supervening disequilibrium arising from the changed circumstances that occur after the conclusion of a contract.[2] Force majeure doctrine and hardship doctrine are two important doctrines relating to supervening disequilibrium. This book will concentrate on hardship rules relating to the supervening disequilibrium.

This chapter provides a background against which good faith will have a role to play in long-term relational supply contracts. Section 3.2 will outline the differences between the force majeure doctrine and the hardship doctrine. Section 3.3 will briefly discuss how different institutions adopted by domestic laws deal with the problems following hardship. Given the fact that the content, scope and approach of these institutions vary due to different legal cultures, this section will only examine them to the extent that they can be applied to deal with issues arising from hardship from a functional perspective. Section 3.4 will examine in detail the CISG

---

[1] Ahmet Cemil Yildirim, *Equilibrium in International Commercial Contracts: with Particular Regard to Gross Disparity and Hardship Provisions of the UNIDROIT Principles of International Commercial Contracts* (Wolf Legal Publishers, 2010) 1. Contractual equilibrium is closed related to the theory of changed circumstances. More details on this theory, see M. T. Rafiei, *Law of Contract: The Effect of Change in Circumstances a Comparative Study* (Universal Law Publishing, 2003) 64–83

[2] Ibid. See also, Schwenzer, Hachem and Kee, above n 73 (Chap. 1), 666–674.

P. Guo, *Good Faith in Long-Term Relational Supply Contracts in the Context of Hardship from A Comparative Perspective*,
https://doi.org/10.1007/978-981-16-5513-5_3

rules and the UNIDROIT Principles in order to trace the development of the hardship doctrine in international commercial law and international contract practice. Section 3.5 will address the necessity and the importance of the hardship doctrine in the performance of long-term relational supply contracts. Section 3.6 will conclude the chapter.

3.2 Force Majeure and Hardship

For further analysis of the role of good faith in long-term relational supply contracts in the context of hardship, it is worth examining the differences between force majeure and hardship.

The foremost difference between hardship and force majeure lies in the impossibility of fulfilling a contract. In theory it is argued that 'hardship is at stake where the performance of the disadvantaged party has become much more burdensome, but not impossible, while force majeure means that the performance of the party concerned has become impossible, at least temporarily'.[3] This difference in practice may not be as clear as in theory.[4] Relying on the impossibility to distinguish force majeure from hardship is very difficult in certain cases.[5] The distinction between force majeure and hardship can become blurred and too often it is impossible to distinguish force majeure from hardship, as absolute impossibility no longer exists, and most supervening events just render the performance, to a greater or lesser extent, onerous rather than impossible for the party invoking force majeure or hardship.[6]

In addition, the hardship doctrine and the force majeure doctrine serve different purposes and therefore may operate in different ways. The party who invokes force majeure doctrine intends to obtain relief by being exempted from fulfilling his or her contractual obligation, including secondary obligations to pay damages for breach, whereas the party who invokes the hardship doctrine seeks to have the contract adapted or terminated.[7] In other words, the invocation of the hardship doctrine gives the party facing hardship an opportunity to perform his or her obligations in an adapted form, which would allow the contract to continue. In contrast, by invoking the force majeure doctrine, the disadvantaged party has no choice to continue

---

[3] Dietrich Maskow, 'Hardship and Force Majeure' (1992) 40 *American Journal of Comparative Law* 657, 663–4.

[4] Marcel Fontaine and Filip De Ly, *Drafting International Contracts: An Analysis of Contract Clauses* (Martinus Nijhoff Publishers, 2009) 456.

[5] Berger and Erdelyi, above n 74 (Chap. 1), 70.

[6] Ingeborg Schwenzer, 'Force Majeure and Hardship in International Sales Contracts' (2009) 39 *Victoria University of Wellington Law Review* 709, 725. Under certain circumstances, 'onerous' may be comparable to absolute impossible. See Berger and Erdelyi, Ibid.

[7] Michael Bridge, 'The CISG and the UNIDROIT Principles of International Commercial Contracts' (2014) 19 *Uniform Law Review* 623, 635.

performing his or her obligations as the obligor will not be required to perform, and the contract will be unenforceable. This distinction between them is the key to understanding the support for the hardship doctrine, and to the virtue of a unified approach to it.

As to legal consequences, the force majeure doctrine is designed to terminate a contract by discharging the parties from having to perform while the hardship doctrine is intended to save a contract by maintaining the performance and at the same time adapting it to the changed circumstance.[8] In practice, 'a force majeure clause will stress suspension of the obligations, while a hardship clause will be centred on re-negotiation.'[9] Hardship clauses usually require that a contract be renegotiated with a view to adapting it to the changed circumstances, and in the event that the renegotiations fail, they often allow a third person to make recommendations or even adapt the contract, while force majeure clauses often provide for the possibility of termination.[10]

The hardship doctrine may be more useful and necessary to certain types of contracts, such as long-term supply contracts, other than one-shot contracts on the sale of goods.[11] Particularly for long-term relational supply contracts, the hardship doctrine may play a significant role in assisting the parties to achieve their long-term commercial interests given the special long-term relationship that they have established and would not wish to break or terminate easily. One of the main purposes of long-term relational supply contracts is to keep the contract alive and maintain the long-term relationship to enable both parties to obtain that for which they have negotiated. Therefore, the hardship doctrine other than the force majeure doctrine is a more appropriate solution for parties who wish to continue their long-term relational supply contracts.

3.3 Hardship Rules in Domestic Laws

National laws regarding supervening disequilibrium can be categorised into two groups: one that is based on the objective theory that emphasises the equilibrium of a contract, and another that rests on the subjective theory that focuses on the intention and expectations of the parties and the change of the circumstances in which the contract was entered into.[12]

---

[8] Yildirim, above n 1, 88–9. See also, Berger and Erdelyi, above n 74 (Chap. 1), 68.

[9] Fontaine and De Ly, above n 4.

[10] Ingeborg Schwenzer (ed), *Schlechtriem and Schwenzer Commentary on the UN Convention on the International Sale of Goods (CISG)* (Oxford University Press, 4th ed, 2016) 1153.

[11] Bridge, 'The CISG and the UNIDROIT Principles of International Commercial Contracts', above n 7, 635.

[12] Yildirim, above n 1, 49. The Chinese Civil Code entered into force on 1 January 2021. It has officially adopted the objective theory and the approach taken by the UNIDROIT Principles. More details on hardship in Chinese contract law, see Peng Guo and Shu Zhang, 'China's Approach to

3.3.1 *Hardship Rules in Civil Law*

3.3.1.1 German Law

The first theory dedicated to dealing with supervening events in German law is the doctrine of *Voraussetzung* which made it possible to give effect to supervening events; however, this doctrine was not incorporated into the German Civil Code.[13]

The most significant and serious supervening disequilibrium situation faced by the German courts and scholars was the high inflation rate in the first half of the twentieth century caused by the two world wars.[14] Several doctrines were established and developed during that period to provide solutions to the problems caused by high inflation.

Among those doctrines, two less influential objective doctrines are the doctrine of *Unzumutbarkeit* and the doctrine of *Erfüllingzeitraum.*[15] The former clarifies a collapse of the foundation of the transaction,[16] whereas the latter focuses on the economic impossibility in cases where circumstances make the production of the goods too much to ask, meaning that it may be too difficult or too costly to provide the goods.[17]

The most influential doctrine is the doctrine of *Wegfall der Geschäftsgrundlage* based on good faith in Article 242 of the German Civil Code.[18] This doctrine was first introduced by legal scholars,[19] then was recognised and applied by different courts,[20] and eventually was codified in the German Civil Code and entered into force in 2002.[21]

The doctrine of *Wegfall der Geschäftsgrundlage* is now called *Störung der Geschäftsgrundlage* in Article 313 of the German Civil Code which reads:

> [i]f the circumstances which have become the foundation of the contract have seriously altered after the conclusion of the contract and if the parties would not have concluded the

---

the Principle of Change of Circumstances under the New Chinese Civil Code: from the CISG model to the PICC model' 2021 37(1-2) *Journal of Contract Law* 86-104; Peng Guo and Linxuan Li, 'The Reform of Contract Rules in China's New Civil Code – Successes or Pitfalls', (2021) 23(2) *European Journal of Law Reform* 242–263.

[13] Konrad Zweigert and Hein Kötz, *Introduction to Comparative Law* (Tony Weir trans, Clarendon Press, 3rd ed, 1998) 518–9 [trans of: *Einführung in die Rechtsvergleichung* (3rd ed, 1996)].

[14] Ibid, 520–4.

[15] Yildirim, above n 1, 59–60.

[16] Norbert Horn, 'Standard Clauses on Contract Adaptation in International Commerce' in Norbert Horn (ed), *Adaptation and Renegotiation of Contracts in International Trade and Finance* (Kluwer Law International, 1985) 111, 135–6.

[17] Zweigert and Kötz, above n 13, 520.

[18] Reinhard Zimmermann, *Breach of Contract and Remidies under the New German Law of Obligations* (Centro di Studi e Ricerche di Diritto Comparato e Straniero, 2002) 13.

[19] See generally B S Markesinis, W Lorenz and G Dannemann, *the German Law of Obligations, the Law of Contracts and Restitution: A Comparative Introduction* (Clarendon Press, 1997) vol 1, 511–544.

[20] Ibid, 544–615.

[21] Ewoud Hondius and Hans Christoph Grigoleit, 'Overview: Concepts Dealing with Unexpected Circumstances' in Ewoud Hondius and Hans Christoph Grigoleit (eds), *Unexpected Circumstances in European Contract Law* (Cambridge University Press, 2011) 55, 145.

> contract, or would have concluded it with a different content if they had foreseen this alternation, then adaptation of the contract can be demanded in so far as adherence to the unaltered contract cannot be expected of one party taking into consideration all the circumstances of the individual case and in particular the contractual or statutory division of risk.[22]

If the requirements of the doctrine are met, an adaptation of the contract can be demanded.[23] If the adaptation is not possible or cannot be expected by a party, the disadvantaged party can withdraw from the contract; in cases of long-term contracts, the disadvantaged party can unilaterally terminate the contract by notice instead of by withdrawal.[24] The consequence of withdrawal is retrospective, meaning that the performance received is subject to restitution, while that of termination is prospective and leaves past performance untouched.[25]

Apart from Article 313, Article 275(2) of the German Civil Code, representing the doctrine of *Unmöglichkeit* that is intended to apply to cases involving factual impossibility, may also be invoked to deal with hardship situations. It reads:

> The debtor can refuse performance in so far as this requires expenditure which is in gross disproportion to the creditor's interest in performance, having regard to the content of the obligation relationship and the requirement of good faith.[26]

As for the consequence of Article 275(2), the disadvantaged party can choose to either perform the original contractual obligations or refuse to perform by using factual impossibility as a defence.[27] If Article 275(2) is raised, the advantaged party can then raise Article 326(1) to release him or herself from the corresponding performance.[28]

3.3.1.2 French Law

The old French Civil Code does not contain any provision dealing with supervening disequilibrium in general and hardship situations in particular.[29] The traditional approach adopted by French courts is that the principle of *pacta sunt servanda* should be respected and intervention in a contract upon the occurrence of the

[22] Basil S Markesinis, Hannes Unberath and Angus Johnston, *The German Law of Contract: A Comparative Treatise* (Hart Publishing, 2nd ed, 2006) 902.

[23] Ewoud Hondius and Hans Christoph Grigoleit, 'Introduction: An Approach to the Issues and Doctrines Relating to Unexpected Circumstances' in Ewoud Hondius and Hans Christoph Grigoleit (eds), *Unexpected Circumstances in European Contract Law* (Cambridge University Press, 2011) 3, 7–8.

[24] Ridder and Weller, above n 14 (Chap. 1), 385–6.

[25] Ibid, 386.

[26] Markesinis, Unberath and Johnston, above n 22, 886.

[27] Ridder and Weller, above n 14 (Chap. 1), 375–6.

[28] Ibid.

[29] Yildirim, above n 1, 57.

supervening disequilibrium should be rigidly confined.[30] The most famous case that reflects the view of the court in this regard is the *Canal de Crappone* case in which the *Cour de cassation* held that a contract price in a long-term relational contract relating to construction, maintenance and management of irrigation channels could not be revised even if the contract price had been fixed more than 300 years before and had become tremendously low on the ground that the contract price had increased tremendously.[31] The court held that 'in no case shall it be for the courts, however fair their decision may seem, to take into account the passage of time and circumstances in order to modify the parties' contracts and to substitute new clauses for those which were freely accepted by the contracting parties.'[32] In later cases, the *Cour de cassation* maintained its position in this regard and confirmed that the courts could not adapt contracts on the basis of equity or for any other reasons.[33]

Only in the field of administrative cases may the courts adapt contracts in the event of a change of circumstances.[34] The aim of the adaptation is to protect the public interest.[35] The doctrine of *imprévision* was established by the *Conseil d'État* in the famous *Compagnie générale d'éclairage de Bordeaux* case in which the court held that, because of the dramatic increase in the price of coal, a request for an increase of gas price in a long-term gas supply contract was justified and accepted. The court took into account the risk that the streets would be unlit and the difficulty and reduced ability of the *Compagnie d'éclairage de Bordeaux* to supply gas to the City of Bordeaux based on the principle of continuity of public services.[36] Although this decision was followed by subsequent cases,[37] unfortunately the doctrine of *imprévision* was confined to administrative cases, particularly those relating to transport, public works and the distribution market,[38] and could not be applied in civil and commercial cases.[39]

---

[30] Ibid.

[31] Ibid, 57–8.

[32] Bénédicte Fauvarque-Cosson, 'Does Review on the Ground of *Imprévision* Breach the Principle of the Binding Force of Contracts' in John Cartwright and Simon Whittaker (eds), *The Code Napoléon Rewritten: French Contract Law after the 2016 Reforms* (Hart Publishing, 2017) 187, 187.

[33] Rodrigo Momberg Uribe, *The Effect of a Change of Circumstances on the Binding Force of Contracts: Comparative Perspectives* (Intersentia, 2011) 46–7.

[34] Fontaine and De Ly, above n 4, 454.

[35] Barry Nicholas, 'Force Majeure in French Law' in Ewan McKendrick (ed), *Force Majeure and Frustration Contract* (Lloyd's of London, 2nd ed, 1995) 21, 28–9.

[36] Ibid.

[37] Uribe, above n 33, 50–2.

[38] Hondius and Grigoleit, 'Overview: Concepts Dealing with Unexpected Circumstances', above n 21, 147.

[39] Yildirim, above n 1, 58.

Although the doctrine of *imprévision* was not recognised by the old French Civil Code,[40] recent case law has recognised this doctrine to a very limited extent.[41] The *Cour de cassation* in a series of cases held that there was a duty for one party to renegotiate if the performance to be rendered by the other party became excessively onerous, leading to a radical change in the equilibrium of the contract.[42] According to the *Cour de cassation*, the duty to renegotiate is based on the principle of good faith and the duty of loyalty.[43]

The contract law section in the old French Civil Code was modernised and came into force on 1 October 2016.[44] The doctrine of *imprévision* is now recognised and established by Article 1195 which reads as follows:

> [i]f a change of circumstances that was unforeseeable at the time of the conclusion of the contract renders performance excessively onerous for a party who had not accepted the risk of such a change, that party may ask the other contracting party to renegotiate the contract. The first party must continue to perform his obligations during renegotiation. In the case of refusal or the failure of renegotiations, the parties may agree to terminate the contract from the date and on the conditions which they determine or by a common agreement ask the court to set about its adaptation. In the absence of an agreement within a reasonable time, the court may, on the request of a party, revise the contract or put an end to it, from a date and subject to such conditions as it shall determine.[45]

It confers on the disadvantaged party the right to request renegotiations of the contract with the advantaged party upon the occurrence of a change of circumstances.[46] In Article 1195, both 'revise' and 'adaptation' are used. However, there is no clear distinction between the two terms. It is argued that the use of these two terms intends to 'distinguish between two situations (the one in which there is a common agreement and the one where there is none) in practice, the distinction between 'adaptation' and 'revision' is difficult to make'.[47]

If the parties fail to reach an agreement within a reasonable time, Article 1195 confers on the court a broad discretion to revise or terminate the contract.[48] The recognition of the doctrine of *imprévision* may play a particularly important role in dealing with issues relating to long-term contracts affected by hardship events in the future. Also, the long-lasting difference between German law and French law in this

---

[40] Hondius and Grigoleit, 'Introduction: An Approach to the Issues and Doctrines Relating to Unexpected Circumstances', above n 23, 145.

[41] Uribe, above n 33, 44.

[42] Ibid, 55.

[43] Ibid, 55–6, 222.

[44] Solène Rowan, 'The New French Law of Contract' (2017) 66 *International and Comparative Law Quarterly* 805, 805.

[45] John Cartwright and Simon Whittaker (eds), *The Code Napoléon Rewritten: French Contract Law after the 2016 Reforms* (Hart Publishing, 2017) 434.

[46] Rowan, above n 44.

[47] Fauvarque-Cosson, above n 32, 192.

[48] Rowan, above n 44.

regard seems to be disappearing.[49] This may lead to the recognition of this doctrine in other civil law countries whose contract laws or civil codes are based on the old French Civil Code. Eventually, there may be a unified attitude towards the hardship issues and a uniform rule to resolve relevant disputes in the civil law system, and it may even affect the approach of the common law to the same issues.

3.3.2 *Hardship Rules in Common Law*

3.3.2.1 English Law

English contract law does not have the concept of hardship. The issues relating to supervening events are dealt with in the doctrine of frustration.[50] *Paradine v Jane*[51] is the landmark case representing the well-established doctrine of absolute contracts which refers to the strict performance of contractual obligations.[52] In *Taylor v Caldwell,*[53] the court for the first time established the doctrine of frustration to deal with an unexpected change of circumstances which resulted in the impossibility of the contract being fulfilled. This doctrine was applied in *Krell v Henry*[54] and other 'coronation cases' and was extended to situations relating to the frustration of purpose. The content of the doctrine of frustration was well articulated by Lord Radcliffe in *Davis Contractors Ltd v Fareham UDC*:

> Frustration occurs whenever the law recognised that without default of either party a contractual obligation has become incapable of being performed because the circumstances in which the performance is called for would render it a thing radically different from that which was undertaken in the contract. *Nom haec in foedera veni.* It was not this that I promised to do.[55]

It is noteworthy that the doctrine of frustration should be applied within very narrow limits.[56] The courts have no power to adapt a long-term contract to an unforeseen change of circumstances, except in exceptional cases stipulated in the Law

[49] It is argued that the reform of French contract law in this regard is affected not only by national laws but also European projects on the harmonisation of European contract law and the UNIDROIT Principles. Fauvarque-Cosson, above n 32, 205.

[50] See generally, Andrew Burrows, *A Restatement of the English Law of Contract* (Oxford University Press, 2016) 164–8.

[51] 82 Eng. Rep. 897 (K.B. 1647).

[52] The case was criticised that it did not establish the doctrine of absolute contract and was misunderstood. John Wladis, 'Common Law and Uncommon Events: The development of the Doctrine of Impossibility of Performance in English Contract Law' (1987) 75 *Georgetown Law Journal* 1575, 1579–86.

[53] 122 Eng. Rep. 309 (Q.B. 1863).

[54] [1903] 2 K.B. 740.

[55] [1956] AC 696, 728–9.

[56] *Tsakiroglou v Noblee Thori* [1962] A.C. 93, 115 per Lord Simonds; *J Lauritzen AS v Wijsmuller BV* (The Super Servant Two) [1990] 1 Lloyd's Rep. 1, 8 per Bingham LJ.

Reform (Frustrated Contracts) Act 1943.[57] If frustration is established, the contract is terminated automatically and the parties, accordingly, are discharged from the performance of any further obligations; if frustration is not established, the parties must continue to perform the contract.[58] Also, a party may be compensated upon the termination under the Law Reform (Frustrated Contracts) Act 1943.[59]

The strict and narrow application of the doctrine of frustration cannot produce a satisfactory adaptation of the contract which the commercial community would consider as fair.[60] However, no mechanism is available to the courts for them to adapt a contract based on a change of circumstances.[61] Hence, a more flexible approach or mechanism is needed.[62]

3.3.2.2 Australian Law

Like the English contract law, the hardship concept does not exist in Australian contract law. The English contract law's approach to dealing with hardship issues was inherited by Australia contract law. The doctrine of frustration in general and Lord Radcliffe's definition of frustration have been adopted by Australian courts.[63] The scope of the doctrine covers impossibility of performance and frustration of purpose.[64] But it does not apply to impracticality.

Rules regarding the consequences of frustration are the common law rules in Australia which are modelled on the English common law rules in this regard.[65] If a contract is frustrated, termination occurs automatically, and the parties are discharged from all future obligations under the contract.[66] It is noteworthy that New

[57] J Arthur Mcinnis, 'Frustration and Force Majeure in Building Contracts' in Ewan Mckendrick (ed), *Force Majeure and Frustration Contract* (Lloyd's of London, 2nd ed, 1995) 195, 213.

[58] Ewan McKendrick, *Goode on Commercial Law* (Penguin Books, 5th ed, 2016) 154.

[59] Ewan McKendrick, 'The Consequence of Frustration-The Law Reform (Frustrated Contracts) Act 1943' in Ewan Mckendrick (ed), *Force Majeure and Frustration Contract* (Lloyd's of London, 2nd ed, 1995) 223, 223–244.

[60] McKendrick, above n 58.

[61] Uribe, above n 33, 132.

[62] McKendrick, above n 58.

[63] *Codelfa Construction Pty Ltd v State Rail Authority of New South Wales* (1982) 149 CLR 337; *Veremu Pty Ltd v Ezishhop.Net Ltd* [2003] NSWCA 317; *oOh! Media Roadside Pty Ltd v Diamond Wheels Pty Ltd* [2011] VSCA 116

[64] John W Carter, *Contract Law in Australia* (LexisNexis Butterworths, 6th ed, 2013) 760–5.

[65] Ibid, 786–794.

[66] John Gooley, Peter Radan and Ilija Vickcvich, *Principles of Australian Contract Law* (LexisNexis Butterworths, 3rd ed, 2014) 511.

South Wales,[67] Victoria[68] and South Australia[69] have statutes regulating the consequences of frustration as well.[70]

3.3.2.3 American Law

In American law, the hardship issues are dealt with by the doctrine of frustration[71] and the doctrine of commercial impracticability.[72] The doctrine of frustration deals with supervening events that make the exchange worthless to one of the parties while the doctrine of commercial impracticability deals with supervening events which impede performance.[73] The doctrine of frustration was inherited by American law from English Law and appears in the Uniform Commercial Code (hereinafter: the UCC)[74] and in the Restatement (Second) of Contracts (hereinafter: the Restatement 2nd).[75] It applies to cases where the contracts are substantially frustrated.[76]

Apart from the doctrine of frustration, the doctrine of impracticability has been incorporated in the UCC[77] and in the Restatement 2nd.[78][79] The underpinning policy of this doctrine is 'to use equitable principles in furtherance of commercial standards and good faith'.[80] Although there is no explicit definition of impracticability, based on the official comments to the UCC and the Restatement 2nd, impracticability can be defined as an excused performance as a result of an unavoidable event that causes a party to suffer severe, unreasonable and unpredictable hardship.[81] Also, the

---

[67] *Frustrated Contracts Act* 1978 (NSW).

[68] *Australian Consumer Law and Fair Trading Act 2012* (Vic).

[69] *Frustrated Contracts Act* 1988 (SA).

[70] Carter, above n 64, 794–809; Gooley, Radan and Vickcvich, above n 66, 513–8.

[71] The doctrine of frustration is used in a sense that it consists of the doctrine of impossibility and the doctrine of frustration of purpose. The usage and application of the three terminologies, possibility, impracticability and frustration of purpose, is not always clear. Sukhnam Digwa-Singh, 'The Application of Commercial Impracticability under Article 2-615 of the Uniform Commercial Code' in Ewan Mckendrick (ed), *Force Majeure and Frustration Contract* (Lloyd's of London, 2nd ed, 1995) 305, 310–2.

[72] Comment, 'Relief from Burdensome Long-Term Contracts: Commercial Impracticability, Frustration of Purpose, Mutual Mistake of Fact, and Equitable Adjustment' (1982) 47 *Missouri Law Review* 79, 80, 82–3.

[73] Ibid, 82–3, 92–3.

[74] § 2-615 of Uniform Commercial Code.

[75] § 265 and § 266(a) of Restatement (Second) of Contracts.

[76] Comment, 'Equitable Reformation of Long-Term Contracts – The "New Spirit" of ALCOA' (1982) *Utah Law Review* 985, 985–6.

[77] § 2-615 of Uniform Commercial Code.

[78] § 261 of Restatement (Second) of Contracts.

[79] Uribe, above n 33, 160–1.

[80] Comment 6 to § 2-615 of UCC, see Digwa-Singh, above n 71, 305.

[81] Uribe, above n 33, 161–2.

doctrine of impracticability derives from the doctrine of frustration dealing with impossibility in English law; however, impracticability seems to be broader than impossibility.[82]

Generally, in case law, two methods have been applied by the courts to determine impracticability. The first method involves quantitative analysis whereby the court considers the amount of loss, the amount of any increased costs, the whole context of the transaction, and the position of the parties in the relevant market.[83] The second method involves qualitative analysis whereby the court examines the degree to which the performance has been affected.[84] In both methods, the foreseeability, the assumption of risk, the allocation of risk and the existence of severe hardship are important determinants of whether this doctrine applies.[85]

The remedy for impracticability is that the parties are released from further performance. But in practice, 'common law judges historically have refused to spread the burden of a contract discharged because its performance has been rendered commercially impracticable'.[86] Also, although it is argued that a duty to renegotiate exists in the context of impracticability based on the duty to perform in good faith and on the co-operation and flexibility required by the long-term relationship between the parties, this view is not supported by the courts.[87] *Aluminium Co. of America v Essex Group, Inc.*[88] was the first and the only case in which the contract was adapted.[89] In this case, the court asserted that a 'new spirit' of equity would allow judicial adaptation of a long-term contract in the context of hardship.[90] The equitable adaptation is applied to promote the commercial standards and good faith in cases where justice cannot be served.[91]

American law emphasises flexibility while English Law and Australian Law concentrate on the certainty. It is stated that 'English doctrine relies on the source-oriented standard of the parties' agreement or intentions, whereas American law permits 'more content-oriented standards of validity' in the context of hardship.[92]

---

[82] Nottage, 'Changing Contract Lenses', above n 59 (Chap. 1), 395–6.

[83] Uribe, above n 33, 166–9.

[84] Ibid.

[85] 'Relief from Burdensome Long-Term Contracts', above n 72, 83–95.

[86] Trakman, 'Winner Take Some', above n 18 (Chap. 2), 471.

[87] Uribe, above n 33, 177–8; See also John P Bermingham, 'Extending Good Faith: Does the U.C.C. Impose a Duty of Good Faith Negotiation under Changed Circumstances' (1987) 61 *St. John's Law Review* 217, 220–1.

[88] 499 F. Supp. 53 (W.D. Pa. 1980).

[89] Uribe, above n 33, 178–181.

[90] 'Equitable Reformation of Long-Term Contracts', above n 76, 996–9, 1003–7.

[91] 'Relief from Burdensome Long-Term Contracts', above n 72, 104–5.

[92] Luke Nottage, 'Tracing Trajectories in Contract Law Theory: Form in Anglo-New Zealand Law, Substance in Japan and the United States' (2013) 4 *Yonsei Law Journal* 175, 179.

3.4 Hardship Rules Under the CISG and the UNIDROIT Principles

There is a huge difference between civil law and common law jurisdictions when dealing with hardship issues, and even among countries in the same legal tradition.[93] It is very difficult to identify convergence among various jurisdictions as even the legal systems themselves do not have a 'clear, systematic, complete and convincing concept' relating to the legal consequences of hardship situations.[94] Therefore, it is worthwhile examining the rules at the international level to see whether a common framework can be found.

3.4.1 Hardship Rules Under the CISG

The CISG does not contain an article which explicitly stipulates issues on hardship. The aim is to avoid ambiguity, complexity and conflict of the meanings of different terms in domestic laws and to promote the uniform interpretation and application of the CISG. Article 79 of the CISG is the most relevant article which can be used to tackle problems relating to hardship. Article 79 contains a neutral term 'impediment' to mean something similar but not identical. The term 'impediment' is unfamiliar to both civil law and common law lawyers who first encounter it.

Before going into any detail, it is worth citing Article 79 at the outset:

(1) A party is not liable for a failure to perform any of his obligations if he proves that the failure was due to an impediment beyond his control and that he could not reasonably be expected to have taken the impediment into account at the time of the conclusion of the contract or to have avoided or overcome it or its consequences.

(2) If the party's failure is due to the failure by a third person whom he has engaged to perform the whole or a part of the contract, that party is exempt from liability only if:

(a) he is exempt under the preceding paragraph; and
(b) the person whom he has so engaged would be so exempt if the provisions of that paragraph were applied to him.

(3) The exemption provided by this article has effect for the period during which the impediment exists.

(4) The party who fails to perform must give notice to the other party of the impediment and its effect on his ability to perform. If the notice is not received by the other party within

[93] For example, the English law and the New Zealand law are more formal while the US law and the Japanese tend to be more substantive, which illustrates the difference between the Law in Books approach and the Law in Action approach. See Nottage, 'Changing Contract Lenses', above n 59 (Chap. 1).

[94] Ewoud Hondius and Hans Christoph Grigoleit, 'General Comparative Remarks: Converging Tendencies, Remaining Differences and the Unsolved Mystery of Adjustment' in Ewoud Hondius and Hans Christoph Grigoleit (eds), *Unexpected Circumstances in European Contract Law* (Cambridge University Press, 2011) 641, 652–3.

a reasonable time after the party who fails to perform knew or ought to have known of the impediment, he is liable for damages resulting from such non-receipt.

(5) Nothing in this article prevents either party from exercising any right other than to claim damages under this Convention.

Article 79 is essentially an article dealing with exemption in a situation where one party fails to perform his or her contractual obligations by reason of an impediment which is beyond this party's control and which cannot reasonably be foreseen or avoided or overcome.

3.4.1.1 International Interpretation of "Impediment"

Article 79 was drafted to serve international trade and was intended to create its own and special meaning of impediment, rather than to choose from certain existing concepts. The spirit and creation of impediment might be rooted in the existing legal concepts in domestic laws, but it cannot be traced back to any particular domestic legal concept.[95] In order to establish its own system, the CISG deliberately avoided the adoption of or reference to certain domestic legal concepts which are normally applied to deal with similar situations, such as force majeure and frustration.[96] This was intended to prevent misinterpretation and confusion arising from the different understandings of the same or a similar concept in various domestic laws.

Also, the UNCITRAL Working Group intended to guarantee a 'narrow and objective' construction of Article 79.[97] The term 'impediment' was chosen to express and emphasize the objective nature and external character of the impediment envisaged in the CISG.[98]

Therefore, to respect the CISG itself and the efforts of the drafters, Article 79 ought to be interpreted in light of the intention that it should be understood at the international level, be interpreted according to the system in which the CISG is embedded or which it intends to create and be kept separate and independent from various domestic laws in order to avoid misunderstanding.

[95] Fritz Enderlein and Dietrich Maskow, *International Sales Law, United Nations Convention on Contracts for the International Sale of Goods, Convention on the Limitation Period in the International Sale of Goods* (Oceana Publications, 1992) 320.

[96] C M Bianca and M J Bonell (eds), *Commentary on the International Sales Law: the 1980 Vienna Sales Convention* (Giuffrè, 1987) 574.

[97] Peter Schlechtriem and Ingeborg Schwenzer (eds), *Commentary on the UN Convention on the International Sale of Goods (CISG)* (Oxford University Press, 2nd (English) ed, 2005) 812.

[98] Bianca and Bonell, above n 96, 579–580.

3.4.1.2 Article 79 and Hardship

There are different arguments in regard to the relationship between Article 79 and hardship as the terminology 'impediment' was not defined by the drafters of the CISG.[99] It is generally agreed that an impediment under Article 79 includes *force majeure* if the requirements of Article 79 are met.[100] However, it remains debatable whether Article 79 is limited to *force majeure* or whether it can be interpreted flexibly in order to cover hardship rules; there is still no clear answer to this.

There have been heated debates on whether hardship rules should be included in the CISG prior to the finalisation of the texts of the CISG in the drafting process. According to the drafting history, hardship was excluded from the scope of Article 79.[101] The intention of the UNCITRAL Working group was not to confer on the promisor a right to invoke hardship rules.[102] In addition, the rejection of a Norwegian proposal to extend the scope of Article 79 to hardship might indicate that the drafters of the CISG deliberately excluded hardship rules from the CISG.[103] It, therefore, may be inferred that there was some consensus regarding the exclusion of hardship rules from the CISG in general and in Article 79 in particular.[104]

The final wording of Article 79 is a compromise. It seems that the CISG has chosen to give priority to the principle of *pacta sunt servande*[105] and to stick to a strict interpretation of it.[106]

There are three views on the scope of Article 79. The first view is that it is completely impossible to apply hardship rules to contracts governed by the CISG.[107] The silence of the CISG on hardship issues amounts to an implicit and positive exclusion of it and leaves no gap to be filled by the application of other articles in the CISG

---

[99] Roberto Pirozzi, 'The Effect of Changing Circumstances in International Commercial Contracts: The Scaform Case' (2012) 16 *The Vindobona Journal of International Commercial Law and Arbitration* 207, 220.

[100] Schwenzer, *Schlechtriem and Schwenzer Commentary on the UN Convention on the International Sale of Goods (CISG)*, above n 10, 1136–7.

[101] Joern Rimke, 'Force Majeure and Hardship: Application in International Trade Practice with Specific Regard to the CISG and the UNIDROIT Principles of International Commercial Contracts' *Pace Review of the Convention on Contracts for the International Sale of Goods (1999–2000)* (Kluwer Law International, 2001) 197, 217–8.

[102] Schlechtriem and Schwenzer, above n 97, 823.

[103] Alejandro M Garro, 'CISG Advisory Council Opinion No 7 – Exemple of Liability for Damages under Article 79 of the CISG' in Ingeborg Schwenzer (ed), The CISG Advisory Council Opinions (Eleven International Publishing, 2017) 167, 183.

[104] Ibid.

[105] Hans-W Micklitz and Leticia Diez Sanchez, 'The Politics of Fairness in CISG' in Ingeborg Schwenzer (ed), *35 Years CISG and Beyond* (Eleven International Publishing, 2016) 269, 283–4.

[106] Stefan Kröll, Loukas Mistelis and Pilar Perales Viscasillas (eds), *UN Convention on Contracts for the International Sale of Goods (CISG)* (C H Beck, 2011) 1088.

[107] Paulo Nalin, 'International Fair Trade (Fair Trade in International Contracts and Ethical Standard)' in Ingeborg Schwenzer (ed), *35 Years CISG and Beyond* (Eleven International Publishing, 2016) 317, 339.

for the incorporation and application of the hardship doctrine.[108] The second view claims that on the basis of court decisions and arbitral awards as well as academic writings, it is more or less generally accepted that Article 79 covers the issues with regard to hardship, as hardship may be considered as a particular set of cases under the general *force majeure* provisions.[109] The CISG Advisory Council expressed the same view in its Advisory Opinion.[110] This view provides, not only sufficient flexibility to reach just and equitable decisions and guarantee legal certainty, but also promotes the application of good faith and fair dealing in international sales law.[111] The third view suggests that one cannot determine with sufficient certainty that the CISG regime was designed and actually widely used for the purpose of dealing with the hardship issue on the basis that the corresponding remedies deriving from the application of the hardship doctrine, such as renegotiation or adaption of contracts did not seem to be available to the parties under the CISG.[112] In addition, it is posited that the text and the legislative history of Article 79 leave room for debate on whether or not it covers hardship.[113] Even if Article 79 includes hardship, there is still a concern that the CISG does not provide explicit rules regarding those cases of hardship that amount to an impediment and the remedies that are available to the aggrieved party.[114] This view seems more reasonable due to the vagueness of the consequences of hardship and the absence of remedies available in Article 79.

Moreover, although hardship is not expressly provided for under the CISG, there are still views on how hardship rules can be invoked under Article 79.[115] The CISG Advisory Council favours the direct application of Article 79 to deal with hardship issues.[116] Another view is that the CISG rules imply the hardship doctrine and the application of hardship rules is feasible via Article 7(2).[117] Schlechtriem argues that the CISG has a shortcoming in relation to hardship which is not fully covered by Article 79, although it is possible to develop a similar doctrine under Article 7(2) by invoking the general principles of the CISG to address the shortcoming. Those prin-

[108] Bridge, 'The CISG and the UNIDROIT Principles of International Commercial Contracts', above n 7, 635–7.

[109] See, eg. Schwenzer, 'Force Majeure and Hardship in International Sales Contracts', above n 6, 713, 715.

[110] Alejandro M Garro, above n 103, 181. Recently, the CISG Advisory Council has published an opinion on "Hardship under the CISG", see CISG Advisory Council Opinion No. 20, Rapporteur: Prof. Dr. Edgardo Munoz, 2020, www.cisgac.org. On the comparison of the hardship rules under the CISG and in the Chinese Civil Code, see Peng Guo, Shu Zhang and Linxuan Li, CISG and Chinese Contract Law Reform in the New Chinese Civil Code: Impacts, Interactions and Implications (2021) 37(3) *Journal of Contract Law* 192, 203–5.

[111] Schwenzer, 'Force Majeure and Hardship in International Sales Contracts', above n 6, 725.

[112] Rimke, above n 101, 218–227.

[113] Brunner, above n 70 (Chap. 1), 110.

[114] Schwenzer, 'Force Majeure and Hardship in International Sales Contracts', above n 6, 713.

[115] Clayton P Gillette and Steven D Walt, *The UN Convention on Contracts for the International Sale of Goods: Theory and Practice* (Cambridge University Press, 2nd ed, 2016) 302–315.

[116] Alejandro M Garro, above n 103, 186–7.

[117] Nalin, above n 107.

ciples include good faith which requires that both parties attempt to adapt the contract in the case of unforeseeable developments.[118] Yet another view is that Article 79 can be interpreted to cover hardship in accordance with Article 7(1) by using the UNIDROIT Principles and the PECL as complementary tools.[119] However, it is argued that 'hardship is not a term nor principle which can be imported into the CISG via the [UNIDROIT] Principles' because they do not have the same structure or approach regarding the hardship topic.[120] Also, the use of the UNIDROIT Principles or other non-legislative documents as complementary sources to address the shortcomings of the CISG are criticised as they contravene an express rule in Article 7(2) and may increase the non-uniform interpretation and application of the CISG in the name of pursuing a uniform interpretation and application.[121]

The theoretical basis for the inclusion of hardship in the CISG is the Convention's strict application of the principle of *pacta sunt servanda* which is inconsistent with the principle of *clausula rebus sic stantibus*[122] that is designed to rebalance the interests between the parties when a balance is altered by unforeseeable circumstances.[123]

In judicial practice, the obligor is, by and large, required to assume the risk of occurrence of hardship events.[124] Until 2008, no single court or tribunal case had been reported in which a party, be it a buyer or a seller, had been exempted from the liabilities by reason of hardship under an international sales contract governed by the CISG.[125] However, the Belgian Supreme Court in 2009 held that the CISG covered the hardship issue by using the gap-filling provisions of Article 7.[126] Also, in one case, the Polish Supreme Court applied Article 79 to discharge the seller from his obligations due to hardship.[127] In other cases relating to Article 79, hardship rules have been invoked, and these cases have been decided in various countries such as Spain, Netherland, Belgium, the United States, Germany, Russia, France and China, in different years.[128]

---

[118] Harry M Flechtner (ed), 'Transcript of a Workshop on the Sales Convention: Leading CISG Scholars discuss Contract Formation, Validity, Excuse for Hardship, Avoidance, Nachfrist, Contract Interpretation, Parol Evidence, Analogical Application, and Much More' (1999) 18 *Journal of Law and Commerce* 191, 236–7.

[119] Pirozzi, above n 99, 219.

[120] Bruno Zeller, *Damages under the Convention on Contracts for the International Sale of Goods* (Oceana Publications, 2nd ed, 2005) 170

[121] Harry M Flechtner, 'Uniformity and Politics: Interpreting and Filling Gaps in the CISG' in Peter Mankowski and Wolfgang Wurmnest (eds), *Festschrift für Ulrich Magnus zum 70. Geburtstag* (Sellier European Law Publishers, 2014) 193, 203–5.

[122] It is a principle which makes the validity of a contract depend on the continuance of the circumstances at the time of its conclusion. Zweigert and Kötz, above n 13, 518.

[123] Micklitz and Sanchez, above n 105, 283.

[124] Kröll, Mistelis and Viscasillas, above n 106.

[125] Schwenzer, 'Force Majeure and Hardship in International Sales Contracts', above n 6, 716.

[126] Anna Veneziano, 'UNIDROIT Principles and CISG: Change of Circumstances and Duty to Renegotiate according to the Belgian Supreme Court' (2010) 15 *Uniform Law Review* 137, 137–149.

[127] Micklitz and Sanchez, above n 105, 284.

[128] For more details, see cases coded as '79B' by the UNCITRAL thesaurus, available at http://www.cisg.law.pace.edu/cisg/text/digest-cases-79.html. Ibid.

3.4.2 Hardship Rules Under the UNIDROIT Principles

Unlike the CISG, hardship issues are explicitly dealt with by Articles 6.2.1, 6.2.2 and 6.2.3 of the UNIDROIT Principles. The hardship doctrine and the relevant articles are an innovation of the UNIDROIT Principles. It is envisaged that they will deal with situations in which the occurrence of an event radically changes the balance of the interests of the parties to a contract. They are designed to meet the need for fairness in international commercial contracts that dominates current contractual, arbitral and judicial practice.[129]

Hardship rules under the UNIDROIT Principles are most likely to be invoked and applied under long-term contracts where it can be difficult, or even impossible, for the parties to predict an event that will occur and to draft corresponding clauses for such events that may have an influence on the original duties of the parties under the contract.[130] Therefore, articles on hardship issues in the UNIDROIT Principles can be of tremendous significance to the parties to a long-term contract who are facing an unforeseen and substantial change of circumstances and who do not have a hardship clause in the long-term contract but intend to continue to perform the outstanding obligations of their contract.[131]

3.4.2.1 Hardship Rules as an Exception

Article 6.2.1 is the starting point for a further examination of articles on hardship rules in the UNIDROIT Principles. Article 6.2.1 reads:

> Where the performance of a contract becomes more onerous for one of the parties, that party is nevertheless bound to perform its obligations subject to the following provisions on hardship.

Article 6.2.1 is titled 'Contract to be observed'. The purpose of this title is to make it clear that, according to the binding nature of the contract, performance must be rendered as long as it is possible and regardless of the burden it may impose on the performing party.[132] Therefore, 'even if a party experiences heavy losses instead of the expected profits or the performance has become meaningless for that party the terms of the contract must nevertheless be respected'.[133] However, the binding nature of contracts is not an absolute principle.[134] Where the supervening circumstances lead to a fundamental alteration of the original equilibrium of the contract

---

[129] Yildirim, above n 1, 2.

[130] Stefan Vogenauer (ed), *Commentary on the UNIDROIT Principles of International Commercial Contracts (PICC)* (Oxford University Press, 2nd ed, 2015) 810.

[131] Ibid, 811.

[132] Comment 1 to Article 6.2.1 UNIDROIT Principles 2016.

[133] Ibid.

[134] Comment 2 to Article 6.2.1 UNIDROIT Principles 2016.

amounting to hardship,[135] an exception to the general rule may come into play. The message delivered by Article 6.2.1 is that the general duty is to perform, and that relief is very much the exception; this has been well received and applied by international arbitration institutes and domestic courts in many cases.[136]

3.4.2.2 Definition of Hardship

The definition of hardship is dealt with in Article 6.2.2 which provides that:

> There is a hardship where the occurrence of events fundamentally alters the equilibrium of the contract either because the cost of a party's performance has increased or because the value of the performance a party receives has diminished, and
>
> (a) the events occur or become known to the disadvantaged party after the conclusion of the contract;
>
> (b) the events could not reasonably have been taken into account by the disadvantaged party at the time of the conclusion of the contract;
>
> (c) the events are beyond the control of the disadvantaged party; and
>
> (d) the risk of the events was not assumed by the disadvantaged party.

Hardship is defined as a situation where the occurrence of events fundamentally alters the equilibrium of the contract, and the events meet the requirements provided for in sub-paragraphs (a) to (d).

3.4.2.3 Elements of Hardship

It can be inferred from Article 6.2.2 that whether or not an event constitutes hardship depends on the seriousness of its consequence and the foreseeability and controllability of its occurrence from the parties' perspective. Even though it is from the parties' perspective, an objective approach should be adopted meaning that the test in respect of foreseeability and controllability is to determine whether a reasonable person situated in the same position as the parties would be able to foresee and control the occurrence of the event that may trigger hardship.

For an event to be considered as resulting in a hardship situation, it must fundamentally alter the equilibrium of the contract as a result of either the increased cost of a party's performance or the decreased value of the performance a party receives.[137] If there is a situation where neither the cost of the performance due has increased nor has the value of the performance owed has decreased owing to the occurrence of a supervening event, the situation may not be considered as hardship. Also, Article 6.2.2 does not clarify the meaning of 'fundamentally'. It is suggested

---

[135] Ibid.

[136] Vogenauer, *Commentary on the UNIDROIT Principles of International Commercial Contracts (PICC)*, above n 130, 813.

[137] Comment 2 to Article 6.2.2 UNIDROIT Principles 2016.

that the word 'fundamentally' rather than 'materially', 'substantially' or other alternative words was employed to impose a higher threshold, thereby narrowing the scope of the hardship doctrine.[138] However, the meaning of 'fundamentally' is left open and can be determined only by taking into account the facts and all other circumstances surrounding the individual case.[139] This eventually becomes an issue of contract interpretation. As good faith in Article 1.7 is a general principle of the UNIDROIT Principles, it should also apply in the interpretation of an issue arising from the application of the UNIDROIT Principles. Therefore, it requires the party who intends to rely on the hardship articles to act in good faith when claiming that an event has resulted in hardship and when requesting renegotiation or resorting to the courts to adapt or terminate the contract on the basis of hardship.

In addition, Article 6.2.2 does not stipulate the extent of the increase of the cost or the decrease of the value of the performance. If, for the disadvantaged party, the performance has not exceeded a certain point, such as becoming substantially more onerous or radically increasing the burden of performing, there is unlikely to be a 'fundamental' alteration in the equilibrium of the contract.[140]

Apart from the requirement that performance has been fundamentally altered, four other elements should be established before the hardship rules apply. The four elements are listed in sub-paragraphs (a) to (d) of Article 6.2.2. These four sub-paragraphs deal mainly with the foreseeability and controllability of an event.

Sub-paragraphs (a) and (b) focus on the timing of the occurrence of the event which should be after the contract was entered into and on the foreseeability of the event which means that the event could not be reasonably foreseen by the disadvantaged party when the contract was concluded. In other words, if the event occurred before or at the time when the contract was made or even if the event happened after the conclusion of the contract, and if the disadvantaged party could have taken it into account, then the disadvantaged party cannot invoke the hardship rules. However, sometimes the event may have developed gradually, and only the final consequence of those gradual changes may constitute hardship.[141] If the change began to occur before the contract was entered into, it would not cause hardship, unless the pace of change increased dramatically during the course of the contract.[142] Although sub-paragraph (b) does not define 'dramatically', an 80% devaluation of a currency may fall within the scope of 'dramatically' on the basis of the illustration provided in this regard.[143]

Sub-paragraphs (c) and (d) regulate the degree of the risk relating to the event, meaning that the event should be outside the control of the disadvantaged party and

---

[138] Vogenauer, *Commentary on the UNIDROIT Principles of International Commercial Contracts (PICC)*, above n 130, 813.

[139] Ibid, 814.

[140] Ibid, 816–7.

[141] Comment 3 to Article 6.2.2 UNIDROIT Principles 2016.

[142] Ibid.

[143] Illustration 3 in Comment 3 to Article 6.2.2 UNIDROIT Principles 2016.

the risk of the event occurring should not be assumed by the disadvantaged party. Unlike the foreseeability in sub-paragraph (b), the word 'reasonably' is not used in sub-paragraph (d) on the assumption of the risk, which may impose a limitation on the possibility of the assumption of the risk. It remains unclear whether or not the objective test is still applicable. In addition, the word 'assumption' makes it clear that the risk may be due to the very nature of the contract.[144] A party who enters into a speculative transaction is deemed to accept some degree of risk, even if he or she may not have been fully aware of the nature and extent of that risk when the contract was concluded.[145]

3.4.2.4 Scope of Hardship

Hardship is relevant only with regard to performance yet to be rendered. Once a party has performed his or her obligations, the party is no longer entitled to invoke a substantial increase in the costs of the performance or a substantial decrease in the value of the performance as a result of a change of circumstances that occurs after the performance.[146]

If the fundamental alteration of the equilibrium of the contract occurs at a time when the performance has been only partially rendered, hardship can play a role only in resolving issues in relation to the part of the performance still to be rendered.[147] Another important point is that hardship is normally of special relevance to long-term contracts in general and long-term relational contracts in particular.[148]

In cases where the facts of a situation can at the same time be considered as both hardship and force majeure, it is for the disadvantaged party to decide which remedy to pursue. On the one hand, if the party invokes the force majeure rules in Article 7.1.7, it means that an excuse for non-performance is being sought; on the other hand, if the party invokes hardship rules, this suggests that the party intends to renegotiate the terms of the contract in order to maintain the contract.[149]

3.4.2.5 Effects of Hardship

Effects of hardship are dealt with in Article 6.2.3 of the UNIDROIT Principles which reads:

[144] Comment 3 to Article 6.2.2 UNIDROIT Principles 2016.

[145] Ibid.

[146] Comment 4 to Article 6.2.2 UNIDROIT Principles 2016.

[147] Ibid.

[148] Comment 5 to Article 6.2.2 UNIDROIT Principles 2016.

[149] Comment 6 to Article 6.2.2 UNIDROIT Principles 2016.

(1) In case of hardship the disadvantaged party is entitled to request renegotiations. The request shall be made without undue delay and shall indicate the grounds on which it is based.

(2) The request for renegotiation does not in itself entitle the disadvantaged party to withhold performance.

(3) Upon failure to reach agreement within a reasonable time either party may resort to the court.

(4) If the court finds hardship it may, if reasonable,

(a) terminate the contract at a date and on terms to be fixed, or

(b) adapt the contract with a view to restoring its equilibrium.

A two-step approach is provided for considering the effects of hardship. The first step is renegotiation, and if it fails, the second step is adaptation of the contract, or its termination. There is no explicit obligation imposed on the non-disadvantaged party to be positively engaged in renegotiations with the disadvantaged party.[150] Whether it is a mandatory duty could be in dispute. If could be inferred that the duty may be of a mandatory nature, as comment 5 in this article states that 'once the request has been made, both parties must conduct the renegotiations in a constructive manner…' It is also argued by scholars that the renegotiation by its very nature is compelled.[151] The 'request' seems to impose a duty on the other party to renegotiate.[152] Schlechtriem agrees that, firstly, the parties 'have to' renegotiate and if they cannot reach an agreement, they can then turn to the court which may adapt the contract to the changed circumstances, or terminate the contract.[153]

In addition, if the court decides to adapt a contract in response to the hardship situation, are the parties obliged to accept the adjustment? It seems that when the economic balance of the contract is substantially and severely disrupted by the hardship situation, a judge-made adjustment can be imposed on parties.[154]

3.5 The Recognition of Hardship in Long-Term Relational Supply Contracts

In long-term contracts, particularly in long-term relational supply contracts, it is possible that the circumstances will change substantially, when performance of the contracts is due.[155] All the rules discussed above regarding supervening disequilibrium, be it in the domestic laws or in the international convention or soft laws, are

---

150 Vogenauer, *Commentary on the UNIDROIT Principles of International Commercial Contracts (PICC)*, above n 130, 819.

151 Perillo, above n 11 (Chap. 1), 25–6.

152 Flechtner, 'Uniformity and Politics', above n 121, 200.

153 Flechtner, 'Transcript of a Workshop on the Sales Convention', above n 118, 235.

154 John O Honnold and Harry M Flechtner, *Uniform Law for International Sales under the 1980 United Nations Convention* (Kluwer Law International, 4th ed, 2009) 628.

155 Fontaine and De Ly, above n 4, 453.

of practical significance for the parties to a long-term relational supply contract facing problems relating to the possibility of changes in circumstances for the duration of their long-term relational supply contract.[156]

In theory, it is argued that the stability of contracts shall be kept and that the necessary flexibility of contracts shall be guaranteed as well,[157] as the parties have the desire to recognise that hardship events may alter the nature of their obligations under the long-term relational supply contract.[158] In practice, the parties often attempt to strike a balance between flexibility and stability.[159] They insert different clauses into the contracts to allow for the adaptation of their contracts[160]; on the other hand, they often restrict the mechanism with regard to the adaptation of contract terms. The worst scenario is when there is no explicit clause in the contract providing for adaptation. This section of the book will show that the parties to a long-term relational supply contract intend to maintain their contracts by adaptation and will often insert a hardship clause to achieve this goal.

3.5.1 Maintain or Abandon the Contract in the Context of Hardship?

When facing a hardship situation, the parties to a long-term relational contract are more likely to keep their contract alive and maintain their ongoing relationship by reaching an agreement to adapt the contract terms. In the context of hardship, the adaptation of a contract could be a more convenient and more efficient solution than its termination.[161] For example, a long-term supply contract that requires a minimum number of deliveries may be affected by an economic crisis, and the purchaser who is compelled to reduce his production substantially may obtain the consent of the other party to reduce the agreed minimum by invoking hardship rules.[162] Schmitthoff expressed a similar view regarding long-term construction and supply contracts.

> Long-term contracts for the construction of works or installations, the periodic supply of goods or the regular performance of services may produce a problem which is unlikely to

[156] Yildirim, above n 1, 50.

[157] Horn, 'The Concepts of Adaptation and Renegotiation in the Law of Transnational Commercial Contracts', above n 10 (Chap. 1).

[158] Aubrey Diamond, 'Force Majeure and Frustration under International Sales Contracts' in Ewan Mckendrick (ed), *Force Majeure and Frustration Contract* (Lloyd's of London, 2nd ed, 1995) 257, 265.

[159] Keith J Crocker and Scott E Masten, 'Pretia Ex Machina? Prices and Process in Long-Term Contracts' (1991) 34 *The Journal of Law and Economics* 69, 73.

[160] Examples include a hardship clause, a gross inequity clause, a price adjustment clause or a renegotiation clause.

[161] Yildirim, above n 1, 50–1.

[162] Fontaine and De Ly, above n 4, 455.

> be encountered in an ordinary transaction aimed at the execution of a single object. In the course of performing a long-term contract economic, political or social circumstances may change fundamentally in a manner entirely unforeseen and unforeseeably by the parties. That fundamental change may constitute an event entitling either of them to contend that the contract is frustrated or to invoke a force majeure clause under which he may claim suspension or termination of the contract. But that is not the intention of the parties. They wish to continue their contractual relationship and to implement it but to wish to adapt the contract to the changed circumstances.[163]

For long-term relational supply contracts, the mutual trust and confidence of the parties and the relational nature of their contract render the preservation of their contractual relationship particularly important.

3.5.2 *Hardship Clauses in Long-Term Relational Supply Contracts*

In long-term international commercial contracts, clauses anticipating fundamental changes in circumstances surrounding the contracts are widely used, such as force majeure clauses.[164] Since the second half of last century, hardship situations have occurred much more frequently with the concurrent or subsequent changes in economic, political and social circumstances. The two world wars, the closure of the Suez Canal, the oil crisis in the 1970s, and the fall of the Eastern Bloc were times when there was an increasing and significant need for the adaptation of long-term contracts.[165]

Hence, hardship clauses have been included to substitute for or complement the traditional, widely-used force majeure clauses.[166] Hardship clauses have been included in long-term relational supply contracts due to the vulnerability of such contracts over the long period of performance.[167] The insertion of hardship clauses in international commercial contracts increased dramatically due to the ethical concerns about the protection of weaker parties in international commerce, the changes in the global political and economic situations, and the influence of the oil crisis.[168]

To avoid the courts' or the arbitral tribunals' inability to offer satisfactory solutions to adapt long-term relational supply contracts to meet the needs of the parties and to accommodate the changes required by emerging hardship situations, a hardship clause is used to make contracts more flexible so that they can be adapted when

[163] Clive M Schmitthoff, 'Hardship and Intervener Clauses' in Chia-Jui Cheng (ed), *Clive M Schmitthoff's Select Essays on International Trade Law* (Martinus Nijhoff Publishers and Graham and Trotman, 1988) 415, 415.

[164] Horn, 'Standard Clauses on Contract Adaptation in International Commerce', above n 16, 130.

[165] Yildirim, above n 1, 51.

[166] Horn, 'Standard Clauses on Contract Adaptation in International Commerce', above n 16, 131.

[167] Fontaine and De Ly, above n 4, 459.

[168] Yildirim, above n 1, 11.

hardship occurs.[169] They not only define the limits of contractual liability, but also offer a complementary mechanism to allocate risks and duties to the parties and to guide the parties in reaching a flexible resolution to issues arising from hardship via renegotiation.[170]

3.6 Conclusion

This chapter offers an overview of hardship rules in domestic laws and in international instruments. There rules serve as a background for the further analysis of the application of good faith in a long-term relational supply contract.

In both civil law and common law systems, the principle of *pacta sunt servanda* has a solid foundation.[171] Problems arising from the hardship events entail an exception to the strict application of this principle. Different domestic laws have been developed and adopted by various institutions to deal with such problems. In the CISG, whether or not Article 79 applies to hardship cases is still debatable. What is clear is that Article 79 is 'ill-suited' to dealing with cases with regard to hardship.[172] In the UNIDROIT Principles, Articles 6.2.1 to 6.2.3 deal explicitly with hardship issues. If hardship is established, the parties have a duty to renegotiate, and if the renegotiation fails, the court can terminate or adapt the contract. It is noteworthy that this stance diverges from the approach taken by the UNIDROIT Principles.[173]

For a long-term relational supply contract, in the case of hardship, the parties are mainly interested in an adaptation of their contract by means of renegotiation to accommodate the new circumstances, and if the contract cannot be adapted, they might prefer to be released from their obligations. Therefore, it may be desirable and necessary for them to insert a hardship clause into their contract which clearly provides solutions to hardship situations.

[169] Ibid, 51.

[170] Horn, 'Standard Clauses on Contract Adaptation in International Commerce', above n 16, 131.

[171] Perillo, above n 11 (Chap. 1).

[172] Schlechtriem and Schwenzer, above n 97, 823–4.

[173] Schwenzer, Hachem and Kee, above n 73 (Chap. 1), 666–674.

Chapter 4
Good Faith in Domestic Laws and International Instruments

4.1 Introduction

Civil law countries tend to apply the principle of good faith when dealing with hardship issues; this is evident in German law and French law. In regard to common law countries, American law has adopted the doctrine of impracticability based on good faith, while English law and Australian law seem to adhere to the principle of *punta sunt servanda*. At the international level, the UNIDROIT Principles in this regard are clearly affected by civil law traditions while the status of the CISG remains blurred.

In practice, good faith is perhaps the most important principle in the process of long-term contracting.[1] The good faith issue frequently arises '[b]ecause a contract is an exchange expressed imperfectly and projected into an uncertain future'.[2] For example, in a long-term coal supply contract which has an open term on quantity, when issues regarding quantity arise, it is argued that good faith should be applied by the court when determining the appropriate quantity or the way in which the coal should be produced and supplied.[3]

It is worth noting that good faith is recognized and accepted as being a notoriously complicated topic. The long-standing problem of good faith is that it is difficult, or to some extent impossible, to give it an accurate or exact definition or to address clearly what it means. The aim of the analysis of good faith in this chapter is not to define good faith itself. It is to propose an innovative understanding of good faith from a functional perspective. Traditionally, domestic laws and international

[1] Nystén-Haarala, above n 31 (Chap. 1), 32.

[2] Steven J Burton, 'Breach of Contract and the Common Law Duty to Perform in Good Faith' (1981) 94 *Harvard Law Review* 369, 371.

[3] Goldberg, 'Discretion in Long-Term Open Quantity Contracts', above n 23 (Chap. 1), 319–320.

P. Guo, *Good Faith in Long-Term Relational Supply Contracts in the Context of Hardship from A Comparative Perspective*,
https://doi.org/10.1007/978-981-16-5513-5_4

instruments focus too much on the meaning of good faith and its scope of application. From a functional perspective, the various levels and many facets of good faith is more important than its meaning. This chapter will identify the manifestations of good faith in the context of hardship and to examine whether good faith is an appropriate tool that can be widely adopted to resolve problems arising from long-term relational supply contract upon the occurrence of hardship at the international level.

Section 4.2 will discuss good faith in different domestic contract laws. Section 4.3 will investigate good faith in the CISG and the UNIDROIT Principles. Section 4.4 will propose a framework in which good faith has various levels and many facets. Good faith in either domestic laws or international legal instruments, to a large degree, fits in the framework. The various levels and many facets of good faith show its flexibility in dealing with hardship issues in general, and those relating to a long-term relational supply contract in particular. Section 4.5 will offer the conclusion that good faith should be used to deal with hardship issues and that it can provide better solutions.

4.2 Good Faith in Domestic Laws

The understanding of good faith may be deeply rooted in national culture in general and in the contract law rules that have been developed by national courts in particular. Good faith reflects, to a great extent, a cultural identity of an individual, or more pervasively, a national legal system.[4] More precisely, it can be understood that 'different domestic approaches towards the notion of good faith not only reflect concerns about purely technical matters; rather, they go to the root of the understanding of the judicial function and the role of contract law that prevail in the respective jurisdictions'.[5]

A court which is often confronted with one kind of contract will devise and create contractual doctrines different from another court often dealing with another kind of contract.[6] There may be an even greater difference between common law and civil law. A vivid statement may illustrate this point: '[w]hether Napoleon's jibe be true or not, it certainly seems that the English law of contract was designed for a nation of shopkeepers. If that be so, the common lawyer might retort, then the French system was made for a race of peasants.'[7] In the contemporary context, it

---

[4] Simon Whittaker, '"General Principles" and "Underlying Principles" in the Proposed Common European Sales Law and Their Role in Its Interpretation' in Jacobien Rutgers and Pietro Sirena (eds), *Rules and Principles in European Contract Law* (Intersentia, 2015) 99, 111.

[5] Vogenauer, *Commentary on the UNIDROIT Principles of International Commercial Contracts (PICC)*, above n 130 (Chap. 3), 208. On the comparison of good faith in Chinese contract law, Australian contract law and the CISG, see Peng Guo and Shu Zhang, 'Is the CISG an Appropriate Option for Australian and Chinese Businesses? A Good Faith Perspective' (2019) 23(1) *Vindobona Journal of International Commercial Law and Arbitration* 81–104.

[6] M P Ellinghaus, 'An Australian Contract Law?' (1989) 2 *Journal of Contract Law* 13, 20.

[7] Sir Otto Kahn-Freund, Claudine Lévy and Bernard Rudden, *A Source-book on French Law: System, Methods, Outlines of Contract* (Clarendon Press, 2nd ed, 1979) 318.

would be more accurate to state that the English contract law is suitable for 'hard-nosed international business executives' while the French contract law is preferable for consumers.[8] The notion of good faith according to civil law and common law will be discussed separately.

4.2.1 *Good Faith in Civil Law*

4.2.1.1 German Contract Law

Article 242 of the German Civil Code provides that '[t]he debtor is obliged to perform in such a manner as good faith requires, regard being had to general practice'.[9] Another translation reads as '[t]he debtor is bound to perform according to the requirements of good faith, ordinary usage being taken into consideration'.[10] At first glance, it seems that good faith applies only to the performance of the contract by the debtor. However, in practice, good faith has been recognised by German courts as a general principle of German contract law.[11] Good faith is a principle that serves as the basis of all obligations arising from a contract.[12] The principle of good faith is so general that the whole system of German private law might be taken as an embodiment of it and could be administered based on it only.[13]

Scope of the Application of Good Faith

On the basis of this principle, the German courts have created an elaborate structure of rules governing contracts.[14] The principle of good faith probably has the broadest scope of application as it applies to every civil and commercial case.[15] It permeates

[8] Hein Kötz, 'Towards a European Civil Code: The Duty of Good Faith' in Peter Cane and Jane Stapleton (eds), *The Law of Obligations: Essays in Celebration of John Fleming* (Clarendon Press, 1998) 243, 257.

[9] Markesinis, Unberath and Johnston, above n 22 (Chap. 3), 120.

[10] Werner F Ebke and Bettina M Steinhauer, 'The Doctrine of Good Faith in German Contract Law' in Jack Beatson and Daniel Friedmann (eds), *Good Faith and Fault in Contract Law* (Clarendon Press, 1995) 171, 171.

[11] Ibid.

[12] Nathalie Hofmann, 'Interpretation Rules and Good Faith as Obstacles to the UK's Ratification of the CISG and to the Harmonization of Contract Law in Europe' (2010) 22 *Pace International Law Review* 145, 160.

[13] Peter Schlechtriem, *Good Faith in German Law and in International Uniform Laws* (Centro di Studi e Ricerche di Diritto Comparato e Straniero, 1997) 1.

[14] E Allen Farnsworth, 'Good Faith Performance and Commercial Reasonableness under the Uniform Commercial Code' (1963) 30 *University of Chicago Law Review* 666, 678–9.

[15] Ulrich Magnus, 'Harmonization and Unification of Law by the Means of General Principles' in Morten M Fogt (ed), *Unification and Harmonization of International Commercial Law: Interaction*

every corner of German contract law including formation, validity, content, performance, hardship, remedies for non-performance, and even exists outside contract law.[16] Article 157 of the German Civil Code explicitly emphasises that contracts are to be interpreted as required by good faith.[17] Due to the wide scope of application, good faith has led to various 'diverse', 'complex' and 'subtle' developments that can be used to meet the needs of changes.[18] In the name of good faith, it is possible to find a source for every solution or approach imaginable or envisaged, and good faith can be regarded as a legal anchor for even the wildest views and consequences.[19]

Functions of Good Faith

Different civil law scholars have listed the functions from different perspectives. Good Faith is considered to have three important functions: concretisation/interpretation, supplementation and correction/limitation; and on rare occasions a fourth one is created to be distinguished from the third, emphasizing differences between the correction/limitation of a right for one's own improper behaviour and the correction/limitation of a right of an innocent party.[20] This view is supported by certain scholars.[21] Other scholars argue that there are three basic functions of good faith from another perspective: legal basis of interstitial judicial law-making; basis of legal defences in private law suits; and statutory basis of reallocation of risks in private contracts.[22] There are also other approaches to categorise the functions of the principle of good faith more generally in the context of the German Civil Code. According to one approach, good faith may have three functions: first, extension and creation of rights and duties; second, prohibition of the abusive exercise of formal rights; third, transformation and relief of contractual obligations due to changed circumstances; and each of these may have several sub-categories.[23]

---

or Deharmonization? (Kluwer Law International, 2012) 161, 162.

[16] Martijn Hesselink, 'The Concept of Good Faith' in Arthur S Hartkamp et al. (eds), *Towards a European Civil Code* (Kluwer Law International and Ars Aequi Libri, 4th ed, 2010) 619, 628–635.

[17] Article 157 (Interpretation of Contracts) stipulates that 'Contracts are to be interpreted as required by good faith and having regard to custom.' Markesinis, Unberath and Johnston, above n 22 (Chap. 3), 872.

[18] Ibid, 122.

[19] Schlechtriem, above n 13, 8.

[20] Hesselink, above n 16, 627.

[21] See, e.g., Uli Foerstl, *The general Principle of Good Faith under the CISG: A functional Approach to Theory and Practice of the United Nations Convention on Contracts for the International Sale of Goods* (VDM Verlag Dr. Müller, 2011) 21–4.

[22] Ebke and Steinhauer, above n 10, 171–2.

[23] Uwe Diederichsen and Karl-Heinz Gursky, 'Principles of Equity in German Civil Law' in Ralph A Newman (ed), *Equity in the World's Legal Systems: A Comparative Study dedicated to René Cassin* (Établissements Émile Bruylant, 1973) 277, 279–296.

However, civil law courts can give the principle of good faith new functions in order to meet the needs of new and changing situations and emerging challenges.[24] Judges have relied on good faith not only to solve significant economic and social problems arising after the two world wars and after the reunification of Germany, but also to deal with conflicts between rigorous individualism and the changed social and moral attitudes of the society.[25] To a great extent, judges play a central role in the interpretation and application of the principle of good faith, as German law has followed the Roman tradition whereby it is part of a judge's function to decide whether the parties have performed their contractual obligations according to the requirements of good faith.[26] Also, the courts are able to develop new doctrines to deal with omissions from the German Civil Code by applying good faith to fill in the gaps.[27] The extensive interpretation and application of the principle of good faith by the courts have shown that the courts are willing to apply it in a very flexible way in order to adjust it where its strict interpretation or application would result in inequitable consequences, and to customise and adapt it accordingly to keep pace with the rapid, unprecedented changes in society.[28]

It should be borne in mind that, although German judges, to a certain degree, can apply the principle of good faith at will, they are bound to respect some of the values embedded in good faith. Three institutional levels of values can be distinguished: at the highest level is the set of values found in the German constitution; values derived from other parts of the German legal order are at the second level; and the values reflected in collective conviction which means the belief that every reasonable person would consider as fair and decent are at the third level.[29]

It is reasonable to conclude that good faith is one of the most salient characteristics of German contract law. At the risk of exaggeration, good faith could be considered as a catholicon.

4.2.1.2 French Contract Law

Good Faith Before the Reform of the French Civil Code

Article 1134 of the old French Civil Code provides that '[c]ontracts must be executed in good faith'.[30] It can be seen that, prior to the reform of French contract law, good faith was only relevant to the performance of contracts. Good faith was only

---

[24] Raphael Powell, 'Good Faith in Contracts' (1956) 9 *Current Legal Problems* 16, 32.

[25] Kötz, above n 8, 244.

[26] Powell, above n 24.

[27] Hugh Beale, 'Relational Values in English Contract Law' in David Campbell, Linda Mulcahy and Sally Wheeler (eds), *Changing Concepts of Contract: Essays in Honour of Ian Macneil* (Palgrave Macmillan, 2013) 116, 126.

[28] Diederichsen and Gursky, above n 23, 296.

[29] Schlechtriem, above n 13, 18–20.

[30] Barry Nicholas, *The French Law of Contract* (Clarendon Press, 2nd ed, 1992) 153.

indirectly related to the formation of contracts and pre-contractual liability.[31] In practice, the application of good faith in Article 1134 was not generalised by the French courts.[32] Explicit reference to good faith was relatively rare.[33] The courts had, only in limited situations, applied Article 1134 expressly, as they were reluctant to give up control on a principle that was so general that could be invoked in almost every situation.[34] Even in cases where *imprévision* occurs, the *Cour de cassation* had rejected that it could justify adjustment or termination of contract,[35] and had retained the strict application of good faith: '[i]n no case is it open to the courts, no matter how equitable their decision may seem to them to be, to take time and circumstances into account in order to modify the agreement of the parties and substitute new terms for those which have been freely accepted by those parties'.[36] Since 1992 the *Cour de cassation* has slightly eased the restrictions on the application of the principle of good faith by imposing on the advantaged party a duty to renegotiate in good faith in the context of hardship.

On the other hand, administrative contracts were treated differently as the protection of public interest was a substantial factor that the courts would take into account. As a result, the *Conseil d'Etat*, taking a different approach from the *Cour de cassation*, affirmed the application of good faith in the context of *imprévision*,[37] and that contracts of an administrative nature could be adapted to restore the original equilibrium[38] or could be terminated by judges upon the request of the party whose performance had become extremely onerous.[39]

Good Faith After the Reform of the French Civil Code

The French contract law was revised and the new law was promulgated in February 2016 and came into force in October 2016. Good faith is dealt with in the first paragraph of Article 1104 of the new French Civil Code which provides that '[t]he contracts must be negotiated, formed and performed in good faith'.[40] Article 1104 is included in the initial section and recognised as a general principle of French law of

31 Ibid.

32 Daniel Tricot, 'La bonne foi dans les Principes d'UNIDROIT' (2017) 22 *Uniform Law Review* 116, 119.

33 Denis Tallon, *Le Concept de Bonne Foi en Droit Français du Contrat* (Centro di Studi e Ricerche di Diritto Comparato e Straniero, 1994) 2.

34 Nicholas, above n 30, 153–4.

35 Peter Rosher, 'French Contract Law Reform' (2016) 17 *Business Law International* 59, 60.

36 Nicholas, above n 30, 209.

37 Ibid, 209–210.

38 José Angelo Estrella Faria, 'The Influence of the UNIDROIT Principles of International Commercial Contracts on National Laws' (2016) 21 *Uniform Law Review* 238, 268.

39 Rosher, above n 35, 60.

40 Cartwright and Whittaker, above n 45 (Chap. 3), 412.

contract.[41] It seemed that good faith as a general principle now extended to contract negotiation and contract formation.[42] The scope of the application of the principle of good faith had been officially extended. To put it another way, the incremental recognition of the application of good faith in contract formation by the courts in case law was codified and added to the French Civil Code.[43] Also, the second paragraph of Article 1104 emphasises that '[t]his provision is a matter of public policy'.[44]

Good faith was an evolving concept,[45] evident in the reform of the French contract law. Under French contract law, good faith is now not just a general principle of contract law, as it was raised to a new height and given a new role as public policy. Given the new and stronger role of good faith, it is important and interesting to await and see how the courts apply it.

4.2.2 *Good Faith in Common Law*

4.2.2.1 American Contract Law

In the United States,[46] there is a generally accepted concept of good faith.[47] Good faith was included in both the UCC and the Restatement 2nd. An obligation of good faith is embodied in both the UCC and the Restatement 2nd and imposed on the parties to a contract.[48] Old Section 1-203 of the UCC stated '[e]very contract or duty within this Act imposes an obligation of good faith in its performance or enforcement'.[49] In 2001, in the revised section on good faith, Section 1-304 stipulates that '[e]very contract or duty within the Uniform Commercial Code imposes an obligation of good faith in its performance and enforcement'.[50] It is argued that 'there is no obligation in all of the UCC and in general contract law of more overall importance than the general obligation of good faith'.[51]

---

[41] Rowan, above n 44 (Chap. 3), 812–3.

[42] Estrella Faria, above n 38, 265.

[43] Rosher, above n 35, 61–2.

[44] Cartwright and Whittaker, above n 45 (Chap. 3), 412.

[45] Tallon, above n 33, 5–9.

[46] For the history of the development of the duty to perform in good faith, see Steven J Burton, 'History and Theory of Good Faith Performance in the United States' in Larry Dimatteo and Martin Hogg (eds), *Comparative Contract Law: British and American Perspectives* (Oxford University Press, 2015) 211, 211–5.

[47] Allan E Farnsworth, *The Concept of Good Faith in American Law* (Centro di Studi e Ricerche di Diritto Comparato e Straniero, 1993) 1.

[48] Ibid, 2.

[49] Boris Kozolchyk, *Comparative Commercial Contracts: Law, Culture and Economic Development* (West Academic Publishing, 2014) 973.

[50] Ibid.

[51] Robert S Summers, 'Good Faith Revisited: Some Brief Remarks Dedicated to the Late Richard E Speidel – Friend, Co-Author, and UCC Specialist' (2009) 46 *San Diego Law Review* 723, 726.

Meaning of Good Faith

Regarding the meaning of good faith in American law, Farnsworth argued that there were a 'general definition' and a 'special definition' of good faith in the UCC.[52] At the time when Farnsworth wrote his article, the 'general definition' was stipulated by Section 1-201 (19) of the UCC in which good faith meant 'honesty in fact in the conduct or transaction concerned.'[53] The 'special definition' was contained in Section 2-103(1)(b) which defined good faith in merchant cases as 'honesty in fact and the observance of reasonable commercial standards of fair dealing in the trad.'[54] By adding 'fair dealing' in the 'special definition' to the 'general definition' would render the definition of good faith more suitable for good faith performance.[55] Conversely, Summers argued that the definition contained in Section 1-201 (19) was narrow, while the definition provided in Section 2-103(1)(b) constituted a broader definition.[56]

Section 1-201 (19) was replaced in 2001 by Section 1-201(b)(20) which defines good faith as 'honesty in fact and the observance of reasonable commercial standards of fair dealing'.[57] The honesty factor of good faith remains the same, but good faith extends to cover reasonable commercial standards of fair dealing. It can be seen that the new 'general definition' and the 'special definition', to a large extent, are similar. Therefore, in 2003, the special definition of good faith was removed when Article 2 of the UCC was amended.[58] One possible explanation for the removal is that the general provisions of Article 1 of the UCC had covered almost all the definitions of good faith.[59]

Scholars have different interpretations and understandings of the definitions mentioned above. Farnsworth, Summers and Burton each proposed one of the three most important 'aspects'[60] or 'conceptualisations'[61] of good faith performance, separately. Farnsworth observed that the duty of good faith performance could be used

---

[52] Farnsworth, *The Concept of Good Faith in American Law*, above n 47, 3.

[53] Ibid.

[54] Kozolchyk, above n 49.

[55] Farnsworth, *The Concept of Good Faith in American Law*, above n 47, 3.

[56] Robert S Summers, 'The Conceptualisation of Good faith in American Contract Law: A General Account' in Reinhard Zimmermann and Simon Whittaker (eds), *Good Faith in European Contract Law* (Cambridge University Press, 2000) 118, 122–3.

[57] Kozolchyk, above n 49.

[58] Ibid, 973–4. It should be noted that the UCC withdrew all of the 2003 amendments to Article 2 and none were ever implemented. More details see, https://www.law.cornell.edu/ucc/2/article2 and http://entrepreneur.typepad.com/files/article-2-and-2a-memo.pdf.

[59] The definition of good faith in Article 5 of the UCC is not covered by the general provisions of Article 1 of the UCC. Ibid, 974.

[60] Farnsworth, *The Concept of Good Faith in American Law*, above n 47, 3–5.

[61] Summers, 'The Conceptualisation of Good faith in American Contract Law', above n 56, 125–134.

as a source or basis for courts to imply a variety of terms.[62] Summers argued that good faith should be understood and used as an 'excluder' without general meaning or meanings and that its function is to exclude various and different forms of bad faith.[63] To understand what good faith means, the concept of bad faith must be understood. The approach is first to find out the forms that bad faith takes and list them, and the next step is to work out what particular meaning good faith has as the opposite of a specific bad faith form.[64] Burton believed that good faith should be used to 'effectuate the intentions of the parties, or to protect their reasonable expectations'[65] and that an operational standard, which could be used to distinguish good faith performance from bad faith performance, should and could be elucidated and canvassed.[66] His views are based on a broader understanding of parties' contractual expectation interest, which means that contractual expectation interest should be understood as covering not only the expected interest conferred on one party but also the expected loss incurred by the other party,[67] and on the concept of 'discretion in performance' referring to either party's power to control the terms of performance after the conclusion of a contract.[68] In the context of contract performance, if a party exercises his or her discretion to achieve 'any purpose within the reasonable contemplation of the parties at the time of formation—to capture opportunities that were preserved upon entering the contract, interpreted objectively', the party is regarded as acting in good faith; conversely, if a party exercises his or her discretion to 'recapture opportunities forgone upon contracting', such as the party 'refuses to pay the expected cost of performance', the party is considered as acting in bad faith.[69] All three propositions have obtained support from the courts and have been applied by them.[70] Although there are conflicts among these propositions, Farnsworth argued and tried to prove that all three propositions had been applied, to a certain extent, cumulatively and consistently by courts.[71] There is another argument that the

[62] Farnsworth, *The Concept of Good Faith in American Law*, above n 47, 3.

[63] Robert S Summers, '"Good Faith" in General Contract Law and the Sales Provisions of the Uniform Commercial Code' (1968) 54 *Virginia Law Review* 195, 196, 201, 262.

[64] Ibid, 199–207, 262.

[65] Steven J Burton, 'Good Faith Performance of a Contract Within Article 2 of the Uniform Commercial Code' (1981) 67 *Iowa Law Review* 1, 3.

[66] Burton, 'Breach of Contract and the Common Law Duty to Perform in Good Faith', above n 2, 369–370.

[67] Ibid, 373.

[68] Steven J Burton, 'More on Good Faith Performance of a Contract: A Reply to Professor Summers' (1984) 69 *Iowa Law Review* 497, 501–3.

[69] Burton, 'Breach of Contract and the Common Law Duty to Perform in Good Faith', above n 2, 371–3.

[70] Farnsworth, *The Concept of Good Faith in American Law*, above n 47, 3–5.

[71] Ibid, 5–7.

courts on many occasions do not correctly understand the definition of the duty of good faith and therefore apply it wrongly.[72]

From the perspective of a relational contract, Macneil found that:

> The subject of good faith is of particular interest in terms of perceiving the degree to which scholarly work is promise-centered rather than relationally-centered, because we find two conflicting views, apparently reflecting differing degrees of promise-orientation. Steven Burton advances a promise-centered case: "courts generally do not use the good faith performance doctrine to override the agreement of the parties. Rather, the good faith performance doctrine is used to effectuate the intentions of the parties, or to protect their reasonable expectations, through interpretation and implication." Robert Summers' view, on the other hand, is far more relational. He favours a "contractual morality" approach "of a piece" with other such morality as the "unconscionability doctrine and various general equitable principles."...[73]

Scope of the Application of Good Faith

Another critical issue is the scope of good faith in American contract law. It is noteworthy that the good faith duty stipulated by the UCC and the Restatement 2nd is restrained only in the performance and enforcement of a contract.[74] The reference to good faith in the negotiation of a contract has been omitted by both the UCC and the Restatement 2nd as a duty to negotiate in good faith is not recognized and is often replaced by other concepts.[75] However, some courts have tried to enforce an agreement to negotiate in good faith under certain circumstances.[76] Due to the tendency to recognise an express agreement to negotiate in good faith, it was argued that pressure would be imposed on courts to imply such an agreement in cases where good faith was not expressly mentioned, which would effectively put the parties under a duty to negotiate in good faith.[77]

Even if good faith is explicitly confined to contract performance, its scope is still vague. It is argued that the scope was best articulated by former Justice Posner who stated that the boundaries of good faith performance are like a spectrum with duties of a fiduciary at one end and with intentional tort obligation at the other and that the duty of good faith performance should be floating in the middle of them and needs

[72] Jay M Feinman, 'The Duty of Good Faith: A Perspective on Contemporary Contract Law' (2015) 66 *Hasting Law Journal* 937, 941–9.

[73] Macneil, 'Relational Contract', above n 66 (Chap. 2), 521–2 (citations omitted).

[74] Steven J Burton and Eric G Anderson, *Contractual Good Faith, Formation, Performance, Breach, Enforcement* (Little, Brown and Company, 1995) 115–9.

[75] Farnsworth, *The Concept of Good Faith in American Law*, above n 47, 2.

[76] E Allan Farnsworth, 'Precontractual Liability and Preliminary agreements: Fair Dealing and Failed Negotiations' (1987) 87 *Columbia Law Review* 217, 263–9.

[77] Mark P Gergen, 'Liability for Mistake in Contract Formation' (1990) 64 *Southern California Law Review* 1, 31.

to be specified in order to work out a specific outcome.[78] When deciding an actual case, courts should bear in mind that '[o]n the one side, there is the tort law of fraud to protect the innocent, but we want the contract doctrine to go further than that. On the other side, there is the law of fiduciary obligation, but in the case of ordinary commercial contracts we do not want the law to go that far'.[79] Also, it has been held that the duty of good faith applies to the renegotiation of a contract, especially when the contract is of a long-term and relational nature.[80] The parties to such contracts should renegotiate in good faith to maintain their relationship; the court should examine whether the offers made during the renegotiation are made in good faith, and if one party rejects a good faith offer made by the other party, the court may request that the rejecting party accept the good faith offer.[81]

In addition, Farnsworth argued that both common sense and tradition indicate that good faith performance should be understood from an objective perspective based on decency, fairness or reasonableness.[82] However, the UCC provisions relating to good faith and their application do not always endorse an objective test,[83] whereas the Restatement Second does adopt an objective test.[84] Therefore, it seems that there is no simple 'yes' or 'no' answer to whether the duty of good faith should be understood from a subjective or objective perspective. Both subjective and objective standards have been applied in one way or another by different courts in different cases.[85] The answer, therefore, varies depending on the facts and circumstances of each case.

4.2.2.2 English Contract Law

Status of Good Faith

Centuries ago in England, in the age when the law merchant, administered by merchant judges in the merchant courts, dominated and permeated the merchants' transactions in England and across Europe,[86] good faith was once a general concept and

[78] Todd D Rakoff, 'Good Faith in Contract Performance: Market Street Associates Ltd. Partnership v Frey' (2007) 120 *Harvard Law Review* 1187, 1189–1192.

[79] Ibid, 1191.

[80] L W Newman, 'Problems with Long Term Contracts: A Practical Viewpoint' [1986] *Australian Mining and Petroleum Law Association Yearbook (AMPLA Yearbook)* 487, 493.

[81] Ibid.

[82] Farnsworth, 'Good Faith Performance and Commercial Reasonableness under the Uniform Commercial Code', above n 14, 671–2.

[83] Ibid, 673–4.

[84] Steven J Burton, 'Good Faith in Articles 1 and 2 of the U.C.C.: The Practice View' (1994) 35 *William and Mary Law Review* 1533, 1539.

[85] Burton and Anderson, above n 74, 74–90.

[86] For a brief discussion of the law merchant and the merchant courts, see Peng Guo, 'What can International Arbitration learn from Medieval Merchant Courts?' (2017) 9 *HUFS Global Law*

a commercial custom.[87] During the period when the merchant courts were gradually replaced by the royal courts and the law merchant was absorbed into English common law, good faith eventually vanished,[88] although the Court of Chancery still granted a remedy to a party because of a breach of the obligation of good faith promises.[89] Since the disappearance of the law merchant, although there were various views arguing for or against the adoption of good faith into English contract law,[90] there has been neither an 'overriding general positive duty of good faith imposed on the parties to a contract,'[91] nor a recognition of 'the existence of a general doctrine of good faith'.[92] The only exception was Lord Mansfield's attempt to expand a general duty to perform contracts in good faith from insurance contracts to all contracts.[93] It is also argued that there is no need for a doctrine of good faith in English contract law,[94] and an artificial transplant might result in new divergences and unpredictable issues.[95] There are several practical reasons underlying the non-existence or non-recognition of good faith in English contract law. Firstly, the business world is rough and tough, and it is the parties' own responsibility to look after themselves and to stand on their own two feet.[96] Also, English contract lawyers distrust general principles as they are too vague, too uncertain, or too unworkable.[97] A general doctrine of good faith does not take into account the diversity of contracting against the commercial background.[98] In addition, the enactment of good faith

---

Review 69, 69–81; Leon E Trakman, 'The Evolution of the Law Merchant: Our Commercial Heritage Part I Ancient and Medieval Law Merchant' (1980) 12 *Journal of Maritime Law and Commerce* 1; Leon E Trakman, 'The Evolution of the Law Merchant: Our Commercial Heritage Part II The Modern Law Merchant' (1981) 12 *Journal of Maritime Law and Commerce* 153; Leon E Trakman, 'The Twenty-First-Century Law Merchant' (2011) 48 *American Business Law Journal* 775

[87] Roy Goode, *The Concept of 'Good Faith' in English Law* (Centro di Studi e Ricerche di Diritto Comparato e Straniero, 1992) 3–4.

[88] Ibid, 2.

[89] J F O'Conner, *Good Faith in English Law* (Dartmouth, 1990) 18.

[90] Roger Brownsword, *Contract Law: Themes for the Twenty-First Century* (Oxford University Press, 2nd ed, 2006) 114–130.

[91] Powell, above n 24, 25.

[92] Ewan McKendrick, *Contract Law: Texts, Cases and Materials* (Oxford University Press, 7th ed, 2016) 486.

[93] Kozolchyk, above n 49, 964–5, 971–2.

[94] Michael Bridge, '*Does Anglo-Canadian Contract Law need a Doctrine of Good Faith*' (1984) 9 *The Canadian Business Law Journal* 385, 386, 425–6.

[95] Gunther Teubner, 'Legal Irritants: Good Faith in British Law or How Unifying Law Ends Up in New Divergences' (1998) 61 *Modern Law Review* 11, 14–33.

[96] Goode, above n 87, 2.

[97] Ewan McKendrick, 'Good Faith: A Matter of Principle?' in A D M Forte (ed), *Good Faith in Contract and Property* (Hart Publishing, 1999) 39, 46.

[98] Michael Bridge, 'Good Faith in Commercial Contracts' in Roger Brownsword, Norma J Hird and Geraint Howells (eds), *Good Faith in Contract: Concept and Context* (Ashgate and Dartmouth, 1999) 139, 150.

is unnecessary and may cause trouble, disorder and inconsistency and may be abused by an individual judge.[99] The theoretical reason for the non-recognition of good faith is based on the common law philosophy of utilitarianism and which primarily concerns the economic exchange between parties.[100] This philosophy requires that 'the predictability of the legal outcome of a case is more important than absolute justice.'[101] The achievement of predictability may be at the expense of absolute fairness and may result in harsh consequences such as disputes between parties.[102] That is to say, when the courts are faced with a choice between certainty and justice in a particular case they are likely to choose certainty instead of justice.[103] It can be concluded that in English contract law '[i]n the inescapable and perennial search, common to all legal systems, for the right balance between fairness and justice on the one hand, and certainty and predictability on the other, the scales tipped firmly against fairness and in favour of predictability'.[104]

Piecemeal Solution Approach

The non-existence of a general doctrine of good faith is regarded as a peculiarity of English contract law.[105] This, however, does not necessarily mean that English contract law does not contain any good faith element at all. On the contrary, there are a number of individual cases where the law incorporates an element of good faith, either subjective or objective.[106] Bingham L.J. once stated in *Interfoto Picture Library Ltd v Stiletto Visual Programmes Ltd*, that:

> In many civil law systems, and perhaps in most legal systems outside the common law world, the law of obligations recognises and enforces an overriding principle that in making and carrying out contracts parties should act in good faith. This does not simply mean that they should not deceive each other, a principle which any legal system must recognise; its effect is perhaps most aptly conveyed by such metaphorical colloquialisms as 'playing fair', or 'coming clean' or 'putting one's cards face upwards on the table'. It is in essence a principle of fair and open dealing… English law has, characteristically, committed itself to no

---

[99] Ibid, 140.

[100] Barry Nicholas, *The United Kingdom and the Vienna Sales Convention: Another Case of Splendid Isolation?* (Centro di Studi e Ricerche di Diritto Comparato e Straniero, 1993) 5.

[101] Goode, above n 87, 9.

[102] Ibid.

[103] Nicholas, *The United Kingdom and the Vienna Sales Convention*, above n 100.

[104] H K Lücke, 'Good Faith and Contractual Performance' in Paul Finn (ed), *Essays on Contract* (The Law Book, 1987) 155, 157.

[105] Ole Lando, 'Out on a Limb- Four English Peculiarities in Contract Law' in Andrea Büchler and Markus Müller-Chen (eds), *Private Law national – global – comparative, Festschrift für Ingeborg Schwenzer zum 60 Geburtstag* (Stämpfli Verlag AG Bern and Intersentia, 2011) vol 2, 1001, 1001–5.

[106] Powell, above n 24, 23–5.

> such overriding principle but has developed piecemeal solutions in response to demonstrated problems of unfairness.[107]

His view is accepted and supported by academic writings as well. It is submitted that 'English law does not have anything equivalent to the general concept of good faith found in civil law; we require good faith in particular situations'.[108] Under specific circumstances, doctrines and rules of English contract law may generally conform to the requirements of good faith,[109] and could achieve the same results through approaches that are different from those employed by civil law countries.[110] For example, 'silent' good faith, such as rules relating to co-operation and the implication of contractual terms, is frequented used in such approaches.[111] Also, in the absence of good faith, the doctrine of rectification and the doctrine of estoppel have been developed to deal with certain issues that would have been tackled by good faith in civil law.[112] In addition, equity, the unique body of law or set of doctrines, to a great extent, plays a significant role in achieving a similar solution in cases where good faith dominates the outcome.[113] For example, good faith can be considered as a prerequisite for a party to be granted any equitable remedies by the courts.[114] The prerequisite could be regarded as a manifestation of one of the maxims of equity that 'one who comes to equity must come with clean hands'.[115] Many other doctrines based on the piecemeal approach exist under current English contract law or equity.[116] Therefore, it seems that the piecemeal solutions are preferred by English courts and scholars to an over-arching principle of good faith, in response to specific cases involving unfairness.

---

[107] *Interfoto Picture Library Ltd v Stiletto Visual Programmes Ltd* [1988] 1 All. E.R. 348, at 352 per Bingham L.J.

[108] Goode, above n 87, 6.

[109] McKendrick, *Contract Law*, above n 92.

[110] Goode, above n 87, 9–10.

[111] Michael Furmston and J W Carter, 'Good Faith in Contract Law: A Commonwealth Survey' in the UNIDROIT (ed), *Eppur si muove: The age of Uniform Law, Essays in honour of Michael Joachim Bonell to celebrate his 70th birthday* (the UNIDROIT, 2016) vol 2, 988, 1020–2.

[112] Justice Steyn, 'The Role of Good Faith and Fair Dealing in Contract Law: A Hair-Shirt Philosophy?' (1991) 6 *The Denning Law Journal* 131, 133.

[113] Goode, above n 87, 7.

[114] McKendrick, above n 58 (Chap. 3), 102.

[115] Peter Radan and Cameron Stewart, *Principles of Australian Equity and Trusts* (LexisNexis Butterworths, 3rd ed, 2016) 39.

[116] Neil Andrews, 'Good Faith Beneath the Surface: The Ethical Sensitivity of English Contract Law' in the UNIDROIT (ed), *Eppur si muove: The age of Uniform Law, Essays in honour of Michael Joachim Bonell to celebrate his 70th birthday* (the UNIDROIT, 2016) vol 2, 953, 962–971.

Recent Developments

Certain common law doctrines influenced by equitable concepts such as good faith have been moving away from the traditional adversarial model to an emerging co-operation model focusing on the reasonable expectations of the parties.[117]

Recently, English law has been regarded as having taken a further step in the recognition of a general principle or a duty of good faith.[118] First of all, English courts have slowly begun to recognise a duty of good faith relating to either negotiation[119] or performance[120] of contracts which expressly contain good faith requirements,[121] particularly in cases where there is an agreement to negotiate in good faith.[122] Secondly, there is also a trend to recognize a duty of good faith implied in fact in a certain type of contracts, particularly in long-term relational contracts. The leading case is *Yam Seng Pte v International Trade Corporation Ltd*[123] in which Leggatt J argued that the courts could imply a general duty of good faith in a relational contract such as a long-term distribution contract in *Yam Seng*. The approach taken in *Yam Seng* was followed by *Bristol Groundschool v Intelligent Data Capture*[124] which also related to a relational contract with regard to a joint venture, by *Portsmouth City Council v Ensign Highways Ltd*[125] which involved a relational contract on the maintenance of highways for 25 years, and by *D&G Cars Ltd v Essex Police Authority*[126] which concerned a relational contract with respect to a service contract. The good faith issue reached its climax before the High Court of Justice of England and Wales in another landmark case, *MSC Mediterranean Shipping Co v Cottonex Anstalt,*[127] in which the court admitted the existence of a general principle of good faith in English contract law.[128] Unfortunately, this view

[117] Anthony Mason, 'Contract, Good Faith and Equitable Standards in Fair Dealing' 2000 (116) *The Law Quarterly Review* 66, 72.

[118] Klaus Peter Berger and Thomas Arntz, 'Good Faith as a 'General Organising Principles' of the Common Law' (2016) 32 *Arbitration International* 167, 170.

[119] *Petromec v Petroleo Brasileiro SA Petrobas* [2005] EWCA Civ 891; *Knatchbull-Huguessen v SISU Captial Ltd* [2014] EWHC 1194 (QB).

[120] *Compass Group UK and Ireland Ltd v Mid-Essen Hospital Services NHS Trust Ltd* [2012] EWCA Civ 781.

[121] Christina Perry, 'Good Faith in English and US Contract Law: Divergent Theories, Practical Similarities' (2016) 17 *Business Law International* 27, 34–5.

[122] Leon Trakman and Kunal Sharma, 'The Binding Force of Agreements to Negotiate in Good Faith' (2014) 73 *The Cambridge Law Journal* 598, 617–628.

[123] [2013] EWHC 111 (QB).

[124] [2014] EWHC 2145 (Ch).

[125] [2015] EWHC 1969 (TCC).

[126] [2015] EWHC 226 (QB).

[127] [2015] EWHC 283 (Comm).

[128] Berger and Arntz, above n 118.

expressed by Leggatt J did not gain support from the Court of Appeal of England and Wales,[129] and it was also criticised by contract law scholars.[130]

Although the Supreme Court of the UK, to a certain extent, implied a term of exercising a contractual right in good faith in *Braganza v BP Shipping Ltd*,[131] the attitude of the Supreme Court on good faith remains unclear.[132] It is a developing area relating to long-term relational contracts in particular.[133] Good faith in such contracts takes its meaning from the circumstances.[134] It should be noted that in all the cases discussed above, there is no clear conclusion in regard to the differences between a long-term contract and a relational contract. Also, it is worth noting that a long-term contract is not necessarily a relational contract and vice versa. It has been argued that it is the relational factor of a contract other than the duration of a contract that prompts the courts to consider an obligation based on good faith.[135]

Hopefully, the Supreme Court will take an opportunity to address this issue in more detail in the future.[136] Before that happens, *Walford v Miles*[137] is still a good law in English contract law, which means that an agreement to negotiate in good faith is uncertain and void and therefore will not be enforced by the courts. As for good faith in the performance of contracts, the sooner there is a Supreme Court decision in this regard, the better view we will have on this issue. Therefore, at this stage, it is far too early and too idealistic to claim that there is now a general principle of good faith in English contract law, be it in negotiation or in performance or in both.

---

[129] *MSC Mediterranean Shipping Co SA v Cottonex Anstalt* [2016] EWCA Civ 789.

[130] J W Carter and Wayne Courtney, 'Good Faith in Contracts: Is There an Implied Promise to Act Honestly?' (2016) 75 *Cambridge Law Journal* 608, 609–619.

[131] [2015] UKSC 17.

[132] There is a view that a substantial body of case law is emerging endorsing the implication of a term of exercising a power conferred by a contract in good faith. See Ewan McKendrick, 'Good Faith in the Performance of a Contract in English Law' in Larry Dimatteo and Martin Hogg (eds), *Comparative Contract Law: British and American Perspectives* (Oxford University Press, 2015) 197, 200–1.

[133] Furmston and Carter, above n 111, 1025.

[134] McKendrick, above n 58 (Chap. 3), 103.

[135] Hugh Collins, 'Implied Terms: The Foundation in Good Faith and Fair Dealing' (2014) 67 *Current Legal Problems* 297, 326.

[136] It is suggested that there are three options that the court may take. The first is to stick to the traditional approach that English law does not recognize a general duty of good faith in contract performance. The second is to recognise a general principle of good faith in the performance of contracts. The third is to embrace a general duty of good faith in the performance of contracts and to make substantive change to certain rules of English contract law. See McKendrick, 'Good Faith in the Performance of a Contract in English Law', above n 132, 209–210. However, it does not mean that the Supreme Court is bound to follow one of these options. It may put forward another solution or other solutions.

[137] [1992] 2 AC 128. It is worth noting that in *Walford v Miles,* an agreement to negotiate in good faith was rejected by the House of Lords and was held as unenforceable. See McKendrick, *Contract Law, Contract Law*, above n 92, 488–494.

However, despite the existence of and apparently persistent hostility toward the general principle or duty of good faith, it seems likely that the English courts are more willing and likely to recognise, in long-term relational contracts, an implied duty of good faith in general,[138] and an implied duty of co-operation or of fair dealing on the basis of good faith in particular.[139] The reason is that many long-term relational contracts need more flexibility and require supplementary duties to achieve business efficacy; therefore, the courts are more likely to adopt a contextual approach to impose greater duties of loyalty and co-operation on the parties.[140] It has been argued that where a long-term contract in general or a long-term relational contract in particular, is embroiled in the disputes, it is more likely that good faith will play a more salient role and the courts may take a more flexible approach.[141] But English contract law should not recognise relational contracts as an independent category of contracts, and the courts' power to intervene ought to be limited and applied only to give effect to the contracts.[142] Suffice to say that the relational nature of a long-term contract is not significant and strong enough to encourage the courts to impose paternalistic duties on the parties.[143] However, it is argued that if the parties explicitly agree to act in good faith in their long-term contracts, the courts should respect the choice of the parties and give effect to relevant contract terms.[144]

In addition, the similarities and differences between relational contracts and contracts involving fiduciary relations have not been fully articulated, if there are any. Whether or not equitable doctrines with regard to fiduciary duties can deal with issues arising from relational contracts effectively and comprehensively is still unclear. Although it is accepted that the doctrines on fiduciary duties handle issues relating to contracts which called for close co-operation on the basis of trust and confidence,[145] it is argued that there is a tendency in the English case law which shows that a duty of co-operative good faith can arise during the life-time of the contracts in which the parties are in a position which floats on a scale with an arm's length at one end and fiduciary relationship on the other.[146]

---

[138] *Yam Seng Pte v International Trade Corporation Ltd* [2013] EWHC 111 (QB).

[139] Andrews, above 116, 953, 974.

[140] Hugh Collins, 'Implied Terms', above n 135, 324–330.

[141] This proposition is accepted by certain English scholars. See, e.g., McKendrick, 'The Regulation of Long-Term Contracts in English Law' above n 3 (Chap. 2), 310–333.

[142] Ibid, 316–322, 329–333.

[143] David Campbell, 'Good Faith and the Ubiquity of the 'Relational' Contract' (2014) 77 *Modern Law Review* 475, 475, 490–2.

[144] Lady Justice Arden, 'Coming to Terms with Good Faith' (2013) 30 *Journal of Contract Law* 199, 209–213.

[145] Michael Bridge, 'Good Faith, the Common Law and the CISG' (2017) 22 *Uniform Law Review* 98, 105.

[146] Andrews, above n 116, 953.

English contract law has shown some signs of moving toward a relational approach based on the context of individual cases.[147] However, it still awaits further clarification from the courts to decide whether relational contracts should be treated separately and differently from concrete contracts and to determine whether parties, who are engaged in a contractual relationship which is not at arm's length and short of fiduciary relationship, are under a duty of co-operation based on good faith, be it via the mechanism of interpretation or implied terms.

It seems that the battle between the piecemeal solution approach and the general principle approach is continuing and will continue for a long time and that there is no sign that the general principle approach will gain great support and applause in English contract law which is deeply rooted and constitutes a corner of the foundations of English common law tradition. However, the recognition of the concept of good faith in the Consumer Rights Act 2015, although limited to certain consumer contracts, has forced English contract law to face the subject of good faith more directly.[148] Also, the cases of relational contracts, as we have seen, result in more a heated debate on good faith. Whether Brexit will have any impacts in this regard remains unclear. Hopefully, together they might break the ice and bring about change, in whatever direction it might be, and the change will not come at too great a cost.[149]

4.2.2.3 Australian Contract Law

There are overwhelming cases, books, articles and other material in relation to good faith in Australian contract law. It is pointed out that '[t]he material available on this issue, whether judicial, academic or otherwise, is so voluminous that one is at pains to know where to dive in'.[150] Therefore, it seems impossible to offer an exhaustive list of the materials available in respect of the good faith issue. The task of unveiling good faith is extremely challenging. To attempt to do so would be like swimming in the ocean where one can easily drown. Therefore, it is easier to have only an overview of the core issues associated with this topic.

The status of good faith in Australian contract law is controversial. The controversy lies in the recognition of it in State and Federal courts and the ambiguous and reluctant attitude of the High Court of Australia to recognise it.

---

[147] Beale, above n 27, 130–6.

[148] McKendrick, *Contract Law*, above n 92, 487–8.

[149] Beale, above n 27, 136.

[150] Marilyn Warren, 'Good Faith: Where are We at?' (2010) 34 *Melbourne University Law Review* 344, 345.

The Status of Good Faith in State and Federal Courts

Case law from state and federal courts and academic writings has advocated and recognized that there is an implied duty of good faith in the performance of a contract.

In case law, good faith has been recognised and established by both state and federal courts as an implied term in contract performance.[151] The case of *Renard Constructions (ME) Pty Ltd v Minister for Public Works*[152] opened a Pandora's Box of good faith in Australia. The case caused debates on whether an implied duty of good faith had been adopted.[153] Following *Renard*, many cases in New South Wales recognised the duty of good faith as a term implied either by law[154] or in fact.[155] The implied term approach of the duty of good faith was accepted by other state courts as well.[156] Apart from state courts, the Federal Court of Australia has also recognised the implied duty of good faith in different cases.[157] But it is noteworthy that views against the existence of good faith as an implied duty are expressed in cases as well.[158] In practice, law firms have started to advise their clients to be aware of and pay heed to the potential duty of good faith in the performance of contractual obligations.[159]

The implied duty approach has obtained support from academics.[160] On the basis of the cases, it is stated that '[i]t is undisputed that in Australia an implied duty to exercise good faith is well established at least within the state court systems despite the reluctance of the High Court to speak on this matter' .[161] Similar to English law, there is also academic support for the view that commercial contracts should be

---

[151] Jeannie Paterson, Andrew Robertson and Arlen Duke, *Principles of Contract Law* (Thomson Reuters, 5th ed, 2016) 350.

[152] (1992) 26 NSWLR 234.

[153] See, e.g., Tyrone M Carlin, 'The Rise (and Fall?) of Implied Duty of Good Faith in Contractual Performance in Australia' (2002) 25 *University of New South Wales Law Journal* 99, 104–5.

[154] See, e.g., *Burger King Corp v Hungry Jack's Pty Ltd* (2001) 69 NSWLR 558; *Vodafone Pacific Limited v Mobile Innovations Limited* [2004] NSWCA 15.

[155] See, e.g., *Overlook Management BV v Foxtel Management Pty Ltd* [2002] NSWSC 17; *Maitland Main Collieries Pty Limited v Xstrata Mt Owen Pty Limited* [2006] NSWSC 1235.

[156] See, e.g., *Far Horizons Pty Ltd v McDonalds Australia Ltd* [2000] VSC 310; *Esso Australia Resources Pty Ltd v Southern Pacific Petroleum NL* [2005] VSCA 228; *Central Exchange Ltd v Anaconda Nickel Ltd* [2002] WASCA 94; *Tone Tasmania Pty Ltd v Garrott* [2008] TASSC 86; *De Pasquale v The Australian Chess Federation Incorporated* [2000] ACTSC 94.

[157] See, e.g., *Hughes Aircraft Services International v Airservices Australia* [1997] 76 FCR 151; *South Sydney District Rugby League Football Club v News Ltd* [2000] FCA 1541.

[158] See, e.g., *GSA Group v Siebe PLC* (1993) 30 NSWLR 573; *Hunter Valley Skydiving Centre Pty Ltd v Central Coast Aero Club Ltd* [2008] NSWSC 539.

[159] Warren, 'Good Faith', above n 150, 347.

[160] See, e.g., Rich Ladbury, 'Implied Duty of Good Faith: A Comment' [2002] *Australian Mining and Petroleum Law Association (AMPLA) Yearbook* 22, 46.

[161] Bruno Zeller and Camilla Baasch Andersen, 'Good Faith – The Gordian Knot of International Commerce' (2016) 28 *Pace International Law Review* 1, 10.

divided into two groups, relational contracts and non-relational contracts, and that good faith has a role to play in dealing with issues arising from relational contracts.[162] In relational commercial contracts, an implied duty of good faith in their performance and enforcement is possible and feasible by taking the contextual and co-operative approach of analysing contractual relations.[163]

However, there is also a view against the implied duty approach. The shortcomings of viewing good faith as an implied duty in the performance of contracts lie in its uncertainty and unpredictability.[164] Also, good faith is implicit or inherent in contract law rules, therefore, implied duty of good faith is unnecessary and may cause confusion.[165]

The Status of Good Faith in the High Court of Australia

In *Royal Botanic Gardens and Domain Trust v South Sydney City Council*,[166] the High Court of Australia, on the one hand, recognized the significance of a doctrine of good faith; but on the other hand, has not yet determined whether such a doctrine exists, and if it does exist, its content and scope has not been decided. In the dissenting judgement of Kirby J, his honour denied the existence of an implied duty of good faith and fair dealing by stating that:

> However, in Australia, such an implied term appears to conflict with fundamental notions of caveat emptor that are inherent (statute and equitable intervention apart) in common law conceptions of economic freedom. It also appears to be inconsistent with the law as it has developed in this country in respect of the introduction of implied terms into written contracts which the parties have omitted to include.[167]

In the joint judgement delivered by Gleeson CJ, Gaudron, McHugh, Gummow and Hayne JJ in the above-mentioned case, their Honours showed an unwillingness to address this issue by stating that:

> The second matter concerns the debate in various Australian authorities concerning the existence and content of an implied obligation or duty of good faith and fair dealing in contractual performance and the exercise of contractual rights and powers… The result is

[162] Howard Munro, 'The "Good Faith" Controversy in Australian Commercial Law: A Survey of the Spectrum of Academic Legal Opinion' (2009) 28 *The University of Queensland Law Journal* 167, 175–6.

[163] Bill Dixon, 'Common Law Obligations of Good Faith in Australian Commercial Contracts-A Relational Recipe' (2005) 33 *Australian Business Law Review* 87, 95–8.

[164] Elisabeth Peden, 'Good Faith in the Performance of Contract Law' (2004) 42 *Law Society Journal* 64, 64.

[165] Elisabeth Peden, '"Implicit Good Faith"- or Do We Still Need an Implied Term of Good Faith?' (2009) 25 *Journal of Contract Law* 50, 51.

[166] *Royal Botanic Gardens and Domain Trust v South Sydney City Council* (2002) 186 ALR 289.

[167] Ibid, 312.

> that, whilst the issues respecting the existence and scope of a "good faith" doctrine are important, this is an inappropriate occasion to consider them.[168]

Callinan J was of the same opinion, deciding that:

> (I)t is unnecessary to answer the question…: whether both in performing obligations and exercising rights under a contract, all parties owe to one another a duty of good faith; and, the extent to which, if such were to be the law, a duty of good faith might deny a party an opportunistic or commercial exercise of an otherwise lawful commercial right.[169]

Kirby J agreed with the joint reasons and the reasons of Callinan J mentioned above in respect of the unnecessary exploration of the good faith issue.[170]

In the most recent case, *Commonwealth Bank of Australia v Barker*,[171] the High Court did not show any tendency to adopt either a general principle of good faith or an implied term in law on good faith.

It is worth noting that Peden proposes that good faith is applied during the construction of a contract.[172] Peden argues that *Carr v J A Berriman Pty Ltd*[173] shows implicit good faith which means, in other words, that the good faith construction was recognized and adopted by the High Court of Australia.[174] However, there has been no official response to this view from the High Court of Australia.

In *Lange v Australian Broadcasting Corporation*, the High Court of Australia has ruled that:

> There is but one common law in Australia which is declared by this Court as the final court of appeal. In contrast to the position in the United States, the common law as it exists throughout the Australian States and Territories is not fragmented into different systems of jurisprudence, possessing different content and subject to different authoritative interpretations.[175]

The view that there is only one common law in Australia was affirmed by the High Court of Australia in *Lipohar v The Queen*[176] by citing McHugh J's statement in *Kable v Director of Public Prosecutions (NSW)* that:

> [T]here is a common law of Australia as opposed to a common law of individual States is clear.[177]

The High Court of Australia also added that:

---

168 Ibid, 301.

169 Ibid, 327.

170 Ibid, 312.

171 (2014) 253 CLR 169.

172 Elisabeth Peden, *Good faith in the performance of contracts* (LexisNexis Butterworths, 2003) 2.

173 (1953) 89 CLR 327.

174 Peden, '"Implicit Good Faith"- or Do We Still Need an Implied Term of Good Faith?' above n 165, 60–1.

175 (1997) 189 CLR 520, 563.

176 (1999) 200 CLR 485.

177 (1996) 189 CLR 51, 112.

> To assert that there is more than one common law in Australia or that there is a common law of individual States is to ignore the central place which precedent has in both understanding the common law and explaining its basis.[178]

Since there is only one common law in Australia, until the High Court of Australia makes a final decision addressing the good faith issue in a future case, it is difficult to argue that good faith plays a significant role in Australian contract law. Unfortunately, given the High Court of Australia's attitude in the two cases on good faith, the High Court of Australia is not likely to take an opportunity to clarify the status of good faith in the foreseeable future.[179] There may be a long waiting time.

4.3 Good Faith Under the CISG and the UNIDROIT Principles

Both the CISG and the UNIDROIT Principles have provisions with regard to the principle of good faith. However, the principle of good faith plays different roles in the CISG and in the UNIDROIT Principles. In the CISG, there is no provision expressly stipulating that parties to an international sale contract should act in good faith. The principle of good faith is mentioned only in Article 7(1) of the CISG, which reads as follows:

> In the interpretation of this Convention, regard is to be had to its international character and to the need to promote uniformity in its application and the observation of good faith in international trade.[180]

Article 7(1) was drafted to deal with the interpretation of the CISG. The ambiguity of the expression 'the observation of the good faith in international trade' renders the role of the principle of good faith both vague and uncertain in the international uniform sales law. On the other hand, there is another picture of the principle of good faith in the UNIDROIT Principles, in which Article 1.7 expressly states that:

> (1) Each party must act in accordance with good faith and fair dealing in international trade.
> (2) The parties may not exclude or limit this duty.[181]

Compared to the CISG, the UNIDROIT Principles give good faith a formal status as a general principle. The recognition of good faith in the UNIDROIT Principles reflects and reinforces a global trend toward the adoption of good faith as a general

---

[178] (1999) 200 CLR 485, 505.

[179] There are several issues that the High Court needs to address in order to clarify the role of good faith, such as the relationship between good faith and equitable doctrines, the relationship between good faith and a fiduciary duty, the relationship between good faith and unconscionability. J W Carter and Andrew Stewart, 'Interpretation, Good Faith and the 'True Meaning' of Contracts: The Royal Botanic Decision' (2002) 18 *Journal of Contract Law* 182, 193–5.

[180] The CISG art 7(1).

[181] Article 1.7 UNIDROIT Principles 2016.

principle in contract law.[182] It will be of help and of significance to understand the status of good faith at the international level more accurately.

4.3.1 Good Faith Under the CISG

Some issues are too difficult to include in the CISG due to the divergences and inconsistencies of domestic laws. Thus, in order to achieve the goal of a broad and general acceptance of the CISG, the drafters needed to compromise on certain matters.[183] Good faith is undoubtedly one of them. Despite the difficulties, good faith is considered to be contained in Article 7 and is regarded as the most significant article in the CISG.[184]

It is both useful and important to investigate good faith throughout the legislative history of the CISG with a view to discovering and ascertaining the original understanding and appropriate interpretation and application in international trade in general and in long-term relational supply contracts in particular in the context of hardship.

4.3.1.1 Historical and Legislative Background of Article 7 of the CISG

Stage One

In the process of drafting Article 7, there were various drafts and proposals which eventually formed the current version of the article. One early proposal consisted of two paragraphs submitted by the Hungarian representative and a third paragraph proposed by the German Democratic Republic.[185] These paragraphs read as follows:

> Paragraph I: In the course of the formation of the contract the parties must observe the principles of fair dealing and act in good faith. Conduct violating these principles is devoid of any legal protection.
>
> Paragraph II: The exclusion of liability for damage caused intentionally or with gross negligence is void.

---

[182] Vogenauer, *Commentary on the UNIDROIT Principles of International Commercial Contracts (PICC)*, above n 130 (Chap. 3), 205–8.

[183] Stefan Kröll, 'Selected Problems Concerning the CISG's Scope of Application' (2005) 25 *Journal of Law and Commerce* 39, 39.

[184] Phanesh Koneru, 'The International Interpretation of the UN Convention on Contracts for the International Sale of Goods: An Approach Based on General Principles' (1997) 6 *Minnesota Journal of Global Trade* 105, 106.

[185] John O Honnold, *Documentary History of the Uniform Law for International Sales* (Kluwer Law and Taxation Publishers, 1989) 298.

> Paragraph III: In case a party violates the duties of care customary in the preparation and formation of a contract of sale, the other party may claim compensation for costs borne by it.[186]

In the course of the discussion relating to the inclusion of good faith in the CISG, the first sentence of paragraph I received significant support from the representatives who agreed that the CISG should contain an article on good faith and fair dealing; however, there were also arguments against the formulation of the proposed article.[187]

> Paragraph I was supported on the basis that it incorporated a desirable standard of business conduct in the process of formation of contracts, a standard which was recognized and codified in many legal systems and there was no reason for not having a similar rule in international trade. Although there might be difficulty ... The existence of a uniform text might encourage future uniformity of interpretation of such matters.
>
> On the other hand, it was noted that the general principle enunciated in the first sentence would not have much effect until it had been judicially interpreted and applied over a long period of time. In addition, the view was expressed that the sentence was too vague and imprecise...[188]

No consensus could be reached on the second and third paragraphs above. Therefore, after considerable deliberation, the Working Group decided to adopt the first sentence of the first paragraph.[189]

Stage Two

The second round of the debate on whether an article with regard to good faith should be included in the CISG caused lengthy and heated discussions during which different views were expressed.

Those who supported an article on good faith argued that good faith was generally and universally recognized and accepted by many domestic legal systems and it was valuable and desirable to include it in a convention governing international trade in particular. The opponents argued that to act in good faith was already implicit in all laws dealing with business activities; hence, there was no need to include such an article in the CISG.[190] In addition, the opponents stated that the draft article did not stipulate the consequences of the failure to observe good faith; whereas the supporters believed that it was unnecessary to specify the consequences of the breach of good faith, and that the gap could be filled by case law developed by the courts in the future application of the CISG.[191] The opponents were concerned that a coherent case law might not be possible due to the uncertainty and

---

[186] Ibid.

[187] Ibid.

[188] Ibid, 298–9.

[189] Ibid, 299.

[190] Ibid, 369.

[191] Ibid.

vagueness of good faith and various legal and social traditions in different domestic laws.[192] Last but not least, the opponents argued that the proposed article on good faith was more like a moral requirement than a legal obligation imposed on the parties.[193] In the light of these different opinions a special Working Group was set up to find a compromise solution.[194]

Stage Three

The special Working Group, after deliberated preparation, proposed a new article on good faith, which states:

> In the interpretation and application of the provisions of this Convention, regard is to be had to its international character and to the need to promote uniformity and to observe good faith in international trade.[195]

The proposal was debated and various amendments were submitted for extensive discussion.[196] After heated debate, the proposed article by the special Working Group was adopted with minor changes. The revised proposal reads as follows:

> In the interpretation and application of the provisions of this Convention, regard is to be had to its international character and to the need to promote uniformity and the observation of good faith in international trade.[197]

Stage Four

During the last stage of the preparation of the article with reference to good faith, minor changes were made before it was finally adopted and read the same as the existing Article 7(1).

In addition, in order to deal with the problems in relation to the unforeseen gaps in the CISG, the current Article 7(2) was added.[198]

> Questions concerning matters governed by this Convention which are not expressly settled in it are to be settled in conformity with the general principles on which it is based or, in the absence of such principles, in conformity with the law applicable by virtue of the rules of private international law.[199]

---

192 Ibid.

193 Ibid.

194 Ibid, 369–370.

195 Ibid, 370.

196 Ibid, 659.

197 Ibid, 370.

198 Bianca and Bonell, above n 96 (Chap. 3), 70–1.

199 The CISG art 7(2).

Finally, Article 7 consisting of two paragraphs, as it is now, was approved by the Diplomatic Conference and was open for signature and ratification. It is argued that 'the result was strange but gained for the principle of good faith a foothold in an international convention for unification of law. It is hoped that this meagre result represents a modest start'.[200]

4.3.1.2 Narrow or Wide Interpretation of Article 7

The adoption of Article 7 of the CISG is not the end of the story in respect of good faith. it is, however, a new start of a battle as to the nature, role, function and other aspects of good faith in the CISG in light of the vague and unclear reference in Article 7, leading to seemingly endless debates and discussions. Article 7 on good faith is, on one hand, a war minus the shooting; on the other hand, a beautiful fairy tale, but difficult to realize.

Since the adoption of Article 7, various scholars have attempted to comment on and analyse its status within the CISG.[201] Different facets and functions of good faith have been identified by scholars.[202] The issue that is of great interest and importance to this book is whether good faith should be applied only in the interpretation of the CISG itself or be applied both to the interpretation of the CISG and to the relationship between the contracting parties.

There is a view that the only role that good faith can play is to interpret the CISG. Honnold believed that the CISG rejects good faith as a general principle and that good faith can solely be used to interpret the CISG itself.[203] Farnsworth, opposing any reference to good faith in the course of drafting the CISG, supported Honnold's view and stated that the CISG should be read literally, which means that good faith should be applied no more than as a guidance for a court in the interpretation of the CISG itself, that good faith does not impose a duty on the parties to act in good faith, and that good faith should not serve as one of the general principles on which the CISG is based.[204] Winship argued that the legislative history of Article

---

[200] Eörsi, above n 35 (Chap. 1), 349.

[201] Ingeborg Schwenzer (ed), *Commentary on the UN Convention on the International Sale of Goods(CISG)* (Oxford University Press, 3rd ed, 2010) 120–144; Schlechtriem and Schwenzer, above n 97 (Chap. 3), 93–110; Bianca and Bonell, above n 96 (Chap. 3), 65–94; Troy Keily, 'Good Faith and the Vienna Convention on Contracts for the International Sale of Goods (CISG)' (1999) 3 *Vindobona Journal of International Commercial Law and Arbitration* 15, 15–40; Paul J Powers, 'Defining the Undefinable: Good Faith and the United Nations Convention on Contracts for the International Sale of Goods' (1999) 18 *Journal of Law and Commerce* 333, 333–353.

[202] See, e.g., Lisa Spagnolo, 'Opening Pandora's Box: Good Faith and Precontractual Liability in the CISG' (2007) 21 *Temple International and Comparative Law Journal* 261, 274.

[203] John O Honnold, *Uniform Law for International Sales* (Kluwer Law International, 3rd ed, 1999) 100.

[204] E Allen Farnsworth, 'Duties of Good Faith and Fair Dealing under the UNIDROIT Principles, Relevant International Conventions, and National Laws' (1995) 3 *Tulane Journal of International and Comparative Law* 47, 55–7.

7 is in favour of the limited reading of the role of good faith.[205] These views are supported by other scholars as well.[206]

In addition, in cases where the CISG is to be interpreted in line with good faith, the meaning and the application of which are limited in international trade in the light of Article 7 (1). Good faith in the CISG needs to be considered, understood and observed in the context of international trade.[207] The drafting history of Article 7(1) reflects the desire to abandon the domestic concepts and rules regarding good faith in the process of the interpretation of the CISG,[208] and to restrain the understanding of good faith from reference to domestic law.[209] Neither should the CISG be read and interpreted through the lenses of domestic law;[210] nor should the interpretation of certain concepts rely on a particular legal system.[211] Recourse to domestic definitions and interpretations of good faith is contrary to the autonomous and international interpretation of the CISG pursuant to Article 7(1); therefore, they cannot be used to interpret the CISG.[212] In several cases, Article 7(1) has been applied broadly to constitute a foundation of the judgments rendered by national courts which have relied on concretized applications of good faith in domestic laws to resolve issues arising from international transactions.[213] This trend is inconsistent with the literal reading of Article 7(1) and may sabotage the integrated and uniform interpretation of the CISG.

However, more scholars believe that good faith should have a broader role in the CISG. Bonell is of the view that good faith is not limited to the interpretation of the CISG itself and that it should be regarded as one of the general principles of the CISG.[214] Schlechtriem argues that good faith is applied not only in the interpretation of the CISG, but also to the legal relations between the parties, but with regard to the later, it is viable only through Article 7(2), by being regarded as one of the general

---

[205] Peter Winship, 'Commentary on Professor Kastley's *Rhetorical Analysis*' (1988) 8 *Northwestern Journal of International Law and Business* 623, 631–3.

[206] See, e.g., John Felemegas, 'Comparative Editorial Remarks on the Concept of Good Faith in the CISG and the PECL' (2001) 13 *Pace International Law Review* 399, 406. He notes that the limited understanding of the role of the principle of good faith in the CISG is clearly showed and supported by the text of the CISG itself and its legislative history.

[207] Bianca and Bonell, above n 96 (Chap. 3), 72–3.

[208] Alexander S Komarov, 'Internationality, Uniformity and Observance of Good Faith as Criteria in Interpretation of CISG: Some Remarks on Article 7(1)' (2005) 25 *Journal of Law and Commerce* 75, 78.

[209] Walt, above n 33 (Chap. 1), 46.

[210] John Honnold, 'The Sales Convention in Action- Uniform International Words: Uniform Application?' (2008) 8 *Journal of Law and Commerce* 207, 208.

[211] Franco Ferrari, 'CISG Case Law: A New Challenge for Interpreters?' (1998) 17 *Journal of Law and Commerce* 245, 246.

[212] Bruno Zeller, 'Good Faith – The Scarlet Pimpernel of the CISG' (2001) 6 *International Trade and Business Law Review* 227, 227–8.

[213] Bridge, 'Good Faith, the Common Law and the CISG', above n 145, 111–2.

[214] Bianca and Bonell, above n 96 (Chap. 3), 85.

principles on which the CISG is based.[215] Kastely argues that good faith in international trade is explicitly stated as a principle of the CISG according to Article 7 and reflected in many other articles in the CISG.[216] In the Secretariat Commentary on the draft provision relating to good faith, it is stated that good faith is a general principle of the CISG by referring to various articles contained in the CISG.[217] Several other scholars support this proposition.[218] Good faith is, therefore, considered to cover not only the application of the CISG itself but also the rights and obligations of the parties to a contract governed by the CISG.[219] The trend to broaden the role of good faith indirectly may in the course of time result in the emergence and recognition of a general duty of good faith according to which parties should act.[220] The risk of considering the principle of good faith as a general principle in the light of Article 7(2) is that good faith may become boundless, and that eventually it may, in meaning everything, mean nothing.[221] Also, good faith as a general principle in the CISG is not widely recognised by the case law.[222]

In addition, since the nature of the CISG is an international treaty, the Vienna Convention on the Law of Treaties (hereinafter: the Vienna Convention) should be considered as well in order to make the role of good faith in the CISG more certain and more transparent. As for the interpretation of international treaties, Article 31(1) of the Vienna Convention stipulates that 'a treaty shall be interpreted in good faith in accordance with the ordinary meaning to be given to the terms of the treaty in their context and in the light of its object and purpose'.[223] Therefore, the CISG, as a treaty, ought to be interpreted in good faith taking into account the ordinary meaning, object, and purpose of its terms both textually and contextually. Zeller argued that taking into account the overlap of the requirement of the application of good faith in the interpretation of an international treaty between the CISG and the Vienna Convention, which may render the emphasis of good faith in Article 7 of the CISG superfluous, good faith, therefore, should be regarded as a standard or an obligation imposed on the conduct of the parties to give its full meaning in a broad sense.[224]

---

[215] Schlechtriem and Schwenzer, above n 97 (Chap. 3), 95.

[216] Amy H Kastely, 'Unification and Community: A Rhetorical Analysis of the United Nations Sales Convention' (1988) 8 *Northwestern Journal of International Law and Business* 574, 597–9.

[217] Honnold, *Documentary History of the Uniform Law for International Sales*, above n 185, 408.

[218] See, eg, Bianca and Bonell, above n 96 (Chap. 3), 85; Kröll, Mistelis and Viscasillas, above n 106 (Chap. 3), 122–3.

[219] Bruno Zeller, 'Good Faith – Is it a Contractual Obligation?' (2003) 15 *Bond Law Review: Festschrift for David Allan and Mary Hiscock* 214, 220–6.

[220] Enderlein and Maskow, above n 95 (Chap. 3), 54–5.

[221] Bridge, 'The CISG and the UNIDROIT Principles of International Commercial Contracts', above n 7 (Chap. 3), 637.

[222] Foerstl, above n 21, 73–105.

[223] *Vienna Convention on the Law of Treaties*, opened for signature 23 May 1969, 1155 UNTS 331 (entered into force 27 January 1980) art 31(1).

[224] Bruno Zeller, 'The Observance of Good Faith in International Trade' in André Janssen and Olaf Meyer (eds), *CISG Methodology* (Sellier, 2009) 133, 136–8.

This view is criticized as it overlooked the restrictive term 'in international trade' in Article 7 that is used to restrain the scope of the promotion of good faith due to the commercial nature of the CISG.[225]

Also, according to Article 31(3) of the Vienna Convention, 'any subsequent practice in the application of the treaty which establishes the agreement of the parties regarding its interpretation' shall be taken into account in the interpretation of a treaty. Therefore, it is necessary and useful to refer to case law relating to the application of Article 7 of the CISG in practice. However, references to case law cannot offer more assistance in determining the role of good faith. The role of good faith in case law is amorphous as some cases follow the narrow approach that good faith applies only to the interpretation of the articles of the CISG, whereas other cases take the broad approach that good faith applies to the interpretation of the CISG itself and to the contracts governed by the CISG alike.[226] What makes it more complicated is that there are several sub-applications of good faith under the broad approach, meaning that good faith can be applied as dicta, as an alternative basis for a result achieved on other grounds, as an additional consideration which supports the achieved result, and as an independent ground for a result.[227]

In the CISG, good faith guides the interpretation of the unified law texts, of individual contracts and of the entire contractual relationship.[228]That good faith can apply in the interpretation of the CISG is not disputed by reason of the fact that the CISG expressly stipulates that in its interpretation good faith in international trade should be observed. It leaves no room for any argument that the CISG ought not to be interpreted in accordance with good faith. In addition, the parties to a contract for the international sale of goods can reach an agreement regarding the terms of their own contract in line with the principle of party autonomy. When the CISG is chosen by the parties as the law governing their contract in case of disputes, they are bound by the provisions contained in the CISG. Therefore, article 7 will apply to their contractual relationship.

Regarding the possibility of the application of good faith to a contractual relationship between the parties, there may be two approaches. Firstly, both parties can incorporate a term that allows the application of good faith or expressly state that they should act in good faith. In this case, they are not even bound to the strict understanding of Article 7 that good faith should only apply in the interpretation of the CISG. Secondly, if a term pertaining to good faith is not included in the parties' contract, it might be inferred that the parties may implicitly agree to be bound by good faith, since they do not expressly exclude the possibility that they ought to act in good faith. Deciding whether the parties intended to permit the application of

[225] Gillette and Walt, above n 115 (Chap. 3), 132–3.

[226] Ibid, 137–8.

[227] Ibid, 138–144.

[228] Ulrich Magnus, 'Remarks on Good Faith: The United Nations Convention on Contracts for the International Sale of Goods and the International Institute for the Unification of Private Law, Principles of International Commercial Contracts' (1998) 10 *Pace International Law Review* 89, 90–1.

good faith to their contractual relationship is a matter of interpretation. The objective test that what a reasonable person would have considered or would have done if placed in the parties' situation should apply.

4.3.1.3 The Possibility of Opting Out of Good Faith

Ideally, parties to contracts in relation to international trade promise to act in good faith all the time, regardless of where they are and their surrounding circumstances. Given the purpose of the CISG and the peculiar status and vague role of good faith in it, it will be impossible to argue and prove that good faith is a compulsory obligation of the contracting parties that cannot be excluded or avoided. It would be desirable and wise to offer some approaches to the parties who do not intend to act in accordance with good faith to exclude it.

Firstly, the parties can definitely exclude the application of good faith by referring to Article 6 of the CISG which reflects the principles of party autonomy and of freedom of contract. Secondly, a principle from public international law might be of help. In public international law, there is a principle called the principle of the persistent objector, according to which a state that has persistently objected to a rule developed in customary international law during the course of the emergence of the rule is not bound by it; therefore, individual states are permitted to opt out of those new and otherwise general rules of public international law.[229] If a similar rule could apply to good faith, it might offer another way for the parties to opt out subject to the prerequisite that they can prove their persistent objection to good faith and its application. In addition, a rule like the principle of the persistent objector may also applies to states, such as the UK, which persistently object to the concept and the application of good faith when deciding whether or not good faith applies to a state.

It can certainly be argued that such a rule seems to introduce a new vague concept to explain and opt out of an existing unclear concept. However, if such a principle has developed and has been used in public international law, it must have some value and advantages. There is no doubt that finding a feasible approach to the application of the principle of good faith or maybe even to the CISG, the collective wisdom of scholars, judges, arbitrators and lawyers from all around the world is required.

[229] Ted L Stein, 'The Approach of the Different Drummer: The Principle of the Persistent Objector in International Law' (1985) 26 *Harvard International Law Journal* 457, 457.

4.3.2 Good Faith Under the UNIDROIT Principles

The UNIDROIT Principles incorporated the principle of good faith in its first edition published in 1994. It remained unchanged in the following 2004, 2010 and 2016 editions. The official comments added to the articles dealing with the principle of good faith have expanded to assist the potential user of the UNIDROIT Principles to understand the principle of good faith better. It should be noted that the UNIDROIT Principles display a great tendency towards civil law concepts in general, and a great preference for good faith in particular, for which the UNIDROIT Principles have been heavily criticised by many common lawyers.[230] In this section, there will be no discussion of the functions of the principle of good faith; rather, the focus is on what good faith requires the parties to do and what it prohibits them from doing.

4.3.2.1 Positive Duty to Act in Good Faith

Article 1.7 cited above imposes a positive duty on the parties to act in accordance with the principle of good faith in international trade. According to the official comment to Article 1.7, the principle of good faith may be regarded as one of the fundamental ideas underlying the UNIDROIT Principles in the light of the fact that many provisions contained in different chapters of the UNIDROIT Principles constitute a direct or indirect application of the principle of good faith in one way or another.[231]

Article 1.7, by establishing the principle of good faith as a general duty that each party must act in accordance with good faith and fair dealing in international trade, makes it clear that the parties' behaviour must be in conformity with the principle of good faith from the birth to the death of the contract.[232]

Unlike the CISG, the drafters of the UNIDROIT Principles purported to extend the application of the principle of good faith to a broader scope. Under the UNIDROIT Principles, it extends to all the stages of an international commercial contract.[233] The principle of good faith applies not only in the process of the conclusion of an international commercial contract but also in the course of the performance thereof. It covers different periods of the contractual relationship between the parties directly or indirectly, ranging from contract negotiations to contract formation, from contract performance to contract non-performance, from contract

[230] Ingeborg Schwenzer, 'Global Unification of Contract Law' (2016) 21 *Uniform Law Review* 60, 67.

[231] Comment 1 to Article 1.7 UNIDROIT Principles 2016. Articles 1.8, 1.9(2), 2.1.4(2)(b), 2.1.15, 2.1.16, 2.1.18, 2.1.20, 2.2.4(2), 2.2.5(2), 2.2.7, 2.2.10, 3.2.2, 3.2.5, 3.2.7, 4.1(2), 4.2(2), 4.6, 4.8, 5.1.2, 5.1.3, 5.2.5, 5.3.3, 5.3.4, 6.1.3, 6.1.5, 6.1.16(2), 6.1.17(1), 6.2.3(3)(4), 7.1.2, 7.1.6, 7.1.7, 7.2.2(b)(c), 7.4.8, 7.4.13, 9.1.3, 9.1.4 and 9.1.10(1) are listed in the Comment 1.

[232] Comment 1 to Article 1.7 UNIDROIT Principles 2016.

[233] Vogenauer, *Commentary on the UNIDROIT Principles of International Commercial Contracts (PICC)*, above n 130 (Chap. 3), 209–210.

re-negotiation to contract adaptation, from contract interpretation to contract termination.[234]

Another difference between the CISG and the UNIDROIT Principles relating to good faith lies in whether good faith applies to the interpretation of both documents themselves. The CISG's attitude is clear in this regard as discussed above, whereas the UNIDROIT Principles are silent on this matter. Article 1.6 of the UNIDROIT Principles deals with the interpretation of the UNIDROIT Principles; however, it does not explicitly state that the principle of good faith can be applied for the purpose of interpretation.[235] The official comment of Article 1.6 nevertheless states that the principle of good faith, despite the fact that it aims at the contractual relationship between the parties, may be regarded as an expression underpinning the purposes of the UNIDROIT Principles[236] and therefore may be applied in the interpretation of the UNIDROIT Principles.[237]

The most salient problem is that the UNIDROIT Principles, like CISG, do not offer a clear definition of the principle of good faith. Although what good faith means still remains a mystery, the fact that good faith is coupled with fair dealing makes it clear that the principle of good faith should be considered and understood in an objective sense, as being synonymous with what is elsewhere in the UNIDROIT Principles referred to as 'reasonable commercial standard of fair dealing'[238] Notwithstanding the vagueness of the meaning, it is at least clear that the parties are under a duty to act in accordance with the principle of good faith in the light of Article 1.7.[239]

Like the CISG, the principle of good faith referred to in the UNIDROIT Principles is confined within international trade. It is clear that in the context of the UNIDROIT Principles, the principle of good faith is to be applied in accordance with an international standard rather than according to the standards originally adopted in national legal systems.[240] This proposition is confirmed by the official comment which states that national standards may probably be taken into account only to the extent that it is clear that they are generally accepted among the various national legal systems.[241] In addition, there is also a considerable and huge distinction in the standard of

[234] Michael J Bonell, *An International Restatement of Contract Law: The UNIDROIT Principles of International Commercial Contracts* (Martinus Nijhoff Publishers, 3rd ed, 2010) 136–150.

[235] Article 1.6 UNIDROIT Principles 2016, which reads as follows:

(1) In the interpretation of these Principles, regard is to be had to their international character and to their purposes including the need to promote uniformity in their application.
(2) Issues within the scope of these Principles but not expressly settled by them are as far as possible to be settled in accordance with their underlying general principles.

[236] Comment 3 to Article 1.6 UNIDROIT Principles 2016.

[237] Magnus, 'Remarks on Good Faith', above n 228, 90.

[238] Bonell, *An International Restatement of Contract Law*, above n 234, 131.

[239] Farnsworth, 'Duties of Good Faith and Fair Dealing under the UNIDROIT Principles, Relevant International Conventions, and National Laws', above n 204, 58.

[240] Bonell, *An International Restatement of Contract Law*, above n 234, 132.

[241] Comment 3 to Article 1.7 UNIDROIT Principles 2016.

business practice among different trade sectors. Even within one given trade sector, differences may still exist and may be more or less stringent in accordance with the socio-economic environment in which the trade is operated by various companies of different size and having various technical skills.[242] This implies that the principle of good faith must be interpreted by virtue of the special conditions of international trade.[243]

By referring to the principle of good faith in international trade, the UNIDROIT Principles, like the CISG, intend to better confine and explain its meaning and scope.[244] The problem arising from this is what the principle of good faith means in terms of international trade. There is no unequivocal answer to this question, just as there is no one definition of good faith. Although it is argued that in some sectors of the international trade, a principle of good faith may exist or be emerging, and may be already well and clearly defined and understood in business circles, no concrete example is given.[245] Neither can the existence of a uniform concept of the principle of good faith that may be valid to contracts of all kinds be discerned at an international level, nor can a concept generally be recognised and accepted for contracts merely of a single kind.[246] The impossibility of defining the principle of good faith in international trade has led to the failure of the attempts of Article 1.7 in the UNIDROIT Principles and Article 7 in the CISG, respectively. In addition, the reference to international trade may cause confusion. To avoid the interference and application of domestic laws, the principle of good faith is confined by the UNIDROIT Principles and the CISG to be understood in the light of international trade, which might be of value and of use; however, to support the principle of good faith in international trade, reference is made to the UNIDROIT Principles and the CISG themselves, which makes the argument a vicious circle that is confusing and unhelpful.[247]

4.3.2.2 Negative Prohibition on Behaviour Against Good Faith

The UNIDROIT Principles are directed, by and large, at redressing behaviour that does not comply with the principle of good faith. Two general rules are stipulated in the UNIDROIT Principles that are designed for, and imposed on, the parties to

---

242 Ibid.

243 Ibid.

244 Giuditta Cordero Moss, 'International Contracts between Common Law and Civil Law: Is Non-State Law to Be Preferred? The Difficulty of Interpreting Legal Standards Such as Good Faith' (2007) 7 *Global Jurist* 28, 30.

245 Ulrich Magnus, 'Comparative editorial remarks on the provisions regarding good faith in CISG Article 7(1) and the UNIDROIT Principles Article 1.7' in John Felemegas (ed), *An International Approach to the Interpretation of the United Nations Convention on Contracts for the International Sale of Goods (1980) as Uniform Sales Law* (Cambridge University Press, 2007) 45, 46.

246 Moss, above n 244, 30–1.

247 Ibid, 32–4.

control their behaviour in their contract. If the parties' behaviour is not compatible with either of the rules, what they have done is considered as a contravention of what the principle of good faith requires.

On the one hand, a typical instance of the parties' behaviour contrary to the principle of good faith is the so-called rule of 'abuse of rights', which is characterised by a party's malicious behaviour that occurs when a party exercises a right merely with a view of damaging the other party or of achieving a purpose other than the one for which it had been granted, or when the exercise of a right is disproportionate to the originally contemplated consequences.[248]

On the other hand, the behaviour of the parties is also controlled by the rule of 'inconsistent behaviour' contained in Article 1.8 of the UNIDROIT Principles, which reads:

> A party cannot act inconsistently with an understanding it has caused the other party to have and upon which that other party reasonably has acted in reliance to its detriment.

This indicates that a duty has been imposed on a party that he cannot cause detriment to the other party by acting inconsistently with an understanding in relation to their contractual relationship which the other party has been lead to have and upon which the other party has reasonably acted in reliance.[249]

The understanding may be the outcome of a representation, of a conduct, or of silence when a party would reasonably expect to be informed by the other party of the existence of an error, a misunderstanding or a misrepresentation that was being relied on.[250]

In addition, as long as the understanding concerns the contractual relationship of the parties in one way or another, this understanding for the purposes of Article 1.8 is not limited to any particular subject-matter and it may relate not only to a matter of fact but also to a matter of law or to a matter of intention, or to the parties' behaviour under their contract.[251]

There is, however, a significant restriction on the understanding that it must be one upon which, in the light of the circumstances of the contract, the other party actually can and reasonably does rely.[252] To decide whether the reliance is reasonable is a matter of interpretation which should take into account the nature and the terms of the contract, the communications and conduct of the parties, the nature and surrounding circumstances of the parties' dealings and the expectations they could reasonably have.[253]

The prohibition provided in Article 1.8 may lead to the creation of rights and to the loss, suspension or modification of rights otherwise than by agreement of the parties by reason of the fact that the understanding on which the parties purport to

---

[248] Bonell, *An International Restatement of Contract Law*, above n 234, 133.

[249] Comment 1 to Article 1.8 UNIDROIT Principles 2016.

[250] Bonell, *An International Restatement of Contract Law*, above n 234, 134.

[251] Comment 2 to Article 1.8 UNIDROIT Principles 2016.

[252] Ibid.

[253] Ibid.

rely upon may itself be inconsistent with their agreed or actual rights under the contract.[254]

The rule of 'inconsistent behaviour' is reflected in many articles of the UNIDROIT Principles, which provide specific guidelines for the parties' behaviour in order to maintain its consistency. For instance,

> [A]n offer cannot be revoked… if it was reasonable for the offeree to rely on the offer as being irrevocable and the offeree has acted in reliance on the offer.[255]

Moreover,

> A contract in writing which contains a clause requiring any modification or termination by agreement to be in a particular form may not be otherwise modified or terminated. However, a party may be precluded by its conduct from asserting such a clause to the extent that the other party has acted in reliance on that conduct.[256]

In addition,

> [W]here the principal causes the third party reasonably to believe that the agent has authority to act on behalf of the principal and that the agent is acting within the scope of that authority, the principal may not invoke against the third party the lack of authority of the agent.[257]

These are several applications of the general rule prohibiting the parties' inconsistent behaviour.

Apart from the two general rules on 'abuse of rights' and 'inconsistent behaviour' discussed above, Article 2.1.15 concerns a significant application with regard to a concrete issue in the UNIDROIT Principles with a view to advancing the principle of good faith, albeit negatively. It does not promote the principle of good faith directly; instead, it prohibits bad faith relating to the negotiation process. Article 2.1.15 provides that:

> (1) A party is free to negotiate and is not liable for failure to reach an agreement.
> (2) However, a party who negotiates or breaks off negotiations in bad faith is liable for the losses caused to the other party.
> (3) It is bad faith, in particular, for a party to enter into or continue negotiations when intending not to reach an agreement with the other party.[258]

According to Article 2.1.15, parties have some freedom when negotiating a contract. They are able to not only freely decide when and with whom to enter into negotiations in order to conclude a contract, but also freely determine how and for how long to proceed in order to reach an agreement.[259] Although the parties are free to enter into negotiations and to decide on the terms to be negotiated and contained in their contract, their freedom is not unlimited, which means their behaviour must

---

[254] Ibid.

[255] Article 2.1.4(2) UNIDROIT Principles 2016.

[256] Article 2.1.18 UNIDROIT Principles 2016.

[257] Article 2.2.5 UNIDROIT Principles 2016.

[258] Article 2.1.15 UNIDROIT Principles 2016.

[259] Comment 1 to Article 2.1.15 UNIDROIT Principles 2016.

not be contrary to the principle of good faith provided in Article 1.7.[260] For instance, once an offer has been made, a party cannot break off negotiations abruptly and without justification at will.[261] Whether a party may simply break off negotiations depends on the contract and the surrounding circumstances of the case, in particular, the extent to which the other party, based on the behaviour of the first party, has reasonably believed that the negotiations will lead to a positive outcome, and also on the number of agreed issues to be incorporated into their future contract.[262] Therefore, one party's misuse of the negotiation process to the detriment of the other party contravenes the duty to act in accordance with the principle of good faith imposed on the parties by Article 1.7 and is, accordingly, prohibited by Article 2.1.15.

No clear definition of bad faith is provided by Article 2.1.15. It offers only one particular example of negotiating in bad faith in paragraph (3) where a party enters into or proceeds with negotiations with the other party in spite of the fact that he or she does not intend to conclude a contract. In addition, another example of bad faith in negotiation is mentioned in the official comments where:

> [O]ne party has deliberately or by negligence misled the other party as to the nature or terms of the proposed contract, either by actually misrepresenting facts, or by not disclosing facts which, given the nature of the parties and/or the contract, should have been disclosed.[263]

These examples are probably insufficient to define and understand what bad faith means in the UNIDROIT Principles and therefore may have a negative impact on the application of Article 2.1.15 and eventually Article 1.7.

Article 1.7 is silent on the consequences of the failure of the parties to act in accordance with good faith. Also, the illustrations in the Official Comments to Article 1.7 do not address this issue explicitly. Only one illustration may implicitly indicate a consequence.

> Under a contract for the sale of high-technology equipment the purchaser loses the right to rely on any defect in the goods if it does not give notice to the seller specifying the nature of the defect without undue delay after it has discovered or ought to have discovered the defect. A, a buyer operating in a country where such equipment is commonly used, discovers a defect in the equipment after having put it into operation, but in its notice to B, the seller of the equipment, A gives misleading indications as to the nature of the defect. A loses its right to rely on the defect since a more careful examination of the defect would have permitted it to give B the necessary specifications.[264]

It seems that one probable consequence of the parties' failure to act in good faith is 'the loss of a right that would otherwise have been available to that party.'[265]

---

[260] Comment 2 to Article 2.1.15 UNIDROIT Principles 2016.

[261] Comment 3 to Article 2.1.15 UNIDROIT Principles 2016.

[262] Ibid.

[263] Comment 2 to Article 2.1.15 UNIDROIT Principles 2016.

[264] Illustration 7 to Article 1.7 UNIDROIT Principles 2016.

[265] Vogenauer, *Commentary on the UNIDROIT Principles of International Commercial Contracts (PICC)*, above n 130 (Chap. 3), 224.

Whether there may be other consequences remains unclear from the text of the UNIDROIT Principles.[266]

4.3.2.3 Exclusion of the General Principle of Good Faith

The general principle of good faith is one of the fundamental ideas on which the UNIDROIT Principles is based and is given a mandatory nature by the UNIDROIT Principles. This means that the parties must act in accordance with good faith; hence, the parties may not contractually exclude or limit it.[267] Three articles[268] in other chapters of the UNIDROIT Principles are referred to as examples for specific application of this general prohibition with respect to exclusion or limitation of the principle of good faith between the parties.[269]

Although it may be impossible for the parties to exclude or limit their duty to act in good faith,[270] the UNIDROIT Principles do not impose restrictions on the parties' ability to set a higher standard than that required by the principle of good faith relating to their behaviour under the contract. Nothing will keep the parties from imposing, in their contract, a duty on themselves in relation to the observation of more stringent standards of behaviour.[271] That is to say, the parties are definitely free to add a term in relation to higher standards of their behaviour to their contract, although they cannot deviate from their general duty to observe the principle of good faith.[272] It seems that the UNIDROIT Principles set only a bottom line requirement for the behaviour of the parties; although this cannot be breached, no corresponding highest requirement has been established.

In addition, even another fundamental idea, the principle of freedom of contract,[273] contained in the UNIDROIT Principles cannot be an exception for the parties to exclude or limit the principle of good faith contractually. Article 1.5 of the UNIDROIT Principles states that:

> The parties may exclude the application of these Principles or derogate from or vary the effect of any of their provisions, except as otherwise provided in the Principles.

This implies that party autonomy is limited in the light of the fact that the UNIDROIT Principles stipulate provisions from which the parties may not

---

[266] It is argued that the loss of a right is the only consequence. Vogenauer argues that '[t]he only consequence attached to Art 1.7 is the non-application of a particular contractual term or a black letter rule for the PICC.' Ibid, 223–4.

[267] Comment 4 to Article 1.7 UNIDROIT Principles 2016.

[268] Articles 3.1.4, 7.1.6 and 7.4.13 UNIDROIT Principles 2016.

[269] Comment 4 to Article 1.7 UNIDROIT Principles 2016.

[270] Article 1.7 UNIDROIT Principles 2016.

[271] Comment 4 to Article 1.7 UNIDROIT Principles 2016.

[272] Bonell, *An International Restatement of Contract Law*, above n 234, 150.

[273] Article 1.1 UNIDROIT Principles 2016 deals with freedom of contract, which reads as follows:
The parties are free to enter into a contract and to determine its content.

derogate.[274] The principle of good faith is one of the expressly stated mandatory articles of the UNIDROIT Principles; therefore, the parties cannot deviate from the principle of good faith by referring to the principle of freedom of contract.[275]

However, it may seem surprising and controversial that some articles provided in a restatement of law[276] or soft law[277] instrument without binding nature, such as the UNIDROIT Principles, claim to be mandatory.[278] Can these mandatory articles, which are contained in the UNIDROIT Principles, such as Article 1.7 in respect of the principle of good faith, really place limitations on the parties' freedom of contract?[279] What if the parties, who choose the UNIDROIT Principles as the governing law of their contract, nevertheless disregard the mandatory articles and their limitations and exclude the application of one or more of them, such as Article 1.7?[280] Although it is rather unlikely that parties would ever agree, for example, not to be bound by the principle of good faith, if it did happen, it would not be difficult to answer the question.[281]

> On the one hand, given the formally non-binding nature of the UNIDROIT Principles, the parties are of course free not only to disregard them as a whole but also expressly to stipulate that they do not intend to be bound by some of their individual provisions including those the Principles themselves consider mandatory. On the other, it is clear that if the parties refer to the UNIDROIT Principles as the law governing their contract but at the same time strike out some of their mandatory provisions, they put themselves outside the system of the UNIDROIT Principles, with the consequence that the Principles will no longer apply as the law governing the contract but will bind the parties only at the contractual level.[282]

It seems that the parties could eventually free themselves from the restraints which require them to act in accordance with the principle of good faith, but they will risk losing the protection and fairer consequences that the UNIDROIT Principles purport to offer.[283]

Fairness is another fundamental idea of the UNIDROIT Principles,[284] so any attempt to exclude the principle of good faith may cause conflict between the two fundamental tenets of the UNIDROIT Principles.

---

[274] Bonell, *An International Restatement of Contract Law*, above n 234, 94.

[275] Ibid, 94–6.

[276] Bonell, 'The UNIDROIT Principles of International Commercial Contracts and CISG – Alternatives or Complementary Instruments?', above n 34 (Chap. 1), 29–30. Bonell argues that the nature of the UNIDROIT Principles is a kind of international restatement of contract law.

[277] Bonell, 'Towards a Legislative Codification of the UNIDROIT Principles?', above n 38 (Chap. 1), 245. Bonell agrees that the UNIDROIT Principles are of the nature of soft law.

[278] Bonell, *An International Restatement of Contract Law*, above n 234, 95.

[279] Ibid, 95–6.

[280] Ibid, 96.

[281] Ibid.

[282] Ibid.

[283] Ibid, 151–172.

[284] Michael J Bonell, 'Policing the International Commercial Contract against Unfairness under the UNIDROIT Principles' (1995) 3 *Tulane Journal of International and Comparative Law* 73, 73–91.

What if, instead of expressly excluding the principle of good faith, the parties purport to re-define it in the light of the special purpose of their own contract? And if they could, to what extent, would they be free to do so?[285]

It seems that the parties are allowed to adjust the principle of good faith to fit their contract, given their rights conferred by Article 1.5. The extent to which they are free to re-shape the principle of good faith depends on the nature of their contract and the surrounding circumstances thereof. It is almost impossible to give a clear and unequivocal answer to this question, as it is a matter of contract construction. Nevertheless, in the worst case where the parties' re-definition of the principle of good faith is fundamentally inconsistent with the original spirit of the UNIDROIT Principles, Bonell's proposal mentioned above should apply.

After considering the possibility of the parties opting out of the principle of good faith itself, another question which is worth examining is whether all the special applications of the principle of good faith in the UNIDROIT Principles can be excluded or limited by the parties.[286] The answer is not that simple. This can be done in some cases but not in others. Where the articles contained in the UNIDROIT Principles directly or indirectly restrict the parties' freedom of contract with respect to, for instance, fraud and exemption clauses,[287] it cannot be done in the light of their mandatory nature authorised by the UNIDROIT Principles.[288] However, it can be done in instances where the articles do not provide such restrictions, since the articles are only default rules or background law which purport to apply only where there are no specific terms in the contract in relation to the issues covered by those articles.[289] Although the solutions provided by those articles which do not impose limitations on the parties may be regarded as the most appropriate for the resolution of disputes, the parties can still freely and definitely contemplate having a different duty under the contract and having special written terms added to their contract which can meet their particular expectations and needs in a way that better suits their needs.[290]

Nevertheless, it should be kept in mind that all the specific applications of the principle of good faith, like the principle of good faith itself, can eventually be excluded or limited by the parties in the light of the soft law nature of the UNIDROIT Principles.

---

[285] Bridge, 'The CISG and the UNIDROIT Principles of International Commercial Contracts', above n 7 (Chap. 3), 625. Bridge just raises the questions without offering answers to them.

[286] Bonell, *An International Restatement of Contract Law*, above n 234, 150.

[287] Articles 3.1.4 and 7.1.6 UNIDROIT Principles 2016, respectively.

[288] Bonell, *An International Restatement of Contract Law*, above n 234, 151.

[289] Ibid.

[290] Ibid.

4.4 The Various Levels and Many Facets of Good Faith

Good faith is criticised for its vagueness and uncertainty. From a textual perspective, the criticism may hold true. However, from a contextual perspective, this criticism cannot stand solidly. Good faith can mean different things depending on the circumstances of the cases.[291] It can turn into different concrete duties that lead the parties to a fair and just performance of their contracts. In the context of hardship, it may become a flexible and useful tool that can be used by the judges or the arbitrators to reallocate the emerging risks and re-establish the equilibrium between the parties to achieve fairness and justice in general, and to reach an equitable solution in particular. From a contextual perspective, good faith has many facets and various levels when applied.

4.4.1 Various Levels and Many Facets of Good Faith in General

4.4.1.1 Various Levels of Good Faith

There are at least three levels at which good faith applies. The first level constitutes an overriding level at which good faith is envisaged as a general principle. It permeates all kinds of contracts and every stage of a contract. On the second level, good faith is considered as a basis for several general duties that are imposed on the parties. These duties include, but are not limited to, the duty to co-operate, the duty not to engage in inconsistent behaviour, the duty to use best efforts and the duty not to negotiate or break off negotiation in bad faith. The third level of good faith arises when these general duties at the second level are divided into concrete sub-duties, including, but not limited to, the duty to renegotiate, the duty to disclose, the duty to mitigate, and the duty to adjust contractual price.[292] Also, the duties that arise at the third level of the principle of good faith are closely interrelated. They are normally not based solely on one duty operating at the second level of the principle of good faith. Rather, they derive rather from the combination or the mixed application of related duties arising from the second level. For example, the duty to renegotiate could reflect the duty to co-operate and the duty to use best efforts; and the duty to mitigate could reflect the duty to co-operate and the duty to not engage in inconsistent behaviour.

---

[291] Bruno Zeller, 'Good Faith – Is it a Contractual Obligation?', above n 219, 220.

[292] Many of the duties at this level have been confirmed by international contract practice and arbitral tribunals. See Pascale Accaoui Lorfing, 'La Regegociation Contractuellement Imprevue/The Contractually Unforeseen Renegotiation' (2010) 1 *Revue de Droit des Affaires Internationales/International Business Law Journal* 35, 35–51.

The first level addresses the abstract nature of good faith. At this level, good faith is regarded as an 'umbrella' principle. Both the second and third levels reflect the concrete nature of good faith. The difference between the second and third levels is that the duties on the second level are more general and apply to every contract while the duties on the third level are more concrete and apply to certain specific contracts under certain circumstances, such as in the context of hardship.

4.4.1.2 Many Facets of Good Faith

Good faith also has many facets; therefore, many concrete duties can be deduced from good faith. Good faith can mean different things at different stages of a contract. In the process of the formation of a contract, good faith may mean to negotiate in good faith and a duty not to break off negotiation in bad faith. In the course of the performance of a contract, good faith may become a duty to co-operate, a duty to use best efforts to perform, and an estoppel preventing a party from acting inconsistently. At other stages of a contract, good faith can be understood and reflected in other explicit or implied duties, such as the duty to mitigate.[293]

Moreover, a concrete duty at the second level of good faith may also have many facets. For example, the duty to co-operate can be regarded differently depending on various fact patterns. For some contracts the duty to co-operate may mean a duty to renegotiate while for other contracts the duty to co-operate may turn into a duty to adjust price or ways of delivery. Another aspect regarding the many facets is that good faith can be understood to incorporate or include different aspects of various abstract concepts. It may include 'faith', 'morals', 'honour', 'honesty', 'fairness', 'reasonableness', 'innocent' or lack of 'suspicion'.[294]

The view that good faith has many facets is, to some degree, also manifested in international law in general and in international economic law in particular. Legitimate expectations, *pacta sunt servanda*, estoppel, acquiescence, equity and clean hands doctrines, and the abuse of rights doctrine are all regarded as concretizations of the principle of good faith.[295] Each of them could be a facet of good faith.

The point should be made that this list is by no means exhaustive, as good faith is able to take on a new facet or lose an old facet due to radical or incremental political, economic, social or cultural changes. To a certain degree, good faith is a self-creating, self-evolving and self-reviving system embedded in human relationships and society regardless of time and space. It is important to have a panorama view of good faith. Each of the concepts discussed above reflects only one facet of good faith appropriately at one level.

---

[293] Article 7.4.8 UNIDROIT Principles 2016 and the CISG art 77.

[294] Farnsworth, 'Good Faith Performance and Commercial Reasonableness under the Uniform Commercial Code', above n 14, 669.

[295] Andreas R Ziegler and Jorun Baumgartner, 'Good Faith as a General Principle of (International) Law' in Andrew D Mitchell, M Sornarajah and Tania Voon (eds), *Good Faith and International Economic Law* (Oxford University Press, 2015) 9, 17–35.

4.4.2 *Various Levels and Many Facets of Good Faith in Particular*

Although the notion of good faith has various levels and many facets, this has not been articulated elsewhere; rather, it can be inferred from the role of good faith in both domestic laws and international legal instruments.

4.4.2.1 Various Levels and Many Facets of Good Faith in Domestic Laws

The view that good faith has various levels and many facets is reflected in domestic laws of both civil law jurisdictions and common law jurisdictions.

Civil law jurisdictions often reflect both the various levels and the many facets of good faith. In Germany contract law, good faith is a general principle which could be the first level and the concreted duties arising from it could at least be the second level. Also, the many functions of good faith reflect its many facets as do the institutions created by the courts on the basis of good faith.[296] In the new French contract law, good faith is recognised as a general principle. The first level of good faith is emerging. Future developments will probably show its other levels and many facets. It is likely that the French contract law will adopt the approach taken by the German contract law in this regard. Other civil law jurisdictions also endorse the various levels and many facets of good faith in one way or another.[297]

Common law jurisdictions normally do not recognise good faith as a general principle, but they may, to a certain degree, confirm its many facets. This is evident in American contract law with its general and special definitions of good faith and its different functions.[298] In Australian contract law, good faith is sometimes regarded as equivalent to either reasonableness or a duty to co-operate.[299] It is worth noting that there is a view that '[o]ften the concepts of good faith and co-operation are interchangeable. However, of the two, good faith is clearly a broader idea than co-operation, which is inherent in the former'.[300] It seems that a duty of good faith and a duty of co-operation are on different levels and co-operation is only one manifestation of good faith. Regarding the many facets, it is argued that good faith permeates every aspect of contract law from implication and incorporation of terms to interpretation, from vitiating factors to frustration and to remedies, as it is the

[296] Ole Lando and Hugh Beale (eds), *Principles of European Contract Law, Part I and II, Combined and Revised* (Kluwer Law International, 2000) 117.

[297] See, eg, Ewan McKendrick and Qiao Liu, 'Good Faith in Contract Performance in the Chinese and Common Laws' in Larry A DiMatteo and Lei Chen (eds), *Chinese Contract Law: Civil and Common Law Perspectives* (Cambridge University Press, 2017) 72, 75–82.

[298] On the functions of good faith, see also, Burton and Anderson, above n 74, 115–9.

[299] Paterson, Robertson and Duke, above n 151, 354–7.

[300] Peden, *Good faith in the performance of contracts*, above n 172, 3.

essence of a contract and inherent in all common law principles.[301] Also, good faith is not an independent and certain concept and its content varies and will rely on the particular rule or terms in every individual contract.[302] Good faith may include but not be limited to: '[a]cting for a proper purpose; consistency of conduct; communication of decisions; co-operation with the other party; consideration of the interests of the other party'.[303] Another view is that good faith includes at least three interrelated notions: 'an obligation on the parties to co-operate in achieving the contractual objects (loyalty to the promise itself); compliance with honest standards of conduct; and compliance with standards of conduct which are reasonable having regard to the interests of the parties'.[304] All this shows that good faith has many facets in Australian contract law. Other common law jurisdictions may take a similar approach on this issue.[305]

4.4.2.2 Various Levels and Many Facets of Good Faith Under the CISG and the UNIDROIT Principles

The CISG

The role of good faith remains unclear in the CISG. Whether it is a general principle is controversial. According to the view that good faith is a general principle on which the CISG is based, it may have various levels and many facets. If good faith is such a general principle, then good faith has at least two levels. The first level is the general principle level, and the second level is the level at which there may be many duties as reflected in other articles in the CISG. To be more precise, the first level is manifested in Article 7 on good faith and the second level is shown in Article 21 on late acceptance, Article 37 on the right of the seller to remedy non-conformity of goods, Article 44 on the relief to failure of the buyer to give notice requirements of non-conformity, Article 77 on mitigation of damages, Article 80 on the duty to co-operate and many other articles.[306]

Good faith may have many facets in the CISG as well. It is argued that good faith in the CISG plays a four-fold role consisting of a practice of the parties, a trade usage, a general principle and an interpretive tool on the basis of the various interpretations of good faith which are categorised as: 1. an obligation established by practices of the parties or by the usage of international trade; 2. an interpretive guide; 3. a prerequisite for exercising the rights and remedies provided in the CISG;

[301] Carter, above n 64 (Chap. 3), 22–7.

[302] Ibid, 27.

[303] Ibid.

[304] Mason, above n 117, 69.

[305] See, e.g., John D McCamus, 'The New General "Principle" of Good Faith Performance and the New 'Rule' of Honesty in Performance in Canadian Contract Law' (2015) *32 Journal of Contract Law* 103, 107–117.

[306] See, eg, Kröll, Mistelis and Viscasillas, above n 106 (Chap. 3), 122–3.

4. a substantive principle in resolving problems which are not expressly governed by the CISG; 5. a source of rights and obligations which may contradict or extend those contained in the CISG; and 6. merely an interpretive guide and no general doctrine of good faith serving as a source of any additional rights and obligations.[307] Another summary of views with respect to the role of good faith in the CISG is stated as '1 an aid to interpreting the CISG itself; 2 a general principle to assist in gap-filling; 3 a direct, positive obligation imposed upon parties; 4 a collective term denoting derivative general principles for gap-filling; 5 a product of international usages or practices established by parties; or 6 an independent source of rights and obligations which may contradict or extend the CISG'.[308] The different possible natures and functions of good faith and the many articles in the CISG pertaining to good faith indicate its many facets.

The UNIDROIT Principles

Four levels of good faith can be discerned in the UNIDROIT Principles. The first level of good faith is that there is a general principle of good faith under the UNIDROIT Principles.[309] At the second level, there are many duties imposed by the UNIDROIT Principles on the parties, such as the duty not to engage in inconsistent behaviour,[310] the duty not to negotiate or break off negotiation in bad faith,[311] the duty of confidentiality,[312] the duty of best efforts,[313] the duty to achieve a special result,[314] the duty to co-operate,[315] the duty to preserve rights and others.[316] These concrete duties could be regarded as the explicit manifestations and applications of the principle of good faith at the first level in the UNIDROIT Principles.[317] At the third level, the UNIDROIT Principles have not explicitly provided as many duties as at the second level. The duty to renegotiate is the most important duty at the third

---

[307] Disa Sim, 'The Scope and Application of Good Faith in the Vienna Convention on Contracts for the International Sale of Goods' 2001, available at http://www.cisg.law.pace.edu/cisg/biblio/sim1.html.

[308] Lisa Spagnolo, above n 202.

[309] Article 1.7 UNIDROIT Principles 2016.

[310] Article 1.8 UNIDROIT Principles 2016.

[311] Article 2.1.15 UNIDROIT Principles 2016.

[312] Article 2.1.16 UNIDROIT Principles 2016.

[313] Article 5.1.4 UNIDROIT Principles 2016.

[314] Ibid.

[315] Article 5.1.3 UNIDROIT Principles 2016.

[316] See Article 7.4.8 UNIDROIT Principles 2016 on duty of mitigation of harm and other duties in the Comment 1 to Article 1.7 UNIDROIT Principles 2016.

[317] Article 1.8 UNIDROIT Principles 2016 regarding inconsistent behaviour and Article 5.1.3 UNIDROIT Principles 2016 concerning co-operation between the parties are considered as the application of the general principle of good faith contained in Article 1.7 UNIDROIT Principles 2016.

level. The UNIDROIT Principles provide that parties shall have a duty to renegotiate in the context of hardship.[318] The duty to renegotiate is based on the combination of the duty to co-operate and the existence of a hardship situation or situations, and further on the general principle of good faith.[319] The duty to renegotiate is a more concrete application than the duty to co-operate under the principle of good faith. Hardship is a necessary prerequisite for the invocation of the duty to renegotiate.[320] The duty to renegotiate comes into existence in the context of hardship. Without the occurrence of hardship, there would be no duty to renegotiate based on the duty to co-operate and the general principle of good faith. At the fourth level, several duties derive from the duty to renegotiate. When requesting renegotiations, the disadvantaged party has a duty to indicate the grounds for renegotiations.[321] In the process of renegotiation, it is required that 'both parties must conduct renegotiation in a constructive manner, in particular, by refraining from any form of obstruction and by providing all the necessary information.'[322]

It is worth noting that it is unclear whether refraining from any form of obstruction and providing all the necessary information are also duties under the UNIDROIT Principles. If they are categorised as duties imposed on the parties, it is necessary to establish their relationship to the duty to renegotiate. It seems that they place limitations on the application of the duty to renegotiate or, in other words, in determining the limits of the duty to conduct renegotiations in a constructive manner. They may be regarded only as quasi-duties imposed on the parties. If they are contemplated as duties, the comment would articulate this view expressly as it does in the case of the requirement to indicate the grounds for a renegotiation request. In the Official Comment 3, it is explicitly provided that Article 6.2.3 imposes on the disadvantaged party the duty to indicate the grounds on which the request for renegotiation has been made. Since the kind of wording in general, or the term 'duty' is not used when refraining from any form of obstruction and providing all the necessary information are mentioned in the Official Comment 5, they probably should not be categorised as duties; the best they could reach may be quasi-duties, as they do put certain limitations on the parties' activities. Another assumption may be that since the requirement to indicate the grounds for the negotiation request appears in the black letter

[318] Article 6.2.3 UNIDROIT Principles 2016.

[319] Comments 1 and 5 to Article 6.2.3 UNIDROIT Principles 2016.

[320] There could be two understandings of the status of the term 'hardship' used in 6.2.3. First, 'hardship' could be regarded as the hardship doctrine. In this case, the notion of hardship and the duties and mechanisms relating to it are themselves a manifestation of the general principle of good faith. If this understanding is adopted, then hardship should appear on the second level of good faith, making it parallel with the various duties directly under the general principle of good faith. Second, the 'hardship' term could be regarded as representing a hardship event or events. In this case, a hardship event triggers the duty to renegotiate. Therefore, hardship should be put on the same level as the principle of good faith. It serves as a background against which the general principle of good faith applies and the duty to renegotiate is the concrete manifestation of the general principle of good faith in this context of hardship. This book adopts the second understanding.

[321] Comment 3 to Article 6.2.3 UNIDROIT Principles 2016.

[322] Comment 5 to Article 6.2.3 UNIDROIT Principles 2016.

rule, it is categorised as a duty in the corresponding Official Comment, whereas requirements to refrain from any form of obstruction and to provide all the necessary information exist only in the Official Comment; they may not be regarded as duties under Article 6.2.3. However, this could be one of the reasonable inferences that could be made from the structure and the wording of Article 6.2.3. It should not preclude other reasonable conclusions that may be reached from another perspective.

Also, the relationships among the duty to indicate grounds for request for renegotiations, the duty to renegotiate, the duty to co-operate and the general principle of good faith are also uncertain, insofar as they are not expressly mentioned either in the black letter rules or in the Official Comments. It is only emphasized that 'the disadvantaged party must honestly believe that a case of hardship actually exists and not request renegotiations as a purely tactical manoeuvre',[323] and that 'both the request for renegotiations by the disadvantaged party and the conduct of both parties during the renegotiation process are subject to the general principle of good faith and fair dealing and to the duty of co-operation'.[324] Therefore, based on the Official Comments, the duty to renegotiate in a constructive manner could, to some degree, be regarded as related to the application of the principle of good faith or be understood as a requirement not to renegotiate in bad faith or in a manner that is in conflict with the principle of good faith. It is, therefore, reasonable to infer that, 'renegotiation in a constructive manner' imposes a duty or at least a quasi-duty on a party not to renegotiate in bad faith. This duty, more or less, resembles the duty not to negotiate in bad faith in Article 2.1.15 of the UNIDROIT Principles as being in a conflict with the principle of good faith.[325]

What can be said is that the duties or quasi-duties to refrain from obstructing renegotiations, to provide for information in negotiating, to indicate grounds for renegotiations, to renegotiate, to co-operate and the principle of good faith are interrelated. However, their relationship is far more complex than what might ordinarily be envisaged and articulated.

As to the many facets of good faith, each duty discussed above can be regarded as a facet of good faith. They show different aspects of the principle of good faith; they are the ingredients of the principle of good faith; and they concretise the principle of good faith and make it easier to grasp and understand.

---

[323] Ibid.

[324] Ibid.

[325] Comment 2 to Article 2.1.15 UNIDROIT Principles 2016.

4.5 Conclusion

Good faith is a subject that is both eternal and fashionable[326] and endlessly debated. Also, the notion of good faith illustrates probably one of the sharpest distinctions between the civil law systems and common law systems. Good faith reflects, to a great extent, the cultural identity of an individual national legal system.[327] In civil law jurisdictions, German law and French law have recognised good faith as a general principle of contract law. In common law jurisdictions, the status of good faith varies. American law has recognised a good faith duty in contract performance. English law strongly rejects the concept of good faith. Australian law takes a stance between American law and English law. State and federal courts have, to a certain degree, recognized an implied duty of good faith while the High Court of Australia has refused to address the role of good faith in Australian law.

There were and still are heated debates on the principle and application of a duty of good faith with respect to the CISG in the course of its preparation and in current research and conferences relating to it. However, there is no clear answer or conclusion regarding the definition or the meaning of good faith, its scope, and the extent to which it should be applied. The UNIDROIT Principles provide that the principle underlying a duty of good faith is mandatory in nature and explicitly imposes a duty on the parties to act in accordance with good faith, whereas the role of good faith in the CISG is rather vague and uncertain.

Due to the similarities and differences of good faith in domestic laws and in international legal instruments, it seems better to consider and understand good faith from a functional, contextual and constructive perspective. Considering all the various roles and distinct functions of good faith, it is proposed that good faith has various levels and many facets indicating its flexibility and multi-functionality.

There is a risk that a duty of good faith may be construed to mean everything will eventually mean nothing.[328] However, the shortcomings of a multifaceted good faith are not unsurmountable. If good faith is analysed and regulated carefully, it can be of enormous value in tackling various issues in general, and in long-term relational supply contracts upon the occurrence of hardship in particular.

The most distinctive feature of a long-term relational supply contract is the significance of good faith, as the mutual interests of the parties could be achieved only if they both act in good faith over the course of their ongoing relationship.[329] It could be argued that the proposition regarding the various levels and many facets of good faith may best meet the needs of the parties to long-term relational supply contracts in light of their complexity, uncertainty and ambiguity. Establishing a functional

[326] Tallon, above n 33, 1.

[327] Whittaker, above n 4.

[328] Bridge, 'The CISG and the UNIDROIT Principles of International Commercial Contracts', above n 7 (Chap. 3), 637.

[329] Veronica L Taylor, 'Continuing Transactions and Persistent Myths: Contracts in Contemporary Japan' (1993) 19 *Melbourne University Law Review* 352, 377–8.

relationship among the principle of good faith, the duty of co-operation and the duty of renegotiation and their manifestations in general, and their relationship in long-term relational supply contracts in the context of hardship in particular, requires a flexible approach in order to best understand how they interrelate and to deal with intruding hardship issues. All this will be addressed in the ensuing Chapters.

Chapter 5
Manifestations of Good Faith in the Context of Hardship Under the UNIDROIT Principles and the Way Forward

5.1 Introduction

Chapters 2, 3 and 4, discussed long-term relational supply contracts, hardship and good faith, respectively. Each of these topics is a dimension of the overall theme of this book.[1] This chapter combines all three dimensions and discusses good faith in long-term relational supply contracts in the context of hardship. The rules in the UNIDROIT Principles provide a framework to examine the manifestations of good faith.

Section 5.2 will analyse the manifestations of good faith in the UNIDROIT Principles in the context of hardship, such as the duty to renegotiate. Section 5.3 will discuss the manifestations of good faith from a normative perspective, taking into account the gaps and shortcomings of relevant rules in the UNIDROIT Principles. The substantive and procedural aspects of good faith will be analysed and their application in long-term relational supply contracts experiencing hardship will be considered. Section 5.4 will introduce a double-construction approach that the judges or the arbitrators should adapt when determining whether the parties have acted in good faith. Also, a list of factors to be considered when determining good faith behaviour will be provided. Section 5.5 will draw a conclusion that imposing the duty to renegotiate on the parties and the judges or arbitrators' power to adapt or terminate a contract are appropriate manifestations of good faith in long-term relational supply contracts experiencing hardship.

[1] For details on the three dimensions, see Overview Part of the book.

P. Guo, *Good Faith in Long-Term Relational Supply Contracts in the Context of Hardship from A Comparative Perspective*,
https://doi.org/10.1007/978-981-16-5513-5_5

5.2 Manifestations of Good Faith in the Context of Hardship under the UNIDROIT Principles

When comparing English common law, the CISG and the UNIDROIT Principles, Bridge pointed out:

> This demonstrates...the UNIDROIT Principles have drawn on the best features of the world legal systems. In numerous instances, they have selected the best rather than the majority or the orthodox view. Given the pressures on legal systems to adapt to a changing world, it should be no surprise that modern reforms in a domestic legal system bear a close resemblance to provisions of the UNIDROIT Principles.[2]

This book uses the UNIDROIT Principles as a framework to search for appropriate solutions to hardship issues at the international level. Therefore, it is necessary to analyse the manifestations of the general principle of good faith under the UNIDROIT Principles before discussing them in a broader context. This will determine whether the UNIDROIT Principles reflect the trend of international trade practice and set an example for future legal reforms or harmonisation of laws.

5.2.1 *Renegotiation*

The duty to renegotiate is the most important manifestation and application of the general principle of good faith in the context of hardship under the UNIDROIT Principles.

Since hardship can cause a fundamental disruption to the equilibrium of the contract. As a result, the disadvantaged party may be entitled to request a renegotiation of the original agreed contract terms to adapt them to the situations emerging from the hardship.[3] For example, if the cost of purchase increases dramatically due to an unexpected devaluation of the agreed currency of payment, the purchaser is entitled to request that other party renegotiate the original price to adapt it to the hardship event.[4]

In addition, if the contract has already incorporated a clause regarding the automatic adaptation of the contract, a request for renegotiations is inadmissible. However, if such a clause did not envisage the events resulting in hardship, renegotiation would not be precluded.[5]

The precise time for requesting renegotiations is not provided by Article 6.2.3; the official comment suggests that the exact time depends upon the circumstances

---

[2] Michael Bridge, 'The UK Sale of Goods Act, the CISG and the UNIDROIT Principles' in Petar Sarcevic and Paul Volken (eds.), *International Sale of Goods Revisited* (Kluwer Law International, 2001) 115, 150.

[3] Comment 1 to Article 6.2.3 UNIDROIT Principles 2016.

[4] Illustration 1 to Article 6.2.3 UNIDROIT Principles 2016.

[5] Comment 1 and illustrations 2 and 3 to Article 6.2.3 UNIDROIT Principles 2016.

of the case. The request for renegotiations should be made as soon as possible after the time when hardship comes into existence.[6] When determining whether there has been 'undue delay', the length of the contract and the nature of the event resulting in hardship must be considered.[7]

If the disadvantaged party fails to act in a timely manner, the right to request renegotiation remains unaffected. However, the delay in making the request may impact the determination of the existence of hardship and its consequences for the contract.[8] This raises the question of whether the other party could decline the request for renegotiations if the disadvantaged party makes the request late. Another question is how to decide whether the delay was unavoidable due to the hardship or whether the delay was contrived on purpose. Consequently, a deliberately late request for negotiation or a decline of the last request should be considered a breach of the duty to co-operate and of the general principle of good faith. The answers to these questions would certainly affect the parties' rights and obligations; however, Article 6.2.3 is silent on these matters.

Article 6.2.3 also requires the disadvantaged party to indicate the grounds on which the request for renegotiation is being made, so that the other party can better assess whether or not the request for renegotiation is justified.[9] When the request for renegotiation does not provide sufficient information, the disadvantaged party must provide further necessary information without undue delay.[10] The comment also explains the consequences of an incomplete request and of failure to provide the grounds for the request for renegotiation.[11] However, the comment does not provide any further explanations for a situation where the request for renegotiation is not justified assuming that it is complete and sets forth the grounds. Nor does it cover the other party's right to decline the request. The nature of the request may determine whether or not it must be accepted.

In general, the request for renegotiation does not allow the disadvantaged party to withhold performance by virtue of the exceptional character of hardship and of the risk of possible abuses of the remedy.[12] However, under exceptional circumstances, withholding performance may be allowed.[13] For example, the disadvantaged party may be able to justify the withholding of performance if he or she has entered into a construction contract and a new safety regulation has been adopted

---

[6] Comment 2 to Article 6.2.3 UNIDROIT Principles 2016.

[7] Vogenauer, *Commentary on the UNIDROIT Principles of International Commercial Contracts (PICC)*, above n 130 (Chap. 3), 820.

[8] Comment 2 to Article 6.2.3 UNIDROIT Principles 2016.

[9] Comment 3 to Article 6.2.3 UNIDROIT Principles 2016.

[10] Vogenauer, *Commentary on the UNIDROIT Principles of International Commercial Contracts (PICC)*, above n 130 (Chap. 3), 820.

[11] Comment 3 to Article 6.2.3 UNIDROIT Principles 2016.

[12] Comment 4 to Article 6.2.3 UNIDROIT Principles 2016.

[13] Ibid.

subsequently rendering the performance on his or her part substantially more onerous.[14]

In addition, Article 6.2.3 does not provide a mechanism or procedure for the way in which the parties should renegotiate.[15] It does emphasise that both the request for renegotiations by the disadvantaged party and the conduct of both parties during the renegotiation process are subject to the general principle of good faith and to the duty of co-operation.[16] Therefore, the disadvantaged party must honestly believe that the hardship situation actually occurred and that the renegotiations are not requested as 'a purely tactical manoeuvre'. Additionally, both parties must conduct the renegotiations based on the request in a constructive manner, 'in particular by refraining from any form of obstruction and by providing all the necessary and relevant information.'[17] New articles regarding the long-term contracts in the UNIDROIT Principles, such as 2.1.14 reflect the general principle of *favor contractus*, which is particularly important to long-term relational contracts as 'it is usually in the interests of both parties to keep their original bargain alive rather than to denounce it and to look for alternative goods or services elsewhere on the market'.[18] Constructive renegotiation reflects not only the principle of *favor contractus* but also the principle of good faith.

5.2.2 *Termination or Adaptation*

According to Article 6.2.3 (3), if the parties fail to reach an agreement on the adaptation of the contract to the hardship situation within a reasonable time, either party can resort to the court.[19] This matter has two elements: 'failure to reach an agreement' and 'within a reasonable time'.[20] The failure to reach an agreement may arise from the fact that the non-disadvantaged party completely ignores or denies the request for renegotiations or where both parties have actively participated in renegotiations in accordance with the requirements of the principle of good faith and of the duty of co-operation, they still cannot agree on a positive outcome.[21] 'How long a party must wait before resorting to the court will depend on the complexity of the

[14] Illustration 4 to Article 6.2.3 UNIDROIT Principles 2016.

[15] See Chap. 3, Sect. 3.4.2.

[16] Comment 5 to Article 6.2.3 UNIDROIT Principles 2016.

[17] Ibid.

[18] Michael Joachim Bonell, 'International Investment Contracts and General Contract Law: A Place for the UNIDROIT Principles of International Commercial Contracts?' (2012) 17 *Uniform Law Review* 141, 148.

[19] Comment 6 to Article 6.2.3 UNIDROIT Principles 2016.

[20] Vogenauer, *Commentary on the UNIDROIT Principles of International Commercial Contracts (PICC)*, above n 130 (Chap. 3), 820.

[21] Comment 6 to Article 6.2.3 UNIDROIT Principles 2016.

issues to be settled and the particular circumstances of the case'.[22] The meaning of 'reasonable time' will depend on the facts and circumstances of the individual case.[23]

If a court finds that a hardship situation exists, it may take measures in several different ways.[24] The first choice that a court has is to terminate the contract.[25] The court should indicate the time when termination takes effect 'at a date and on terms to be fixed' by the court.[26] The second choice available is to adapt the contract to balance the interests of the parties. In doing so, the court will seek to make a fair and just allocation of the risk between the parties in general and the distribution of the losses between them in particular.[27] This may involve a price adjustment that takes into consideration the nature of the hardship and 'the extent to which one of the parties has taken a risk and the extent to which the party entitled to receive a performance may still benefit from that performance'.[28]

The two choices above are expressly mentioned in Article 6.2.3 (4) on the condition that it is reasonable to do so. What is reasonable and what is not reasonable is not detailed.[29] However, under certain circumstances, neither termination nor adaptation may appear to be reasonable or appropriate. Therefore, it seems that 'the only reasonable solution will be for the court either to direct the parties to resume negotiations with a view to reaching agreement on the adaptation of the contract, or to confirm the terms of the contract as they stand'.[30] This could be regarded as the implicit remedies available, although it is more likely that the court will adapt the contract itself rather than confirm the existing terms or order the resumption of renegotiations.[31]

There are several potential issues relating to the measures that the courts can take in cases arising from hardship situations. First, the order of all the measures that the courts can take is not absolutely clear. It is obvious that the courts can adapt or terminate the contracts only upon the failure to reach an agreement within a reasonable time after the commencement of the renegotiation. However, it is not clear whether the court is obliged to consider adapting a contract first before it can terminate the

---

[22] Ibid.

[23] Vogenauer, *Commentary on the UNIDROIT Principles of International Commercial Contracts (PICC)*, above n 130 (Chap. 3), 820.

[24] Article 6.2.3 UNIDROIT Principles 2016.

[25] The term termination used here is, to some extent, different from that in termination for breach. Here a court has a degree of discretion and flexibility in determining the time and terms of termination which it does not have in the case of termination for breach. Vogenauer, *Commentary on the UNIDROIT Principles of International Commercial Contracts (PICC)*, above n 130 (Chap. 3), 821.

[26] Comment 7 to Article 6.2.3 UNIDROIT Principles 2016.

[27] Ibid.

[28] Ibid.

[29] Vogenauer, *Commentary on the UNIDROIT Principles of International Commercial Contracts (PICC)*, above n 130 (Chap. 3), 821.

[30] Comment 7 to Article 6.2.3 UNIDROIT Principles 2016.

[31] Vogenauer, *Commentary on the UNIDROIT Principles of International Commercial Contracts (PICC)*, above n 130 (Chap. 3), 821.

contract.[32] Second, the logic of the process of measures that the court can take may be in conflict with the spirit of the general principle of *favor contractus*. The fact that courts may exercise their discretion to direct the parties to resume negotiations or to confirm the terms of the contract reflects the spirit of the general principle of *favor contractus* with a view to keeping the contract alive. But this is subject to one condition: that neither termination nor adaptation is reasonable or appropriate. Termination puts an end to the contract, which opposes the general principle of *favor contractus*. It is fair to argue that termination is a measure that least reflects the spirit of the general principle of *favor contractus*. If the aforementioned reasoning is correct, then why can a measure that violates the spirit of general principle of *favor contractus*, for example, that termination be adopted, be given priority over a measure which is consistent with the spirit of that principle, such as that renegotiation takes place? Is it not logical? Third, there is a gap in Article 6.2.3 in that there is no boundary on the extent of the duty to renegotiate. That is to say no explicit relief from the duty to renegotiate is provided. It seems reasonable and necessary to set a limitation on the duty to renegotiate providing a condition, which, if met and justified, will allow either party to suspend renegotiations.

5.3 Manifestations of Good Faith in the Context of Hardship from a Normative Perspective

The current rules in national laws dealing with hardship vary. Those rules do not offer a robust basis for tackling hardship issues, as indicated by the following statement:

> The existing doctrines on contract change such as frustration, commercial impracticability, 'imprévision', Wegfall der Geschäftsgrundlage, etc., offer hardly any legal ground for renegotiating contracts which do not include a renegotiation clause. But this lack of flexibility is far from representing a satisfactory situation.[33]

The hardship rules in the UNIDROIT Principles also have certain problems or gaps. However, the approach of the UNIDROIT Principles to hardship issues contains important relational characteristics.[34] The relational characteristics are necessary and crucial in the course of the resolution of disputes relating to long-term relational supply contracts in the context of hardship. The UNIDROIT Principles can be used as a framework to find a more satisfactory solution to tackle hardship

---

[32] It is argued that although termination may be regarded as the first remedy, the courts or the arbitral tribunals tend to adapt a contract, where possible, before terminating it. Ibid, 820–1.

[33] Wolfgang Peter, 'International Investment Agreement-Types, Arbitration and Renegotiation' in Fritz Nicklisch (ed), *The Complex Long-Term Contract: Structures and International Arbitration* (C F Müller Juristisch Verlag, 1987) 119, 128.

[34] Speidel, 'The Characteristics and Challenges of Relational Contracts', above n 78 (Chap. 2), 841–3.

issues from a normative perspective. Good faith plays an indispensable role and offers a robust basis for this envisaged solution as it is used in the UNIDROIT Principles.

5.3.1 Substantive Aspects of Good Faith in the Context of Hardship

The importance of mutual trust and confidence between the parties to a long-term relational supply contract in international commercial transactions cannot be underestimated. From a normative perspective, to ensure such confidence, all involved must possess an unambiguous understanding of the requirements of good faith.[35] The most significant manifestations and applications of good faith in long-term relational supply contracts in the context of hardship will be analysed in detail. The duty to renegotiate and the court's or the arbitral tribunal's power to adapt or terminate the contract would benefit the parties and their relationship by enhancing the flexibility, efficiency and stability of the performance of the contract, and reducing the possibility of a dispute.[36]

5.3.1.1 Duty to Renegotiate

Due to the nature and characteristics of long-term relational contracts, a specific rule has been proposed to better tackle potential issues caused by hardship situations. The rule suggests that the parties to a long-term relational contract are (1) under a duty to renegotiate in good faith, (2) to make equitable price and other adjustments when hardship occurs, (3) that the advantaged party is under a duty to accept an equitable adaptation of the terms of the long terms relational contract as proposed in good faith by the aggrieved party, and (4) that the courts may revise the terms of that contract to share loss caused by the hardship.[37] The duty to renegotiate could be regarded as deriving from a general duty of such parties to act in good faith which is widely accepted by many civil law jurisdictions and non-legislative instruments.[38]

At the international level, the CISG is silent on the duty of parties to long term relational contracts to renegotiate. Scholars who support the view that Article 79 of the CISG covers hardship situations argue that the principles of good faith can serve

[35] John Klein, 'Good Faith in International Transactions' (1993) 15 *Liverpool Law Review* 115, 115.

[36] John Y Gotanda, 'Renegotiation and Adaptation Clauses in Investment Contracts, Revisited' (2003) 36 *Vanderbilt Journal of Transnational Law* 1461, 1469–1472.

[37] Eisenberg, 'Why There is No Law of Relational Contracts', above n 52 (Chap. 2), 818–9. This rule is not suggested by Eisenberg and is criticised by him.

[38] Schwenzer, 'Force Majeure and Hardship in International Sales Contracts', above n 6 (Chap. 3), 721.

as the basis for both a duty to renegotiate and a duty to co-operate in order to restore the balance of the contract.[39] As shown above, the UNIDROIT Principles stipulate that, in exceptional circumstances, one party is entitled to require the other party to renegotiate.[40] More generally, in the context of the modern *Lex Mercatoria*, the disadvantaged party facing a hardship event or events is given the right to request the renegotiation and the adaptation of a contract with a view to keeping it alive on the basis of the principle of *clausula rebus sic stantibus*.[41]

The Existence of the Duty to Renegotiate Under a Hardship Clause

A hardship clause normally has two parts: the first part defines the conditions or lists the events in which the clause can be applied, and the second part lays down the legal consequences arising from the materializing of these conditions, as well as the procedure that are to be applied.[42] This section will focus on the second part. This is because it often offers suitable/appropriate/sustainable/justifiable mechanisms, ranging from simple agreement to renegotiate the contract to an extremely complex procedures involving third parties such as arbitrators or experts.[43] In regard to the goal underlying renegotiation, most hardship clauses would refer to the standard of fairness or to the equilibrium of the contract to guide the renegotiations.[44] These conceptions of fairness and seeking to identify the equilibrium of the contract are vague and often of little assistance. Despite this, a 'no profit – no loss' rule based on a combination of the requirements of both conceptions is widely accepted, which means that neither party should gain any profit or suffer a loss due to the hardship event and the ensuing renegotiations.[45] It would be desirable and useful if the parties could make reference to typical international commercial contracts of the same kind, courses of dealing or trade practice and usages, in seeking both fairness and a new relational equilibrium.[46] All this plays a vital role in the analysis of the manifestations of good faith and coherence/sustainability in the context of hardship.

A hardship clause will normally impose on the parties the duty to renegotiate.[47] In international commercial contracts, the most common and favoured way to provide the parties with the right to request renegotiation is by inserting a hardship

---

[39] See, e.g., Uribe, above n 33 (Chap. 3), 193–4.

[40] Article 6.2.3 UNIDROIT Principles 2016.

[41] Yildirim, above n 1 (Chap. 3), 53.

[42] Schmitthoff, above n 163 (Chap. 3), 418.

[43] Fontaine and De Ly, above n 4 (Chap. 3), 473–5.

[44] Horn, 'Standard Clauses on Contract Adaptation in International Commerce', above n 16 (Chap. 3), 138–9.

[45] Ibid, 139.

[46] Ibid.

[47] Schmitthoff, above n 163 (Chap. 3), 419.

clause in the long-term relational supply contracts.[48] In countries where long-term supply contracts are widely used, hardship clauses are not uncommon. For example, since Australia is one of the largest countries to export natural resources worldwide, the international long-term supply contracts normally contain a hardship clause and are broadly used in relevant industries. In long-term supply contracts for liquefied natural gas, there is often a hardship clause providing a basis for a review of all contract provisions affected by hardship.[49] It is argued that:

> To date a typical hardship clause in an Australian export contract has been to the effect that if a party claims 'hardship' or 'a problem arising from unforeseen circumstances', the parties will meet and 'in good faith' ('or in a spirit of mutual understanding and collaboration') use their best endeavours to mitigate the hardship or solve the problem, as the case may be. The clause is often silent on what follows if the parties do not agree on the course of action to be taken to mitigate the hardship or to solve the problem.[50]

In cases where there is no hardship clause in long-term supply contracts for iron ore, after the occurrence of a hardship, the parties may sign a hardship memorandum to reconfirm the spirit of mutual co-operation and assistance, and agree to meet promptly and use their best efforts to find a solution to alleviate the effect of hardship or unfairness.[51] In the United States, in long-term supply contracts for petroleum coke, the parties renegotiate the price in good faith in order to continue their contracts in cases where there is a substantial deviation in contract price from the market price.[52]

Typically, hardship clauses provide a framework for the parties to renegotiate contract terms where either of the parties claims that fulfilling their obligations under the contract would become onerous and difficult due to the hardship.[53] It is argued that the draft of a hardship clause often involves giving consideration to the way that changes in circumstances can be handled appropriately so that the contractual relationship can be maintained.[54]

In the cases of long-term relational supply contracts, typically, the parties tend to hold an economic interest in the ongoing contractual co-operation.[55] If the perfor-

---

[48] Ibid, 417.

[49] Paul Davis, 'Renegotiating Long-Term Energy Supply Contracts with Japanese Buyers' (2014) 38 *Journal of Japanese Law* 29, 32.

[50] C J R McKillop, 'Commentary on Effect of Changed Circumstances on Mineral and Petroleum Sales Contracts' [1984] *Australian Mining and Petroleum Law Association (AMPLA) Yearbook* 361, 387.

[51] Terence Daintith, 'The Design and Performance of Long-Term Contracts' in Terence Daintith and Gunther Teubner (ed), *Contract and Organisation: Legal Analysis in the Light of Economic and Social Theory* (Walter de Gruyter, 1986) 164, 183.

[52] Goldberg and Erickson, above n 28 (Chap. 1), 386–396.

[53] Wright, above n 34 (Chap. 2), 347.

[54] Bobeff, above n 1 (Chap. 2), 350.

[55] Norbert Horn, 'Changes in Circumstances and The Revision of Contracts in some European Laws and in International Law' in Norbert Horn (ed), *Adaptation and Renegotiation of Contracts in International Trade and Finance* (Kluwer Law International, 1985) 15, 26.

mance of such contracts is interrupted, there is a kind of consensus that certain solutions should be found to deal with the emerging issues.[56] Therefore, hardship clauses will often explicitly stipulate that the parties are under a duty to renegotiate the contract in cases of hardship events. They require the parties to meet and negotiate in good faith with a view to alleviating the difficulties caused by the hardship without any sanction or remedy for failure to reach an agreement on alleviation.[57] The following are examples of clauses used in practice which reflect and support this view:

> Example One
> The buyer and seller confirm that a spirit of mutual cooperation and long-term goodwill underlines this agreement and agree that in the event that unforeseen hardships arise afflicting either party, the parties shall meet promptly with the sincere aim of alleviating such hardship in light of all relevant factors.[58]

> Example Two
> In the event of unforeseeable events or events which were excluded from the Parties' forecasts, including any substantial changes to taxes and duties, which could have the effect of undermining the economic basis of the existing market or prejudice one or other of the Parties, the Parties shall come to an agreement, in the spirit in which the present agreement was concluded, to make the necessary adjustments so as to replace one or other of the provisions of the present contract under the conditions of balance comparable to those which existed at the time of entering into the present contract. In the absence of an agreement, the Parties may refer their dispute to arbitration…[59]

> Example Three
> If, after entering into the electricity supply contract, one or other of the parties suffers unexpected harmful consequences as a result of changes in the technical or economic context and such consequences cannot in all fairness be borne by the party concerned, both parties will try to agree on ways of adapting the contract to such changes in all good faith. This possibility does not entitle them to withdraw from the contract and the other rights and obligations resulting from the contract will remain totally unaffected.[60]

> Example Four
> In the event that substantial and unexpected changes of an economic or technical nature affect the energy and/or … market, and such changes are of an exceptional nature and depart greatly from historical situations, making it significantly harder to honour the undertakings made under the present contract, considering the reason why they have been made, the Consumer and the Supplier undertake to consult with each other to find a solution to the problem that upholds their respective interests…[61]

---

[56] Ibid, 27.

[57] Wright, above n 34 (Chap. 2), 348.

[58] Barnett, above n 9 (Chap. 2), 358.

[59] Guy Block, 'Arbitration and Changes in Energy Prices: A Review of ICC Awards with respect to Force Majeure, Indexation, Adaptation, Hardship and Take-or-Pay Clauses' (2009) 20 *ICC International Court of Arbitration Bulletin* 51, 55.

[60] Ibid.

[61] Ibid, 55–6.

Example Five

(a) If at any time or from time to time during the contract period there has been any substantial change in the economic circumstances relating to this Agreement and (notwithstanding the effect of the other relieving or adjusting provisions of this Agreement) either party feels that such change is causing it to suffer substantial economic hardship then parties shall (at the request of either of them) meet together to consider what (if any) adjustment[s] in the prices... are justified in the circumstances in fairness to the parties to offset or alleviate the said hardship caused by such change.

(b) If the parties shall not within ninety (90) days after any such request have reached agreement on the adjustments (if any) in the said prices... the matter may forthwith be referred by either party for determination by experts...

(c) The experts shall determine what (if any) adjustments in the said prices or in the said price revision mechanism shall be made... and any revised prices or any change in the price revision mechanism so determined by such experts shall take effect six (6) months after the date on which the request for the review was first made.[62]

In addition, Model Hardship Clauses confirm the parties' duty to renegotiate in the context of hardship. For example, the ICC hardship Clause 1985 entitles either party to request a revision of the contract.[63] Although the duty to renegotiate is not explicitly mentioned, it would be reasonable to infer that without renegotiations the parties would not be able to reach an agreement on revision. Also, the comments on this model clause on the Trans-Lex database agree that there is a duty for the parties to renegotiate.[64] Unlike the ICC Hardship Clause 1985, in order to avoid potential ambiguities, the ICC Hardship Clause 2003 expressly requires the parties to renegotiate alternative contractual terms in the case of hardship.[65]

It is worth noting that there may be an issue relating to the validity of the hardship clauses requiring renegotiations on the pre-agreed price or other matters in long-term relational supply contracts.[66] Such hardship clauses may be characterised as an agreement to negotiate by the courts or the arbitral tribunals and, therefore, be regarded as vague and unenforceable,[67] if the courts or the arbitral tribunals consider that those clauses give too much discretion to the parties and make it difficult to ascertain the parties' intentions.[68] It could then be treated as if there were no explicit provisions in relation to the renegotiation or the adaptation. Therefore, it is wise and important for the parties to establish a clear mechanism for renegotiations in their contracts.[69] There is no benefit to the parties agreeing to the creation of vague solu-

---

62 *Superior Overseas Development Corporation v British Gas Corporation* [1982] 1 Lloyd's Rep 262, 264–5.

63 ICC Hardship Clause 1985, available at https://www.trans-lex.org/700650/_/icc-force-majeure-and-hardship-paris-1985-/.

64 Comment 6 and Comment 8, available at https://www.trans-lex.org/700650/_/icc-force-majeure-and-hardship-paris-1985-/.

65 ICC Hardship Clause 2003, available at https://www.trans-lex.org/700700/_/icc-force-majeure-clause-2003-icc-hardship-clause-2003-icc-publication-no-650/.

66 William A W Neilson, 'Price Adjustments in Long-term Supply Contracts: The Saga of the Quintette Coal Arbitration' (1991) 18 *Canadian Business Law Journal* 76, 84.

67 McKillop, above n 50.

68 Neilson, above n 66.

69 Ibid.

tions or mechanisms that may be held unenforceable or void by courts or arbitral tribunals.

The Existence of the Duty to Renegotiate Without a Hardship Clause

There is no doubt that arbitrators or judges will apply hardship clauses if they are included in long-term relational supply contracts and are considered valid and enforceable. Issues often arise when there is no hardship clause in such contracts. One strict view is that, if the parties fail to insert a hardship clause in their contract, the principle of *pacta sunt servanda* will prevail over any attempts to rewrite the contract by applying the flexibility of international commercial contract law.[70] The parties cannot rely on the hardship doctrine to dilute the effect of the principle of *pacta sunt servanda*.[71] They need to bear all the consequences following any hardship events. If the parties believed that renegotiations would be desirable and useful, they would have explicitly inserted into the contract a duty to renegotiate or a hardship clause, and if they did not do so, it was because they had rationally decided not to impose such a duty on themselves.[72]

A counterview is that the duty to renegotiate should apply even if the parties fail to insert a hardship clause in their contract.[73] The duty to renegotiate is not based on the existence of the hardship clause, although it can be presumed to be part of the contractual relationship and to rest on good faith.[74] Good faith gives rise to the duty to co-operate which allows parties to modify their original contract in the face of hardship events but in the absence of hardship clauses.[75] A long-term relationship will not work if it was not realised and understood from the outset that renegotiation is necessary and inevitable.[76] It is not realistic to expect a hardship clause in every long-term contract given the diverse aspects, expertise of knowledge and experience, different levels of diligence, and proficiency of the parties in modern international commercial transactions.[77] Even a very experienced international merchant might forget to insert a hardship clause due to certain explainable or unexplainable

---

[70] Klaus Peter Berger, 'The Relationship between the UNIDROIT Principles of International Commercial Contracts and the New Lex Mercatoria' (2010) 1 *Uniform Law Review* 157, 162–3.

[71] Klaus Peter Berger, 'Renegotiation and Adaptation of International Investment Contracts: The Role of Contract Drafters and Arbitrators' (2003) 36 *Vanderbilt Journal of Transnational Law* 1347, 1355–6.

[72] Douglas G Baird, 'Self-Interest and Cooperation in Long-Term Contracts' (1900) 19 *The Journal of Legal Studies* 583, 591–6.

[73] Yildirim, above n 1 (Chap. 3), 87.

[74] Norbert Horn, 'Procedures of Contract Adaptation and Renegotiation in International Commerce' in Norbert Horn (ed), *Adaptation and Renegotiation of Contracts in International Trade and Finance* (Kluwer Law International, 1985) 173, 188.

[75] Lorfing, above n 292 (Chap. 4), 36–44.

[76] Nystén-Haarala, above n 31 (Chap. 1), 35.

[77] Yildirim, above n 1 (Chap. 3), 87.

reasons. However, it does not necessarily mean that the merchant choses deliberately to give up the potential protection provided by a hardship clause.

The counterview is more reasonable considering the complexity of modern international commercial transactions and the different capacities and levels of knowledge of the parties. This is particularly true for parties to long-term relational supply contracts, as they place more value on maintaining their ongoing relationship, on preserving their mutual trust and confidence established, and on preserving their mutual benefits and commercial expectations. The parties to long-term relational supply contracts usually have a strong interest in maintaining their contracts and relationship and would, therefore, expect to engage in negotiations voluntarily.[78] In practice, a clear clause indicating the intention and expectations of the parties is highly desirable; nevertheless, sometimes renegotiation between the parties may occur.[79] For example, in certain long-term contracts between government and transnational corporations, in the absence of renegotiation clauses or hardship clauses, if hardship events occur, the parties should act in good faith to renegotiate.[80]

In addition, the parties do not generally enter into long-term contracts due to their concern for future changes in prices. Instead, they enter into the contracts to obtain and make full use of the advantages of co-operation.[81] Therefore, even if there is no hardship clause, given the relational characteristics of long-term contracts, a duty to renegotiate, based on the mutual trust and confidence between the parties, could arise. For example, for many long-term oil supply contracts, a sudden rise in oil price could see one party experience exorbitant and unexpected advantages by declining to renegotiate.[82] Without renegotiations under such hardship situations, a fruitful co-operation between the parties would rarely be sustained for the duration of the contract.

External factors also support the duty to renegotiate without a hardship clause. It is argued that '[w]e have to acknowledge that the driving forces behind contract renegotiation are of a political and economic nature, reflecting the parties' bargaining power'.[83] Also, the consequences of renegotiation may be independent of the triggering event and determined by other considerations, such as fairness or balance of obligations between the parties.[84] From a relational point of view, good faith, the duty to co-operate and duty to renegotiate rest on explicit or implied understandings

[78] Horn, 'Standard Clauses on Contract Adaptation in International Commerce', above n 16 (Chap. 3), 138.

[79] Ibid, 136.

[80] Horn, 'Changes in Circumstances and The Revision of Contracts in some European Laws and in International Law', above n 55, 27.

[81] Victor P Goldberg, 'Price Adjustment in Long-Term Contracts' 1985 *Wisconsin Law Review* 527, 531.

[82] Horn, 'Standard Clauses on Contract Adaptation in International Commerce', above n 16 (Chap. 3), 136.

[83] Peter, above n 33, 129.

[84] Ibid, 132.

and agreements between the parties, which govern their ongoing relationship over the duration of their long-term relational supply contracts.

The international development of the harmonisation or codification of general contract law supports the duty to renegotiate. Like the UNIDROIT Principles, the TransLex-Principles also recognise the duty to renegotiate.[85]

Similarly, non-legislative codifications of contract law at the European level also endorse the existence of the duty to renegotiate in the context of hardship.[86] Article 6:111 of the PECL provides that the parties are bound to conduct renegotiations with a view to adapting the contract or terminating it.[87] Also, it requires that the parties must conduct renegotiations in good faith, and that every point of dispute between the parties should be raised in renegotiations.[88] Article 89 of the CESL imposes a duty on the parties to enter into renegotiations with a view to adapting or terminating the contract.[89] The party whose performance could be affected by hardship has to enter into renegotiations with the other party.[90] Article III.-1:110 of the DCFR stipulates that the parties can resort to court for judicial intervention only if they have attempted in good faith to achieve a reasonable and equitable adaptation of the terms of the contract by renegotiation.[91] It is not clear whether there is a duty to renegotiate. A comment made on this article confirms that it does not impose a duty to renegotiate but only requires, as a remedy, that the debtor should attempt in good faith to achieve a reasonable and equitable adjustment by renegotiations.[92]

To sum up, a strict insistence on the application of the principle of *pacta sunt servanda* does not respect the nature, the inherent instability and unpredictability or difficult administration imbedded within long-term relational supply contracts.[93] The existence of the duty to renegotiate does not necessarily lead to uncertainty and instability; however, it may provide flexibility and the possibility for the parties to adapt the contract to accommodate the hardship situations.[94] Therefore, a more flexible, pragmatic and dynamic approach is needed to replace the old all-or-nothing

---

[85] Section No. IV.6.7 – Duty to Renegotiate, available at https://www.trans-lex.org/935000/_/duty-to-renegotiate/.

Section No. VIII.2 – Legal Consequences (of Hardship), available at https://www.trans-lex.org/951500/_/legal-consequences/#references.

[86] Uribe, above n 33 (Chap. 3), 198–215.

[87] Article 6:111 (Change of Circumstances), Lando and Beale, above n 296 (Chap. 4), 322–323.

[88] Ibid, 326.

[89] Article 89 (change of circumstance), Reiner Schulze (ed), *Common European Sales Law: Commentary* (Nomos Verlagsgesellschaft, Verlag C H Beck and Hart Publishing, 2012) 415.

[90] Ibid, 423.

[91] Article III. – 1:110 (Variation or Termination by Court on a Change of Circumstances), Christian von Bar and Eric Clive (eds), *Principles, Definitions and Model Rules of European Private Law: Draft Common Frame of Reference (DCFR)* (Sellier European Law Publishers, 2009) vol 1, 710–1.

[92] Comment C to Article III. – 1:110. Ibid, 712–3.

[93] Samuel B Asante, 'Stability of Contractual Relations in the Transnational Investment Process' (1979) 28 *International and Comparative Law Quarterly* 401, 407.

[94] Uribe, above n 33 (Chap. 3), 235.

approach.[95] The arbitrators and judges should change their rigid view upon the duty to renegotiate in the absence of a hardship clause, unless there is clear evidence that the parties intended to exclude such a clause when they entered into their long-term relational supply contracts.

Case Law on the Duty to Renegotiate

In international arbitral case law, it is established that the hardship doctrine is designed to address the supervening disequilibrium based on the principle of *clausula rebus sic stantibus*. It is widely accepted and constitutes part of the modern *Lex Mercatoria*.[96] International contract practice is oriented to recognise a duty to renegotiate based on the principle of good faith.[97]

In ICC award No. 4761, the arbitral tribunal held that the principle *pacta sunt servanda* was limited by the superior principle of good faith[98] and that, therefore, it would be unjust and unfair to force the parties to perform their original contractual obligations in the context of hardship.[99] In ICC award No. 6219, the arbitral tribunal affirmed that the duty to renegotiate is derived not only from the terms of the contract but also from the general principles of international trade law. Furthermore, if the performance of a contract is in serious difficulties, this duty requires the parties to discuss and engage in active co-operation to find ways to overcome the problems.[100] In the ICC award No. 2291, the arbitral tribunal established a link between good faith and the customary character of the duty to renegotiate long-term contracts in the context of hardship,[101] and therefore acknowledged that reasonable renegotiations are usual and customary in international commercial transactions.[102]

In ICC award No. 8365, the arbitral tribunal made the parties' duty to renegotiate very clear by ruling that:

---

[95] Berger, 'Renegotiation and Adaptation of International Investment Contracts', above n 71, 1377–8.

[96] Yildirim, above n 1 (Chap. 3), 90–1.

[97] Horn, 'Changes in Circumstances and The Revision of Contracts in some European Laws and in International Law', above n 55, 28.

[98] ICC Award No. 4761, available at https://www.trans-lex.org/204761/_/icc-award-no-4761-clunet-1987-at-1012-et-seq/.

[99] Guy Robin, 'Le Principe de La Bonne Foi dans Les Contrats Internationaux/The Principle of Good Faith in International Contracts' (2005) 6 *Revue de Droit des Affaires Internationales/International Business Law Journal* 695, 718.

[100] ICC Award No. 6219, available at https://www.trans-lex.org/206219/_/icc-award-no-6219-clunet-1990-at-1047-et-seq/#1a.

[101] Piero Bernardini, 'Is the Duty to Cooperation in Long-Term Contracts a Substantive Transnational Rule in International Commercial Arbitration' in Emmanuel Gaillard (ed), *Transnational Rules in International Commercial Arbitration* (ICC Publishing, 1993) 137, 140.

[102] ICC Award No. 2292, available at https://www.trans-lex.org/202291/_/icc-award-no-2291-clunet-1976-at-989-et-seq/.

> The arbitral tribunal decides that the applicable rules of the *lex mercatoria* should comprise principles such as the one that contracts must prima facie be executed in conformity with the stipulations contained therein (*pacta sunt servanda*), the one that contracts must be executed in good faith, the one that in case that unforeseen difficulties arise after the conclusion of the contract the parties must negotiate in good faith to overcome them...[103]

ICC awards No. 9994 and No. 10021 again discussed and recognised the existence of a duty to renegotiate in the context of hardship.[104] In ICC award No. 9994, the arbitral tribunal expressly stated that good faith imposes on the parties the duty to seek an adaptation of the contract in the cases of hardship in order to ensure that its performance does not cause the ruin of one of the parties, particularly when a long-term contract is involved; and the arbitral tribunal confirmed that the rule also prevails in international commercial law.[105] In one ICSID case, an arbitrator referred to Articles 6.2.2 and 6.2.3 of the UNIDROIT Principles as an expression of an international standard for a long-term contract which would require the parties to negotiate the contract with a view to achieving an adaptation in the event of hardship.[106]

At the national level, there are also cases dealing with the duty to renegotiate in the context of hardship. In a 2009 Belgian case *Scafom International BV v Lorraine Tubes S.A.S.*,[107] the Belgian Supreme Court held expressly that there is a duty to renegotiate an international sales contract in the case of hardship.[108] This case involved several contracts between a Dutch buyer and a French seller for the delivery of steel tubes. After the conclusion of the contracts, the price of the steel unexpectedly rose by 70% and there were no price adjustment clauses in the contracts. The seller invoked the hardship doctrine to request a renegotiation of the contract price and the buyer rejected it. Since the governing law, the CISG, is silent on the hardship issue, the Belgian Supreme Court applied the UNIDROIT Principles to bridge the gap and held that the seller had the right to make a request for renegotiations on the contract price.[109]

In another case regarding a long-term gas supply contract to provide gas for producing electricity, the algorithm for the determination of the price of the gas, devised ten years earlier, indexed the price of the gas 100% to the price of the coal. The price

[103] ICC Award No. 8365, available at https://www.trans-lex.org/208365/_/icc-award-no-8365-clunet-1997-at-1078-et-seq/#1b.

[104] Julie Dewez et al., 'The Duty to Renegotiate an International Sales Contract under CISG in Case of Hardship and the Use of the UNIDROIT Principles' (2011) 1 *European Review of Private Law* 101, 132. More details on ICC Award No. 9994, see http://www.unilex.info/case.cfm?pid=2&do=case&id=1062&step=Abstract; on ICC Award No. 10021, see http://www.unilex.info/case.cfm?pid=2&do=case&id=832&step=Abstract. The duty to renegotiate has also been discussed or affirmed in non-ICC cases, such as in an Ad hoc Arbitration, available at http://www.unilex.info/case.cfm?pid=2&do=case&id=757&step=Keywords and a case decided by Centro de Arbitraje de México (CAM), available at http://www.unilex.info/case.cfm?pid=2&id=1149&do=case.

[105] Yildirim, above n 1 (Chap. 3), 105.

[106] Available at http://www.unilex.info/case.cfm?pid=2&do=case&id=1667&step=Abstract.

[107] Hof van Cassatie, 19 June 2009, No. C.07.0289.N.

[108] Julie Dewez et al., above n 104, 120–1.

[109] Available at http://cisgw3.law.pace.edu/cisg/wais/db/cases2/090619b1.html#ctoc.

of oil went up, causing an increase in gas and oil prices. The parties found themselves in a hardship situation and the upset in the balance of the contract made it necessary for them to renegotiate the contract.[110]

In the American *Westinghouse* case,[111] a contract price of two billion dollars was to be adapted and the possible bankruptcy of the supplier was as stake, so the parties conducted renegotiations for the long-term supply contract and the case was settled.[112] In a French case, the duty to renegotiate in the context of hardship stipulated by the UNIDROIT Principles was also affirmed by the court.[113] Several Japanese cases have given support to this view in which the courts at different levels have made it clear that the parties should renegotiate in good faith before they can resort to the court to terminate the contract based on the principle of good faith.[114] The inability of parties to renegotiate settlements between them and their resort to the court for aid signal their failure to maintain their relationship.[115]

There may be other cases in which the original contracts were renegotiated without the existence of a hardship clause where certain hardship situations compelled the parties to maintain their contractual relationship based on a mutual understanding.[116]

5.3.1.2 Power of Adaptation or Termination

Renegotiation is the mechanism by which parties tend to solve problems between themselves. However, when the renegotiation cannot provide an appropriate solution, the intervention of a third party may become necessary. For the purpose of this book, a third party is regarded as a court or an arbitral tribunal.[117] What the third party can do to resolve the problems is to adapt or terminate the contract.[118]

---

[110] Block, above n 59, 56–8.

[111] *Florida Power and Light Company v Westinghouse Electric Corporation*, 517 F. Supp. 440 (E.D. Va. 1981).

[112] Horn, 'Procedures of Contract Adaptation and Renegotiation in International Commerce', above n 74, 190.

[113] Available at http://www.unilex.info/case.cfm?pid=2&do=case&id=2121&step=Abstract.

[114] Haley, above n 15 (Chap. 2), 151–5.

[115] Ibid, 176.

[116] Fontaine and De Ly, above n 4 (Chap. 3), 459.

[117] The discussion on the differences between the procedural intervention and contractual intervention regarding the third party intervention is beyond the scope of this book. More analysis on the differences between them, such as those between an arbitrator and a valuer or certifier, from a comparative perspective, see Horn, 'Procedures of Contract Adaptation and Renegotiation in International Commerce', above n 74, 175–6.

[118] Hondius and Grigoleit, 'Introduction: An Approach to the Issues and Doctrines Relating to Unexpected Circumstances', above n 23 (Chap. 3), 10.

Recognition of Adaptation and Termination

A hardship clause normally allows the parties to refer to arbitration or mediation in cases where no agreement can be reached regarding alleviating the consequences of hardship.[119] Hardship clauses often indicate precisely the circumstances under which the parties are entitled to have recourse to arbitration or litigation.[120] The arbitrator or court's power to adapt or terminate the parties' contract can be exercised only in cases where the parties' renegotiations fail and therefore they cannot reach an agreement to resolve the issues arising from the hardship events. At the international level, apart from the UNIDROIT Principles, the TransLex Principles recognise the possibility of adaptation or termination by the courts or the arbitral tribunals.[121] At the European level, the PECL, the DCFR and the CESL all support judicial intervention upon the failure of renegotiations between the parties.[122] At the national level, apart from Germany and France,[123] article 17(1) of the Russian Act on Production Sharing Contracts also allows the adaptation of the contract between the parties without an explicit agreement, if the requirements of a 'significant change of circumstances' are met.[124]

The aim of the judicial intervention is to assist the parties to restore the economic aim of the transaction by taking their interests into account.[125] This is of particular significance to the parties to long-term relational supply contracts facing hardship, as such contracts are 'based on the expectancy that both parties have that the contractual relationship will produce its effects over the course of time, thus allowing room for incompleteness, longevity and (perhaps eventually) either renegotiation or judicial intervention'.[126] As a result of adaptation, such contracts would 'survive and continue to be capable of bona fide performance by the parties'.[127] The parties' interests are so interwoven over the long period of the performance of their contracts that it is very difficult, if not impossible, to suddenly separate their interests. Upon the occurrence of hardship, the situations become more complicated, and the

---

[119] Wright, above n 34 (Chap. 2), 348.

[120] Yildirim, above n 1 (Chap. 3), 86.

[121] Section No. VIII.2 – Legal Consequences (of Hardship).

[122] Article 6:111 of the PECL, Article III. – 1:110 of the DCFR and Article 89 of the CESL.

[123] See relevant parts on hardship in German law and French law in Chap. 3.

[124] Berger, 'Renegotiation and Adaptation of International Investment Contracts', above n 71, 1356. Several former European communist countries, such as Bulgaria and Hungary, allowed the adaptation imposed on the courts or arbitral tribunals as well. See Zhivko Stalev, 'Arbitration to adapt Long-Term International Economic Contracts to Changed Circumstances' in Pieter Sanders (ed), *New Trends in the Development of International Commercial Arbitration and the Role of Arbitral and Other Institutions, ICCA Congress Series* (Kluwer Law International, 1983) vol 1, 199, 201–2.

[125] Schulze, above n 89, 424.

[126] Demetrio Maltese and Marco Farina, 'Theory of the Firm and Organisational Contracts: The Remedial Aspects of Good Faith' (2016) 27 *European Business Law Review* 51, 54.

[127] D A J Vaughan and D W Shenton, 'Arbitration in Long-Term Contracts' (1977) 5 *International Business Lawyer* 41, 41.

parties need the assistance of a third party to resolve issues in a satisfactory manner unless they achieve this via renegotiations between themselves.

In addition, even if there is no hardship clause in a long-term relational supply contract, the courts or the arbitral tribunals can still adapt or terminate the contract. The issues caused by hardship events cannot be ignored given the increasing significance of long-term business transactions in the field of international commerce and economic co-operation.[128]

There are several reasons underlying the view that judicial intervention is an appropriate means of dealing with issues in the context of hardship. First of all, the parties are facing the same hardship issues with or without the hardship clause. If the courts or the arbitral tribunals can adapt or terminate the contract according to a hardship clause, they can do so without a hardship clause. The nature of the hardship events and the nature of the issues do not change regardless of a hardship clause. The parties need a fair and equitable solution to resolve the issues between them. The lack of a hardship clause should not prevent a court or arbitral tribunal from granting appropriate relief. It should, nevertheless, be noted that judicial intervention ought to be confined to certain circumstances.[129]

Secondly, it is impossible for the parties to predict and allow for all possible risks for the long period of the performance of the contract. Hence, good faith and fairness would require the parties to share unforeseen and unallocated losses.[130]

Also, the relational nature of the long-term relational supply contract does not depend on a hardship clause. At the time of the conclusion of the contract, although the relationship between the parties is fixed, it is not fixed indefinitely. In the context of hardship, it may be unfair to go back to the original contract.[131] The relational realities and circumstances of the contract will lead the parties to reasonably expect that the contract would be adapted in the case of hardship.[132]

Moreover, the desire to maintain the ongoing relationship, mutual trust and confidence between the parties sometimes make the judicial intervention necessary. The parties intend to protect their reputation in the relevant industry by accepting adaptation in the event of hardship.[133] The interdependency and mutual reliance based on the ongoing relationship will prompt the parties to resolve disputes.[134] Due to the complexity and uncertainty of predicting and regulating future risks, it is

---

[128] Giorgio Bernini, 'Report: Adaptation of Contracts' in Pieter Sanders (ed), *New Trends in the Development of International Commercial Arbitration and the Role of Arbitral and Other Institutions, ICCA Congress Series* (Kluwer Law International, 1983) vol 1, 193, 193.

[129] Hans Henrik Edlund, 'Imbalance in Long-Term Commercial Contracts' (2009) 4 *European Review of Contract Law* 427, 444.

[130] Robert A Hillman, 'Court Adjustment of Long-Term Contracts: An Analysis under Modern Contract Law' (1987) *Duke Law Journal* 1, 3.

[131] Macaulay, 'Relational Contracts Floating on A Sea of Custom? Thoughts about the Ideas of Ian Macneil and Lisa Bernstein', above n 116 (Chap. 2), 803.

[132] Hillman, 'Court Adjustment of Long-Term Contracts', above n 130, 3–4.

[133] Ibid, 5.

[134] Gillette, above n 5 (Chap. 2), 554–6.

extremely difficult for the parties to allocate all conceivable risks upon entering into their contracts; therefore, the parties will often, predictably, reach an agreement to adapt their contract in light of the occurrence of unforeseen events in order to restore a 'cooperative equilibrium'.[135] Parties to long-term relational contracts will be more willing to do this to achieve a long-term cooperative goal and to obtain the particular advantages derived from mutual co-operation.[136] They will continue to co-operate in maintaining and developing their long-term, ongoing relationship as long as the benefits that derive from the co-operation sustains their continuing relationship and exceeds the benefit of alternatives, such as litigation. Also, from an economic perspective, it is important for the parties to maintain their mutual trust and confidence in each other and to co-operate on the basis of them.[137] If parties cannot find a good solution via renegotiations but still intend to maintain their relationships, judicial intervention may offer a more satisfactory solution than the strict and formalistic application of certain contract terms.

In addition, the reality of business will encourage the parties to seek the appropriate judicial intervention. In the case of hardship, the increased costs as well as the possibility of losing mutual gains and cooperative interest may encourage the parties to agree on court or arbitral tribunal offered solutions. Ultimately, this is a consideration of balance. Most parties to a long-term relational supply contract would give more weight to the long-term benefits than to the short-term losses caused by hardship events. On the one hand, if the parties to a long-term relational contract, bearing good faith in mind, act in a co-operative, honest and committed way, then mutual trust and confidence between the parties may be enhanced and mutual interests may be advanced, thereby reducing potential transaction costs. On the other hand, the break-up of a cooperative contractual relationship will probably result in more harm and economic loss than the costs of establishing a new business relationship.[138] Parties will perform a less favourable and less advantageous contract to obtain future benefits and co-operation.[139] This may also protect the parties' reputation and may eventually bring in other business opportunities with third parties who respect the reputation of their potential business partners.[140] Judicial intervention is a better and more flexible way to protect and promote those long-term benefits and reputation.

Finally, the possibility of judicial intervention may provide a strong incentive for the parties to renegotiate and reach an agreement to deal with issues arising from

---

[135] Robert E Scott, 'Risk Distribution and Adjustment in Long-Term Contracts' in Fritz Nicklisch (ed), *The Complex Long-Term Contract: Structures and International Arbitration* (C F Müller Juristisch Verlag, 1987) 51, 53–4.

[136] Ibid, 55.

[137] Ibid, 65–82.

[138] Nystén-Haarala, above n 31 (Chap. 1), 35.

[139] Stewart Macaulay, 'An Empirical View of Contract' (1985) *Wisconsin Law Review* 465, 467.

[140] Hugh Beale and Tony Dugdale, 'Contracts between Businessmen: Planning and the Use of Contractual Remedies' (1975) 2 *British Journal of Law and Society* 45, 47–8.

hardship events.[141] In *Florida Power and Light Company v Westinghouse Electric Corporation*,[142] the court believed that 'the parties themselves are in a far better position to find an equitable solution'[143] therefore, a special master was appointed to assist the parties to reach an agreement to adapt their long-term supply contracts and the case was successfully settled by the parties themselves. Similarly, in *McGinnis v Cayton*,[144] the court stated that 'long-term contract problems that arise because of fundamental shifts in the balance or equities of the original relationships are best resolved by the parties. Courts should do all they can to encourage settlement and private resolution'.[145] The court also held that '[w]hen that does not work, courts should make themselves available to provide just and equitable resolutions with the primary goal being to maintain the integrity of the long-term contractual relationship'.[146] To avoid an external rebalancing of the contractual relationship imposed by the court, the parties will make efforts to conduct renegotiation, during the process of which, good faith will 'have a deterrent effect in terms of litigation and an enticement effect in terms of co-operation'.[147]

Therefore, the adaptation or termination of contracts by the courts or the arbitral tribunals should be available as last-resort remedies. However, it should be noted that there is a view against judicial intervention where there is no hardship clause. The argument is that the courts or the arbitral tribunals should not be allowed to intervene to adapt or terminate the contract where the parties can protect themselves by the insertion of a hardship clause.[148] In addition, the intervention of judges or arbitrators is usually both costly and difficult for courts to determine unobservable factors. An ancillary result is that the margin for error in judges so deciding is high.[149]

Scott stated three objections to the relational approach in dealing with hardship issues relating to long-term relational contracts: firstly, the court's incompetency and the difficulty in finding a fair or equitable resolution to the disputes, meaning the courts are asked to do what it cannot possibility achieve; secondly, there is no clear standard for what is fair or equitable; and thirdly, including a hardship clause that advocates adaption of a contract may adversely affect parties' incentive to uphold their agreement and set a bad example to similar parties.[150] Scott's

---

[141] Macaulay, 'An Empirical View of Contract', above n 139, 475–6.

[142] 517 F. Supp. 440 (E.D. Va. 1981).

[143] 517 F. Supp. 440 (E.D. Va. 1981), 461 per Merhige J.

[144] 312 S.E.2d 765 (W. Va. 1984).

[145] 312 S.E.2d 765 (W. Va. 1984), 780 per Harshibarger J.

[146] 312 S.E.2d 765 (W. Va. 1984), 779 per Harshibarger J.

[147] Maltese and Farina, above n 126, 62.

[148] Mckendrick, 'The regulation of long-term Contracts in English Law', above n 3 (Chap. 2), 332.

[149] Janwillem (Pim) Oosterhuis, 'Commercial Impracticability and the Missed Opportunity of the French Contract Law Reform: Doctrinal, Historical and Law and Economics Arguments- Comment on Lutzi's Introducing *Imprévision* in to French Contract Law' in S Stijns and S Jansen (eds), *The French Contract Law Reform: A Source of Inspiration?* (Intersentia 2016) 113, 117–8.

[150] Scott, 'The Case for Formalism in Relational Contract', above n 53 (Chap. 2), 850–1, 858–9.

objections are supported by other scholars.[151] Also, the courts or the arbitral tribunals tend to take a passive approach and refrain from intervening in the parties' contracts and their contractual autonomy.[152] For example, the most important difference between the ICC Hardship Clause 1985 and 2003 lies in whether the arbitrator (third party) has the power to revise or adapt the contract. This power was conferred on the arbitrator in the 1985 edition, although it was not conferred in the 2003 edition as the power regarding the revision or adaptation of the contract had never been applied.[153] Again, it is argued that 'the more complex a contract is and the more the future co-operation of parties is in question, the less a court decision or an arbitral award appears to be an adequate answer.'[154]

However, the ability of the parties to use judicial or arbitral proceedings is necessary in cases where renegotiations have failed, the spirit of co-operation has faded, the relationship has gone sour, and the mutual trust and confidence has broken down.[155] With the development of international commerce, the UNIDROIT Principles' rules on hardship are a significant and influential guide in this regard.[156] Despite certain criticism of the hardship rules in the UNIDROIT Principles,[157] these rules have come to be regarded by scholars as part of a global commercial code due to their precise and detailed attention to this topic.[158] The case law to be discussed in the next section reflects this view.

Case Law on Adaptation and Termination

There are normally two views regarding the development of international case law in relation to adaptation and termination. The first view predominates in international commercial cases. It states that adaptation should play no role in hardship cases, and that the only remedies available to the parties are either termination or suspension.[159] In many ICC cases, the arbitral tribunals refuse to grant relief in cases of hardship. In the ICC award No. 1512, the arbitrator stated that generally relief

---

[151] See, e.g., Hillman, 'Court Adjustment of Long-Term Contracts', above n 130, 19–29.

[152] Schwarts, above n 74 (Chap. 2), 282–3, 290–5, 308–315.

[153] Yildirim, above n 1 (Chap. 3), 83.

[154] Horn, 'Procedures of Contract Adaptation and Renegotiation in International Commerce', above n 74, 189.

[155] Ibid.

[156] Allan E Farnsworth, 'An American View of the Principles as a Guide to Drafting Contract in ICC institute of International Business Law and Practice' in Jean-Paul Béraudo (ed), *The UNIDROIT Principles for International Commercial Contracts: a new lex mercatoria? ICC/Dossier of the Institute of International Business Law and Practice ICC publication no. 490/1* (ICC Publishing, 1995) 88, cited by Yildirim, above n 1 (Chap. 3), 83.

[157] Uribe, above n 33 (Chap. 3), 132.

[158] Ole Lando, 'The CISG and the UNIDROIT Principles in a Global Commercial Code' in Mélanges offerts Marcel Fontaine (2003) 467, cited by Yildirim, above n 1 (Chap. 3), 83.

[159] Nassar, above n 25 (Chap. 1), 230.

should not be granted to the parties facing hardship situations.[160] In the ICC award No. 5953, the arbitrator refused to adapt the contract due to hardship, although a clause inserted in the contract allows the adaptation of the purchase price.[161] In the ICC award No. 8873, the arbitral tribunal held that the articles of the UNIDROIT Principles on hardship which allow adaptation and termination of the contract do not correspond, at least presently, to current practices in international trade.[162] In the ICC award No. 9029, the arbitral tribunal expressed that hardship articles under the UNIDROIT Principles are not a reflection of international trade usages.[163]

However, an increasing acceptance of the second view has gradually emerged with the development of international commerce. It is argued that both adaptation and termination should be provided by the courts or the arbitral tribunals as remedies to the parties affected by hardship events and that good faith has also been used by arbitrators to support the power of adaptation and termination.[164]

In many arbitral cases, arbitral tribunals recognised their power of adaptation and termination. The ICC arbitral tribunal in its award No. 4761 recognised the superior status of the principle of good faith when dealing with hardship issues.[165] In other cases, the ICC arbitral tribunals support the adaptation or termination of a contract in the context of hardship without explicitly referring to the principle of good faith. In the ICC award No. 7365, the arbitral tribunal stated that the tribunal can terminate a contract as a result of hardship events.[166] The ICC award No. 10021 affirmed the termination of a contract by the arbitral tribunal after the failure of renegotiations in the context of hardship.[167] Regarding adaptation, in the ICC award No. 9479 the arbitral tribunal held that it would have the power to equitably adapt a contract according to the hardship provision.[168] In the ICC award No. 2291, it was held that the *Lex Mercatoria* allows the adaptation of a contract in order to maintain the economic equilibrium of the contract, and therefore in almost every international contract 'the price is determined according to the conditions which exist in the moment

160 ICC award No. 1512, available at https://www.trans-lex.org/201512/_/icc-award-no-1512-yca-1976-at-128-et-seq-/.

161 ICC award No. 5953, available at https://www.trans-lex.org/205953/_/icc-award-no-5953-clunet-1990-at-1056-et-seq/.

162 ICC award No. 8873, available at http://www.unilex.info/case.cfm?pid=1&do=case&id=641&step=Abstract.

163 ICC award No. 9029, available at https://www.trans-lex.org/209029/_/icc-award-no-9029-10-icc-bull-no-2-1999-at-88-et-seq/.

164 Yildirim, above n 1 (Chap. 3), 91–2.

165 ICC award No. 4761, available at https://www.trans-lex.org/204761/_/icc-award-no-4761-clunet-1987-at-1012-et-seq/.

166 ICC award No. 7365, available at http://www.unilex.info/case.cfm?pid=1&do=case&id=653&step=Keywords.

167 ICC award No. 10021, available at http://www.unilex.info/case.cfm?id=832.

168 Gotanda, above n 36, 1471.

of the conclusion of the contract and it will vary according to the parameters, which reflect the variations of values of the different elements...'[169]

In an unreported arbitration case between a Chilean company and an Argentinean company, the arbitral tribunal adapted the original contract price due to the unexpected and unpredicted change caused by an alleged gas crisis. In this case, Empresa Eléctrica Guacolda S.A. (hereinafter Guacolda), an electricity generation company concluded a long-term gas supply contract with Empresa Minera Mantos Blancos S.A. (hereinafter Mantos Blancos), a mining company. Due to the restrictions on gas supplies imposed by the Argentinean government which affected the agreed price significantly, Guacolda requested that the contract be terminated or that the contract price be adapted if the request for termination was rejected. Mantos Blancos argued that there was no significant increase in costs on Guacolda's side and the behaviour of Guacolda was opportunistic and against good faith. The arbitrator rejected the request for termination but accepted the request for the adaptation on the basis of the occurrence of an unexpected and unpredictable change of circumstances that affected the electricity market and resulted in a significant imbalance in the equilibrium of the contract. The arbitrator fixed a new price accordingly.[170] However, in another case based on similar facts in the context of the gas crisis, the arbitral tribunal rejected the request for the adaptation of the original contract.[171]

In yet another *ad hoc* arbitration case *Hungarian State Enterprise v Jugoslavenski Naftovod (Yugoslav Crude Oil Pipeline)*, the arbitral tribunal confirmed the possibility of judicial intervention under limited circumstances:

> In long-term contracts the parties must reckon with the fact that circumstances which existed at the time of contract formation can subsequently change. If they explicitly or obviously (sinngemäss) refrain from excluding the influence of such changes on their mutual contractual obligations, then it corresponds to the essence of the contract that it must be fulfilled the way it has been concluded. In this case, each party must basically bear the risks stemming from changed circumstances. The parties have no ground whatsoever to have the contract declared nonbinding, or changed, if their expectations or speculations fail to materialise… Judicial intervention at the request of the debtor is… only admissible if the ration of mutual contractual obligations has been so greatly disrupted owing to changed circumstances that the creditor's insistence on his contractual claim constitutes usurious exploitation of the disproportions and, thereby, also an evident abuse of rights.[172]

Like arbitral tribunals, the courts may also refer to principles of equity and good faith.[173] The principle of good faith is considered as a basis of the power of the court or the arbitral tribunal to adapt or terminate a contract in the event of hardship.

---

[169] ICC award No. 2291, available at https://www.trans-lex.org/202291/_/icc-award-no-2291-clunet-1976-at-989-et-seq/.

[170] Uribe, above n 33 (Chap. 3), 114–6.

[171] Ibid, 113–4.

[172] 'Hungarian State Enterprise v Jugoslavenski Naftovod (Yugoslav Crude Oil Pipeline), Award, 6 July 1983' in Pieter Sanders (ed), *Yearbook Commercial Arbitration 1984* (Kluwer Law International, 1984) vol 9, 69, 70.

[173] Horn, 'Changes in Circumstances and The Revision of Contracts in some European Laws and in International Law', above n 55, 25.

Aluminium Co. of America v Essex Group, Inc. (hereinafter the Alcoa case)[174] is an unprecedented case for the judicial intervention to adapt the contract price in a long-term relational supply contract in the United States. In this case, due to the significant increase in energy costs, Alcoa's losses would exceed 60 million dollars which made the performance of the contract impractical. The court held that Alcoa was entitled to 'some relief' rather than rescission.[175] The court concluded that '[a] remedy modifying the price term of the contract in light of circumstances which upset the price formula will better preserve the purposes and expectations of the parties than any other remedy. Such a remedy is essential to avoid injustice in this case'.[176]

The price adjustment in this judgment is an equitable reformation imposed by judicial intervention.[177] It indicates that the court paid 'close attention to the legitimate business aims of the parties, to their purpose of avoiding the risks of great losses, and to the need to frame a remedy to preserve the essence of the agreement.'[178] It also supports the argument that the characteristics of a long-term relational supply contract in general, and the maintenance the ongoing relationship between the parties should be taken into account by the courts when dealing with issues in the context of hardship. Judicial intervention in long-term relational supply contracts in the event of hardship is not impossible and should not be ruled out automatically.[179] It can achieve the goal of preserving the contract, adapting the contract price and avoiding unpredictable loss and not-bargained-for and unjust enrichment.[180] Although this decision caused controversial discussions among contract scholars, it was not followed in subsequent cases.[181] This decision was endorsed by only two judges in two other cases.[182] Some other courts have indicated that they might adapt a contract in an appropriate manner.[183]

The UNIDROIT Principles were referred to in another two domestic cases. In a Spanish case, the court adapted the contract price to accommodate the

[174] 499 F. Supp. 53 (W.D. Pa. 1980).

[175] Richard E Speidel, 'Court-imposed Price Adjustments under Long-Term Supply Contracts' (1981) 76 *Northwestern University Law Review* 369, 377–8.

[176] 499 F. Supp. 53 (W.D. Pa. 1980), 79.

[177] Speidel, 'Court-imposed Price Adjustments under Long-Term Supply Contracts', above n 175, 377–380.

[178] 499 F. Supp. 53 (W.D. Pa. 1980), 91.

[179] Robert A Hillman, 'Maybe Dick Speidel Was Right about Court Adjustment' (2009) 46 *San Diego Law Review* 595, 602–3.

[180] Richard E Speidel, 'The New Spirit of Contract' (1982) 2 *Journal of Law and Commerce* 193, 207–8.

[181] Stewart Macaulay et al., *Contracts: Law in Action: The Advanced Course* (Carolina Academic Press, 4th ed, 2017) vol 2, 690–700.

[182] *McGinnis v Cayton*, 312 S.E.2d 765 (W. Va. 1984) and *Unihealth v U.S. Healthcare Inc.*, 14 F. Supp. 2d 623 (D. N. J. 1998).

[183] Hillman, 'Court Adjustment of Long-Term Contracts', above n 130, 2.

unforeseeable decrease in marketing investment caused by the 2008 economic crisis.[184] In a Lithuanian case, the court held that the parties should share the consequences of the financial crisis in this case, and decreased the contract price accordingly.[185]

5.3.2 Procedural Aspects of Good Faith in the Context of Hardship

To resolve issues arising from hardship events in a better and more satisfactory manner, it is important to consider the procedural aspects of the hardship doctrine and their interactions with good faith. There is a close relationship between the substantive aspects that are discussed above, and the procedural aspects analysed below. Appropriate procedures can guide the parties in finding a substantively satisfactory solution to hardship situations. If the parties do not follow the procedures, they may lose the right to request renegotiation.

In practice, the procedures that the parties should follow are often detailed in a hardship clause. In the event of hardship, the procedural aspects are regarded by many international, commercial entities as important, useful and necessary as they provide a procedure to follow and may increase the prospect of a prompt and just resolution of the problems.[186]

5.3.2.1 Renegotiation

It has been argued that, in theory, the parties are under a duty to renegotiate. In practice, in cases where a hardship clause is inserted into a long-term relational supply contract, the clause often establishes duties regarding timely written disclosure of information, a reasonable waiting period, and a meeting of the parties.[187] Often, hardship clauses require notification of the hardship events, and a renegotiation process usually follows this notification condition.[188] The renegotiation procedure is preferable where the parties envisage a long-term, relational and complex co-operation and the hardship events occur in the middle of the performance of the long-term relational supply contracts.[189]

---

[184] Available at http://www.unilex.info/case.cfm?id=1949.

[185] Available at http://www.unilex.info/case.cfm?id=1898.

[186] Bobeff, above n 1 (Chap. 2), 348.

[187] Horn, 'Procedures of Contract Adaptation and Renegotiation in International Commerce', above n 74, 174–5.

[188] Yildirim, above n 1 (Chap. 3), 86–7.

[189] Horn, 'Procedures of Contract Adaptation and Renegotiation in International Commerce', above n 74.

In the process of renegotiation, the parties should first discuss and mutually determine the occurrence of one or more hardship events, and then renegotiate the price or other contract terms.[190] Normally, the hardship clause will require the parties to renegotiate in good faith, but cannot provide a standard or test to determine whether there is a breach of duty to renegotiate.[191] Therefore, it is often difficult to both argue and prove that either party has not acted in good faith. Accordingly, liability for damages or costs can be only recognized under the most exceptional circumstances.[192] The difficulty of determining whether the parties have renegotiated in good faith and in a proper way increases when there is no hardship clause providing the renegotiation procedure. This section of the book will discuss several important aspects of the renegotiation procedure based on the framework provided for in the UNIDROIT Principles.

Reasonable Time

The first issue relating to the duty to renegotiate is to determine whether there is any time limit on the invocation of the hardship clause prior to requesting negotiations. The ICC Hardship Clause 2003 stipulates that the parties should start a renegotiation within reasonable time of the invocation of the clause.[193] The PECL, the DCFR and the CESL are silent on this issue. Nor do the UNIDROIT Principles regulate this issue in the black letter rules. Also, neither Article 6.2.3 of the UNIDROIT Principles or the ICC Hardship Clause 2003 set a limit on the length of the process of renegotiations. The PECL and the CESL do not explicitly mention it either. However, they both have similar wording that if the parties fail to reach an agreement within reasonable time, they may resort to the court. Therefore, it is reasonable to infer that the renegotiation process should be concluded within a reasonable time.

In practice, the hardship clauses often do include provisions regarding notice or limitation of time. A common format is that the disadvantaged party affected by hardship should, in a reasonable time such as within 30 days, give notice to the party indicating the intention to invoke the hardship clause. The parties should then attempt to reach an agreement, in a reasonable time such as within 90 days from the receipt of the notice.[194]

Although Article 6.2.3 of the UNIDROIT Principles does not mention time or notice, its official comment stipulates that the disadvantaged party should request renegotiations without undue delay.[195] It does not detail what is meant by 'undue

[190] Horn, 'Standard Clauses on Contract Adaptation in International Commerce', above n 16 (Chap. 3), 138.

[191] Ibid.

[192] Ibid.

[193] ICC Hardship Clause 2003, above n 65.

[194] Schmitthoff, above n 163 (Chap. 3), 420.

[195] Comment 2 to Article 6.2.3 UNIDROIT Principles 2016.

delay,' it simply states that the request should be made as quickly as possible after the alleged hardship has occurred.[196] In cases where the disadvantaged party fails to act without undue delay, the right to request renegotiations is not lost.[197] However, the failure may affect the determination of 'whether hardship actually existed and, if so, its consequences for the contract'.[198] It appears that if the courts or the arbitral tribunals find hardship despite the fact that the advantaged party fails to act without undue delay, the undue delay will affect the consequences for the contract. But how can this be so? And if they do not find evidence of hardship, does the undue delay not affect the contract and its consequences? The wording of the comment suggests otherwise and may be unreasonable as it raises these questions: How can an undue delay not affect the consequences of the contract if hardship could not be found because of it? Would the parties' failure to act without undue delay be regarded as opportunistic behaviour and would the failure affect the contract?

The logical reasoning would be that it is possible that the delay in requesting renegotiation is a factor, if not a main one, that may cause the courts or arbitral tribunals to decide that the alleged hardship did not exist at all, and this may affect the consequences of the contract. What would happen if the courts or the arbitral tribunal did find that the hardship did not exist based on the delay in making the request for renegotiations? Based on the wording of Article 6.2.3, apparently they cannot adapt or terminate the contract, as they may only do so if they find hardship and if it is reasonable.[199]

The issue is, then, whether the courts or the arbitral tribunals can force the parties to perform their contract without any change. This issue has been raised before, although not in the context of the finding of non-existence of hardship due to failure to act without undue delay. Furthermore, it is argued that the courts may impose the continuation of the contract without any change based on the reasoning that:

> This may seem to more consistent with the wording of the provisions of the Principles as well as its official comments, on the other hand, the possibility of the court to order the continuation of the contract would lead to a situation where the damaged party has to continue to carry the burden of hardship, which seems to be contrary to the rationale of the Principles provisions on hardship.[200]

It is reasonable to argue that the courts or the arbitral tribunals can force the parties to continue to perform the contract, because if no hardship is found, then the basis for the invocation of Article 6.2.3 no longer exists; hence, there is no basis for changing the disadvantaged party's course of action.[201] This argument cannot be

[196] Ibid.

[197] Ibid.

[198] Ibid.

[199] Article 6.2.3 UNIDROIT Principles 2016.

[200] Ugo Draetta, 'Les Clauses de Force Majeure et de Hardship dans les Contrats Internationaux/ Hardship and Force Majeure Clauses in International Contracts' (2002) 3–4 *Revue de Droit des Affaires Internationales/ International Business Law Journal* 347, 350.

[201] The argument is based on the assumption that hardship is the only basis for the cause of action of the disadvantaged party. If he or she has another basis or another cause of action, the courts or

used against the imposition of performance since, if there is no hardship, there is no burden of hardship for the disadvantaged party to carry, at least according to the courts or the arbitral tribunals; therefore, it will not be inconsistent with the rationale or the spirit of the provisions on hardship.

Grounds for Renegotiations

The official comment to Article 6.2.3 also provides that the disadvantaged party is under a duty to indicate the grounds on which the request for renegotiations is made.[202] And failure to provide such grounds may also affect the determination of the existence of hardship.[203] The reasoning of the result of failure to set forth grounds for the request for renegotiations would be the same as the failure to request for renegotiation without undue delay. If the disadvantaged party fails to provide grounds on which the hardship impacts their ability to continue the contract, the courts or the arbitral tribunals may determine that there is no hardship. If so, they then can force the parties to continue the performance of the contract without making any change to it.

Procedural Significance of Affirmation of the Contract

If the above reasoning is correct, then there actually is an implied procedure that is mentioned only in the official comment to Article 6.2.3. The implied procedure is that the courts or the arbitral tribunals have powers to affirm the contract; therefore, they can order the parties to maintain the contract as is and continue to perform it, on the condition that there is no hardship and therefore no basis for the disadvantaged party to request renegotiations.

Also, there is a risk that adaptation and termination may not fully deal with the opportunistic behaviours of the parties. There are two basic kinds of opportunistic behaviours relating to relational contracts: first, a party may refuse necessary renegotiations; second, a party may request unnecessary renegotiations.[204] The powers exercised by the courts or the arbitral tribunals to adapt or terminate the contract may prevent the first kind of opportunistic behaviour, but may encourage the second kind. If the courts or the arbitral tribunals had the power to affirm the contract, then the unnecessary renegotiations would be better prevented, if not entirely controlled.

In addition, the most important foundation of a long-term relational supply contract is the mutual trust, confidence and ongoing relationship between the parties. This foundation requires the prevention of opportunistic behaviours at the highest

---

the arbitral tribunals need to deal with them further.

[202] Comment 2 to Article 6.2.3 UNIDROIT Principles 2016.

[203] Ibid.

[204] Smythe, above n 59 (Chap. 2), 249–251.

level. It seems, therefore, reasonable and logical to confer on the courts or the arbitral tribunals the powers not only to adapt or terminate such a contract, but also to affirm it on the basis of varying circumstances surrounding the hardship.

The last thing which is noteworthy is that if the disadvantaged party has made a request for renegotiations without undue delay and has indicated the grounds for such a request, what happens if the advantaged party does not conduct renegotiations at all? In this case, the disadvantaged party can always resort to a court or an arbitral tribunal,[205] and the courts or the arbitral tribunals probably will not affirm the contract, but will consider other means of dealing with the issues arising from the hardship.

Compelling Reasons as a Boundary on the Duty to Renegotiate

One party should not be, or be regarded as being, superior to the other party and use that power, either economic or political, to deprive the other party of obtaining the expected benefits of the long-term relational contract. Conversely, there should be some limits on the application of the principle of good faith. The proposed article on termination for compelling reasons has not been approved by the governing council of the UNIDROIT and, therefore, has not been included in the 2016 edition of the UNIDROIT Principles.[206] However, the 'compelling reason' concept has substantial merits and a mechanism based on a compelling reason might have a role to play if it were given a different function, such as limiting the scope of the duty to renegotiate.

The concept of a compelling reason may be used to deal with some potential issues arising from hardship. According to the articles tackling hardship issues under the UNIDROIT Principles, the parties have a duty to renegotiate in the context of hardship.[207] Moreover, if the renegotiation fails, the parties may resort to the court which may subsequently modify or terminate their contract.[208] Considering the general principle of good faith set out in Article 1.7 of the UNIDROIT Principles, the parties should act in good faith, including when they renegotiate. If both parties have genuinely renegotiated in good faith and failed to reach a satisfactory solution, a compelling reason may provide an exception to further renegotiations, or even as an exception to renegotiations in the first place. If a party can demonstrate that there is a compelling reason for not renegotiating the contract with the other party and the compelling reason is real and genuine, they should be offered the opportunity to resort to the court. However, if it turns out that the compelling reason is not real or

---

[205] James Otis Rodner, 'Hardship under the UNIDROIT Principles of International Commercial Contracts' in Gerald Aksen et al. (eds), *Global Reflections on International Law, Commerce and Dispute Resolution: Liber Amicorum in Honour of Robert Briner* (ICC Publishing, 2005) 677, 689.

[206] For a detailed discussion on the drafting history, see Peng Guo, 'Termination for a Compelling Reason under the UNIDROIT Principles: Status Quo and the Way Forward' 21 *International Trade and Business Law Review* 1, 2–6.

[207] Articles 6.2.2 and 6.2.3 UNIDROIT Principles 2016.

[208] Ibid.

genuine, the other party may invoke whatever remedy is suitable and reasonable. Therefore, the better terminology in this case may be 'discharge from renegotiations for a compelling reason'.

This is the envisaged dependent and indirect function of the right to be discharged from renegotiating for a compelling reason. It is dependent insofar as it is a collateral right that is attached to the duty to renegotiate. It offers an exception where a party may avoid renegotiation or suspend further renegotiations if the other party does not renegotiate in good faith. If a party can prove the existence of a compelling reason to justify the discharge from not renegotiating, that party can resort to the court to adapt or terminate the contract accordingly. It is then for the court to determine if there is a compelling reason to discharge the parties from renegotiating the contract. If the court so concludes, it may adapt or terminate the contract. If the court is not satisfied that there is a compelling reason, it may direct the parties to start, or resume, renegotiations. The court may also apply other remedies for abusing the right to discharge from renegotiations for a compelling reason, including monetary compensation to the other party. This judicial approach is fundamentally different from the proposed exceptional remedy that would allow a party to terminate the relationship themselves and also, not paying compensation to the other party.[209] To this extent, discharge from renegotiations for a compelling reason could be regarded as having an indirect function which intends to keep the parties in the contractual relationship until the matter is formally resolved. This is unlike the affirmative function in the proposed provisions which allows, if not encourages, either party to simply claim the existence of a compelling reason, terminate and get out of the contract.[210]

To use a compelling reason as a limitation on renegotiation in the context of hardship may not be ideal; however, it does have several advantages. To begin with, it would avoid many criticisms that it has attracted. For example: 1. neither party would have a discretionary termination right with immediate effect; 2. the supervision of courts could mitigate abuse and unnecessary litigation; and 3. addressing the issues on boundaries for a compelling reason, hardship, force majeure and frustration is unnecessary at this stage. Moreover, the restrictive role of a compelling reason would appear only in the comments relating to the hardship rules. This would not cause as dramatic a change to the structure of the UNIDROIT Principles as a new black letter rule might. In addition, the dependent and collateral role would reflect the value of providing a commercially feasible and fair measure for assessing and determining the boundaries of a duty to renegotiate, and in particular to renegotiate in good faith. This new approach may be a suitable and reasonable step to take at present and invite broader acceptance of this innovative notion in future.[211]

---

[209] Guo, above n 206, 6–16.

[210] Ibid.

[211] Ibid, 16–8.

Procedural Consequences of Renegotiations

First, if the court or the arbitral tribunal finds that hardship cannot be established, then there is no need or basis for renegotiations and they can affirm the original contract terms and order specific performance.

Secondly, if the parties reach an agreement after renegotiations, they can act according to the new agreement.

Thirdly, if the parties fail to reach an agreement, it is reasonable to investigate why the renegotiations have not been successful. If there is a genuine deadlock between the parties, the court or the arbitral tribunal should determine if adaptation or termination is appropriate.[212] Alternatively, the courts or the arbitral tribunals may order the advantaged party to engage in renegotiations in good faith,[213] if the failure of renegotiations is due to the advantaged party refusing to renegotiate with the disadvantaged party without a compelling reason or that the advantaged party did not renegotiate in good faith. Only if the renegotiations fail again, can the courts or the arbitral tribunals proceed with mediation, adaptation or termination.[214] However, if a compelling reason is established, the courts or the arbitral tribunals proceed directly with procedures relating to the adaptation and the termination.

5.3.2.2 Adaptation

Potential Issues with Adaptation

It is argued that '[o]nce the issues of renegotiation have been formulated, the outcome of the renegotiation process depends on the bargaining positions and negotiation skills of the parties. But the renegotiation may be unsuccessful, and the ensuing dispute brought to arbitration'.[215] Upon the failure of renegotiations, the courts or the arbitral tribunals can adapt their contract. The UNIDROIT Principles confer on the courts or the arbitral tribunals the power to adapt the contract, as ICC hardship Clause 1985 did, although the 2003 edition does not.[216] At the European level, the

---

[212] Mediation or non-binding mini trial are considered as creative, efficient and appropriate ways to for the courts to consider in the process of dispute resolution relating to long-term contracts. Hillman, 'Court Adjustment of Long-Term Contracts', above n 130, 19; Adolfo Alvarado Velloso, 'Conciliation and Arbitration' in Fritz Nicklisch (ed), *The Complex Long-Term Contract: Structures and International Arbitration* (C F Müller Juristisch Verlag, 1987) 475, 498; Hoellering, above n 22 (Chap. 1), 526–7.

[213] Hillman, 'Court Adjustment of Long-Term Contracts', above n 130, 19.

[214] There is an argument that none of these solutions are perfect and may cause different problems. However, providing a solution in advance is better than nothing. See Fontaine and De Ly, above n 4 (Chap. 3), 489–490.

[215] Peter, above n 33, 125.

[216] It is argued that most businessmen would not agree to give the courts the power to adapt a contract as they believe that the parties should have control over the adaptation of a contract. This is the reason why adaptation by the court is not included in the ICC hardship Clause 2003. see

PECL, the CESL and the DCFR allow the court to adapt the contract upon the failure to reach an agreement via renegotiations.[217]

There are three questions remaining unclear. Firstly, is the request by either party or both parties necessary for the court or the arbitral tribunal to adapt the contract? Secondly, how do the court or the arbitral tribunal determine when to adapt and when to terminate, and which one should be the priority? Thirdly, if a party requests an adaptation, can the court or the arbitral tribunal order termination, and vice versa?

The answer to the first question is in the negative. Only article 89 of the CESL provides, that upon request by either party, a court may adapt the contract so that it aligns with what the parties would reasonably have agreed to at the time of entering into the contract had they taken into account the occurrence of a hardship event.[218] The UNIDROIT Principles, the PECL and the DCFR do not mention this issue explicitly. Once the matter is referred to the court or the arbitral tribunal, they have control of the proceedings and can make an order as appropriate. The discretion of the court or the arbitral tribunal should not be limited by the request of either or both parties.

In regard to the second question, the answer may depend on the aim of the adaptation. Adaptation is intended to restore the equilibrium of the contract,[219] distribute the losses and gains in a just and equitable way,[220] make the obligations of the parties reasonable and equitable,[221] or align the terms of the contract with what the parties would reasonably have agreed to had they considered the hardship.[222] From a normative perspective, it seems that the goal of the adaptation is to reach a solution that reflects fairness, equity and justice, regardless of the different wording. Therefore, the criteria that the court or the arbitral tribunal should adopt to determine whether to adapt the contract or terminate depend on whether adaptation can achieve fairness, equity and justice. If it is able to achieve these, then the court or the arbitral tribunal should adapt the contract; if it cannot, then it is preferable to terminate the contract.

Regarding the order of adaptation and termination, many factors should be considered. Although the termination may be regarded as the easiest solution, it may not be the most appropriate one, particularly in cases relating to long-term relational supply contracts. In such contracts, adaptation would be preferable to termination, taking into account the nature of long-term relational supply contracts, the ongoing relationship of the parties, the mutual trust and confidence of the parties, the parties'

Bortolotti, 'Reference to the UNIDROIT Principles in Contract Practice and Model Contracts', above n 42 (Chap. 1), 63.

[217] Article 6:111 of the PECL; Article III. – 1:110 of the DCFR; Article 89 of the CESL.

[218] Schulze, above n 89, 415.

[219] Article 6.2.3 UNIDROIT Principles 2016.

[220] Article 6:111 of the PECL.

[221] Article III. – 1:110 of the DCFR.

[222] Article 89 of the CESL.

interest in maintaining the contract, and, often, the public interest or the interests of third parties.

Regarding the third question, the courts or the arbitral tribunals should first consider whether an adaptation can achieve its goal. If it can achieve it, the court or the arbitral tribunal should take reasonable measures to adapt the contract, even if either party requests a termination. If it cannot do so, the court or the arbitral tribunal should terminate the contract, even if either party requests an adaptation.

Boundaries on Adaptation

Parties often face conflicts during the performance of a long-term relational supply contract. Parties expect to maintain a mutual, ongoing co-operation in their contractual relationship yet, they also want the freedom to arrange allocation of risk between them.[223]

Although 'the feasibility and worthwhile nature of a contract or relationship between the parties may come to be viewed differently'[224] the law should act 'not simply to facilitate exchanges, but to regulate relations of dependence and to prevent abuses of trust'.[225] The power of the courts or arbitral tribunals to adapt or terminate contracts may undermine the entrenched status of doctrines on freedom of contract and autonomy of parties.

Therefore, adaptation should not exceed certain boundaries. Firstly, it should not seek to extend a relationship between the parties that has irreparably broken down.[226] Whether or not that breakdown has occurred will depend significantly on whether the mutual trust and confidence between the parties is still sufficiently strong enough to bind them. When that is not the case, it may be inappropriate for the judiciary to adapt the contract. Worth noting is that a complete breakdown will normally render a contract incompatible with the requirements of an existing contract as the parties can no longer co-operate. Partial breakdowns will usually not do so and do justify legal intervention.[227] Furthermore, and as a functional matter, in cases where there is irreconcilable differences or the adaptation create them, it would be impractical or unrealistic for courts or arbitral tribunals to adapt the contract.[228] The test for the complete breakdown of the relationship is that it is so lacking in merit that it is manifestly unreasonable for the parties to be willing to maintain the relationship.

---

[223] Rakoff, above n 78 (Chap. 4), 1191.

[224] Bell, above n 2 (Chap. 2), 198.

[225] Hugh Collins, *The Law of Contract* (Weidenfeld and Nicolson, 1986) 45.

[226] Macneil, 'Relational Contract Theory', above n 67 (Chap. 2), 893.

[227] Ibid, 905–6.

[228] In Japanese law, case law has developed from good faith allowing simple termination if there is a 'transactional breakdown' of the parties' relationship in long-term contracts, especially in distributorships and franchise contracts. Luke R Nottage, 'Form and Substance in US, English, New Zealand and Japanese Law: A Framework for Better Comparisons of Developments in the Law of Unfair Contracts' (1996) 26 *Victoria University Wellington Law Review* 247, 272–3.

Secondly, the judiciary should not adapt a contract so extensively as to rewrite the contract, including by formulating the rights of the parties.[229] It is argued that any adaptation of the contract cannot lead to 'a new and completely different contract being imposed on the parties'.[230] The test on whether the contract has been rewritten could be that '[i]t was not this that I promised to do'.[231]

Procedural Consequences of Adaptation

If the courts or arbitral tribunals decide to adapt a contract, then the parties should perform their obligations under the adapted contract. If they refuse to accept the adapted contract and not perform, they will breach the contract and be liable for damages.

If the courts or arbitral tribunals decide not to adapt a contract, they will proceed with the termination stage.

5.3.2.3 Termination

In the context of hardship, it is not appropriate to terminate long-term relational supply contracts without renegotiations and consideration of the possibility of adaptation.[232] The termination of a long-term relational supply contract should be regarded as the last resort after the parties have done everything reasonable to resolve issues arising from hardship events.[233] The re-stabilisation of the contractual relationship and the maintenance of the contract are the main issues that should be addressed.[234] Not only do the nature and characteristics of long-term relational supply contracts demand these results; they are also required because of the closely interwoven interests and intimately connected ongoing relationship between the parties.

Parties seeking to terminate contracts should demonstrate that they have acted in good faith in performing, including by properly performing their duties to

[229] The adaptation is closely connected with and largely based on the interpretation of the terms in the original contracts. It should be borne in mind that there is a real and significant distinction between interpreting a contract and rewriting one, and that judges should not impose their understandings of commercial common sense and contract terms on the parties and adapt the parties' contract based on such understandings. Sir George Leggatt, 'Making Sense of Contracts: the Rational Choice Theory' (2015) 131 *Law Quarterly Review* 454, 473.

[230] Uribe, above n 33 (Chap. 3), 253.

[231] *Davis Contractors Ltd v Fareham UDC* [1956] AC 696, 729.

[232] Stalev, above n 124, 199.

[233] Horn, 'Standard Clauses on Contract Adaptation in International Commerce', above n 16 (Chap. 3), 137; As to the CESL, it is argued that this right to terminate should not be regarded as an ultimate remedy. Schulze, above n 89, 424.

[234] Stalev, above n 124, 199.

co-operate and to use best efforts. Only after they have attempted reasonably to preserve the contractual relationship, can they seek relief from their future obligations on the grounds of hardship.

Questions arise as to whether good faith can be used to impose a duty of specific performance and whether it could be the basis for the determination of damages due to a breach of good faith. The answer to these questions is in the affirmative. Good faith may have a 'corrective and harmonizing' role in this regard.[235] Specific performance could be regarded as the manifestation of a duty of co-operation in some cases. In addition, good faith could also be used as a basis for determining the damages for a bad faith breach, as long as it is applied in the context of hardship. It is beyond the scope of this book to consider the nature of such damages.

5.4 Determination of Good Faith Behaviour

In settling disputes arising from hardship, good faith is a powerful interpretative, substantive and integrative tool that can be used by judges or arbitrators to ensure the balance between the parties is equitable and fair.[236] It is necessary for the courts or the arbitral tribunals to determine whether the parties have acted in good faith, and in particular, whether they have engaged in the renegotiations in good faith. To determine the good faith behaviour of both parties to long-term relational supply contracts, it is inevitable that courts or arbitral tribunals will play a significant role in the interpretation of the contract and examine the ongoing relationship between the parties, and the circumstances of the contract.

5.4.1 Double Construction Approach

It is extremely difficult for courts or arbitral tribunals to balance the mandated task of reaching a 'win-lose' decision that advances the features of relational contracting practice.[237] There are so many factors involved when making a decision in a case involving a long-term relational supply contracts in the context of hardship.

Macneil's relational contract theory seems to best suit the application of good faith in long-term relational supply contracts. Macneil argued that neither motives of pure self-interest, nor moral considerations like fairness and honesty should govern the parties' behaviour. He states that they should be regulated by 'more particularised norms generated by the contractual relation itself and related to the relation

[235] M Sornarajah, 'Introduction' in Andrew D Mitchell, M Sornarajah and Tania Voon (eds), *Good Faith and International Economic Law* (Oxford University Press, 2015) 1, 3.

[236] Maltese and Farina, above n 126, 55–6.

[237] Rickett, above n 49 (Chap. 2), 378.

in a functional way'.[238] In the case of the interpretation of a long-term relational supply contract, a relational approach which requires sensitivity to the characteristics, such as the length, the nature or the basis of the ongoing relationship, is necessary.[239] The relationship between the parties should be the focus and used as a starting point to determine the parties' behaviour. Without this relationship, the behaviour would never have occurred. The relationship, therefore, forms a basis for the adoption of a double-construction approach. This approach proposes that both the contract itself and the relationships relating to the contract, viewed horizontally or vertically, determine the rights and duties of the parties to a long-term relational supply contract on the basis of good faith. This involves considering the terms of the contract, the intention, and the expectations of the parties. In addition, not only the ongoing relationship between the parties, but also other relevant economic or social relationships that the parties have or that may impact the contract should be considered. In this sense, 'good faith must mean a real commitment to the laws which govern contracts, to the contract itself, and, most importantly, to the other party's aims and objectives, provided these are understood'.[240]

In particular, the mutual trust and confidence established between the parties to a long-term relational supply contracts requires the courts or arbitral tribunals to consider their relationship in determining their reasonable duties in the performance of a contract. In cases where a take or pay contract plays a key role as a financing tool for the development of a new project, it is generally required that:

> The buyer must continue to make the minimum scheduled payments under the contract even where the failure in performance by the seller amounts in law to fundamental breach. The buyer will generally be motivated to submit such seemingly unconscionable impositions because he is a sponsor/participant in the project and the arrangement constitutes in reality 'off balance sheet' debt of the buyer in relation to his project participation. The buyer is in effect assuming the throughout risk attaching to the project (i.e. the risk of the breakdown in either production or sales) by guaranteeing the cash flow necessary to service the project debt financing. In turn the buyer may seek to project his exposure by accepting security over the project which allows him to take over the facilities and means of production in the case of default of the seller.[241]

Also, co-operation plays an important role in the maintenance and development of the mutual trust and confidence between the parties. Co-operative behaviour requires one party to take into account or even give priority to the interests of the other, and to avoid purely self-interested action of any kind, especially in cases where the parties share certain common interests which require them to act towards each other.[242]

In addition, as the interests of both parties, the potential gain and loss from the performance and the continuance of the contracts are so closely connected, it would

[238] Gudel, above n 95 (Chap. 2), 782.

[239] Hadfield, above n 61 (Chap. 2), 987.

[240] Lücke, above n 104 (Chap. 4), 164.

[241] Wright, above n 34 (Chap. 2), 335.

[242] Collins, 'Competing Norms of Contractual Behaviour', above n 14 (Chap. 2), 69.

be unreasonable and unwise if the relationship between the parties were not taken into account. Also, the intimately interwoven relationship is of particular significance to a weaker party as 'mutual dependence keeps the weaker party from being treated as a disposable commodity'.[243] If the parties realise the importance of their relationship and each party knows that the other party has the same long-term economic incentive to maintain their relationship, they are likely to act in a co-operative manner in the performance of their long-term relational supply contract.[244]

To better determine whether the parties have behaved in a co-operative manner, it is also necessary to consider the relationships that are external to the contracted parties' relationships, but still closely related. In effect '[i]t is only possible to grasp the source of co-operative behaviour in contractual contexts once the extra-contractual normative framework is brought into the picture'.[245] In reality, complex long-term relational contracts are often not isolated contracts, but part of a 'hierarchical', 'pyramidal' or 'tri-dimensional' system of contracts.[246] They affect the parties not only horizontally, but also vertically such as in relation to the industries involved. For example, when determining if a party has acted in good faith in terminating a long-term relational mining supply contract, the court or arbitral tribunal should reasonably take account of the risk of threatening the local mining industry and causing the loss of thousands of jobs arising from that termination. Also, judges or arbitrators should take into account their connections with the local government, including perceived costs and benefits borne by government, should a long-term relationship between the contracting parties fail. The objective judicial or arbitral determination would extend beyond the *per se* construction of the terms of the contract between the parties.

Moreover, principles of law lacking a direct legal effect in some domestic jurisdictions, such as the principle of good faith, may assume importance in respect to the conveyance of information on the subject matter, the interpretation of legislation, and the filling of gaps.[247] The court is required to consider, analyse and evaluate the interests of the parties in the light of the nature of their contract, and the surrounding circumstances of the case, and the applicable law. Where there is a case regarding the construction of a long-term relational supply contract before a court or an arbitral tribunal, the judges or arbitrators should also take into account the double-construction approach to in order to construct the contract in an economically sustainable and fair manner in order to render a viable decision. It is worth noting that in the construction of long-term relational supply contract, the terms, intention of the parties, and the expectations of the parties when the contract was

---

[243] Gidon Gottlieb, 'Relationism: Legal Theory for a Relational Society' (1983) 50 *University of Chicago Law Review* 567, 596.

[244] Collins, 'Competing Norms of Contractual Behaviour', above n 14 (Chap. 2), 84.

[245] Ibid, 93.

[246] Herfried Wöss et al., above n 132 (Chap. 2), 35.

[247] Jürgen Basedow, 'General Principles of European Private Law and Interest Analysis: Some Reflections in the Light of *Mangold* and *Audiolux*' (2016) 3–4 *European Review of Private Law* 331, 351.

entered into should be considered. The relationship between the parties should be treated as an evolving process, the development of which is very important in understanding that relationship. Not only the history of the relationship, but also its current state and its future, must be considered in order to have a comprehensive understanding of it. The evolving understanding of the relationship between the parties would be more in accord with relational contract theory and would provide more reasonable and satisfactory solutions.

Courts or arbitral tribunals should take into account all the circumstances surrounding a contract when deciding whether one party has performed in good faith or in accord with the requirements of the duty to renegotiate and the duty to co-operate. This also applies when adapting the contract for the parties. Special regard should be paid to the commercial contents and interests of the long-term relational supply contract and their impact on the parties, their business practices, and trade, investment and/or industrial structures and relations.

When judges or arbitrators analyse relational contracts and the rights and obligations deriving from them, they often handle different values or interests relating to contractual relationships. This means that they avoid relying solely on the wills and consent of the parties at the time of the conclusion of the contract. They also take into account the political, economic, social and cultural circumstances surrounding contractual relationships and their changes over the long-term relationship, particularly the mutual trust and confidence, good will, and reputations of the parties.[248] Examples include whether the parties should renegotiate oil prices due to anticipated or unanticipated disruptions in oil supplies during an oil crisis and whether the court should enforce a price escalation clause or best endeavour to supply clause in a long-term supply contract by considering both parties' past attitudes, behaviours and relevant practices.[249]

5.4.2 Behavioural Factors on the Determination of Good Faith

Long-term relational contracts require the parties to co-operate to the extent that each party will take into account the interests of the other even when they conflict with their own interests, and will not insist upon the strict performance of contractual obligations of the other party.[250] To some degree, this puts more pressure on the courts or the arbitral tribunals to interpret or adapt the contract in line with the double-construction approach. Also, there is always a danger that any duty imposed by the courts or the arbitral tribunals can be regarded as a judicial rewriting of the contracts, even if this is done in order to protect the disadvantaged party from opportunistic behaviours or to promote a redistribution of resources and interests in

[248] Trakman, 'Pluralism in Contract Law', above n 60 (Chap. 2).

[249] Ibid, 1063–4.

[250] Collins, 'Competing Norms of Contractual Behaviour', above n 14 (Chap. 2), 70.

the name of fairness or equity.[251] Therefore, it is important and reasonable for the courts or the arbitral tribunals to determine whether the parties have acted in good faith in the renegotiations before taking any action to adapt or terminate the contract. It may reduce the burden on the court and avoid rendering it into little more than a mediator of differences between the parties.

Berger has listed the following obligations of the parties in the renegotiation process:[252]

1. Keeping to the negotiation framework set out by the clause,
2. Respecting the remaining provisions of the contract,
3. Having regard for the prior contractual practice between the parties,
4. Making a serious effort to reach agreement,
5. Paying attention to the interests of the other side,
6. Producing information relevant to the adaptation,
7. Showing a sincere willingness to reach a compromise,
8. Maintaining flexibility in the conduct of negotiations,
9. Searching from reasonable and appropriate adjustment solutions,
10. Making concrete and reasonable suggestions for adjustment instead of mere general declarations of willingness,
11. Avoiding rushed adjustment suggestions,
12. Giving appropriate reasons for one's own adjustment suggestions,
13. Obtaining expert advice in difficult and complex consensus proceedings,
14. Responding promptly to adjustment offers from the other side,
15. Making an effort to maintain the price-performance relationship taking into consideration the parameters regarded as relevant by the parties,
16. Avoiding an unfair advantage or detriment to the other side ('no profit- no loss' principle)
17. Prohibition on creating established facts during negotiations except in emergency situations (ban on 'escalation' strategies),
18. Maintaining efforts to reach agreement over an appropriate length of time, and
19. Avoiding unnecessary delays in the consensus proceedings.[253]

Whether the parties have reasonably performed their duties listed above is a significant factor that the courts or the arbitral tribunals should establish when determining whether the requirements of good faith have been satisfied. Apart from what has been identified by Berger, there are other factors that could be taken into account, including those implied in the following UNIDROIT Principles:

1. whether the disadvantaged party has given a notice of the occurrence of the hardship event to the other party within in reasonable time and in reasonable form;[254]
2. whether the disadvantaged party has requested to renegotiate or revise the contract within reasonable time from the occurrence of the hardship event;[255]

[251] Speidel, 'The New Spirit of Contract', above n 180, 208.

[252] His list is based on the existence of a renegotiation clause. However, most of the obligations listed indicate the requirements of the behaviours of the parties in the renegotiation process.

[253] Berger, 'Renegotiation and Adaptation of International Investment Contracts', above n 71, 1365–6, (citations omitted).

[254] Comment 2 to Article 6.2.3 UNIDROIT Principles 2016.

[255] Ibid.

3. whether the disadvantaged party has indicated the grounds on which the request for renegotiations is based;[256]
4. whether the disadvantaged party has withheld the performance;[257]
5. whether the disadvantaged party has assumed the risks of hardship by agreement;[258]
6. whether the disadvantaged party has proposed an adaptation that would be feasible and enforceable if it were accepted by the advantaged party;[259]
7. whether the advantaged party has reasonably considered the proposal made by the disadvantaged party to adapt the contract;[260]
8. whether the advantaged party has failed to accept the proposal;[261]
9. whether the advantaged party's refusal has ignored the hardship and imperilled the ongoing relationship between the parties;[262]
10. whether the disadvantaged party or the advantaged party will suffer excessive prejudice if an agreement resulting from the renegotiations is reached and enforced;
11. whether the disadvantaged party and the advantaged party have intended to share losses and risks caused by hardship;[263]
12. whether the disadvantaged party or the advantaged party has attempted to abuse his or her position;[264]
13. whether the disadvantaged party and the advantaged party have taken into account their mutual trust and confidence and commercial and reliance interests;
14. whether the behaviour of the disadvantaged party and the advantaged party has been in line with the maintenance of the ongoing relationship; and
15. whether the ongoing relationship between the disadvantaged party and the advantaged party has broken down.

It is worth noting that neither list is intended to be exhaustive. The court or the arbitral tribunal can exercise their discretion when taking into account all the surrounding circumstances and factors they consider appropriate to help them reach a conclusion on whether the parties have acted in good faith.

5.5 Conclusion

The manifestations of good faith in the UNIDROIT Principles serve as a framework for the analysis of the manifestations of good faith from a normative perspective. The manifestations are the duty to renegotiate and the powers of the courts or the arbitral tribunals to adapt and terminate the contracts in the context of hardship.

As to the substantive aspects of good faith in the context of hardship, the duty to renegotiate and the possibility of contract termination or adaptation by the courts or

[256] Comment 3 to Article 6.2.3 UNIDROIT Principles 2016.

[257] Comment 4 to Article 6.2.3 UNIDROIT Principles 2016.

[258] Speidel, 'The New Spirit of Contract', above n 180, 206–9.

[259] Ibid.

[260] Ibid.

[261] Ibid.

[262] Ibid.

[263] Trakman, 'Winner Take Some', above n 18 (Chap. 2), 503.

[264] Comment 4 to Article 6.2.3 UNIDROIT Principles 2016.

the arbitral tribunals have been discussed in detail. The imposition on the parties of the duty to renegotiate is intended to alleviate the damages and inconveniences that hardship events may bring to the performance and to give the parties a chance to deal with the hardship issues jointly and cooperatively so as to maintain the long-term relational supply contracts. Also, factors like mutual trust and confidence and co-operation are normally emphasised in the course of tackling issues arising from the hardship events, although the wording could be different. The co-operative and trusting spirit based on good faith is the main consideration.

In addition, when a long-term relational supply contract is disrupted by hardship, it is necessary to both order and analyse the procedure mechanisms relating to renegotiation, adaptation and termination. In particular, the parties affected by the hardship events should first attempt to renegotiate in good faith.[265] Only upon the failure of the renegotiations should they have recourse to the courts or the arbitral tribunals. The courts or arbitral tribunals should first consider whether adaptation is an appropriate and efficient choice, taking into account the characteristics of the long-term relational supply contracts, the ongoing relationship between the parties, and their mutual trust and confidence based on their contract and relationship. The aim of judicial or arbitral adaptation is neither to maintain the contractual relationship indefinitely, nor to impose an immutable term. The aims are rather to provide a contract term that the parties may have bargained over but failed to resolve, to find an equitable and just solution for both parties, and to attempt to sustain their relationship by holding the transaction together.[266] Only if adaptation is unreasonable and inappropriate, can the courts or arbitral tribunals terminate the long-term relational supply contracts as the ultimate remedy. The whole procedure is to guarantee the stability and certainty of the long-term relational supply contracts and to ensure their flexibility and adjustability at the same time.[267]

[265] It is argued that at a minimum, the advantaged party should have a legal duty to renegotiate in good faith. At a maximum, the advantaged party may have a legal duty to accept an equitable adjustment proposed in good faith by the disadvantaged party. Speidel, 'Court-imposed Price Adjustments under Long-Term Supply Contracts', above n 175, 404–5.

[266] Ibid.

[267] Horn, 'The Concepts of Adaptation and Renegotiation in the Law of Transnational Commercial Contracts', above n 10 (Chap. 1), 6–7.

Chapter 6
The Future Solution to Hardship: A Relational and Good Faith Approach

6.1 Introduction

A comparative overview of long-term relational supply contracts, hardship and good faith was provided in Chaps. 2, 3 and 4, respectively. Their interaction in the context of international trade was discussed in Chap. 5 from both positive and normative perspectives. This chapter will argue that a principle of *pacta sunt servanda bona fide* is emerging based on the relational understanding of the parties, and the application of hardship rules and good faith dealings in international trade contracts. This principle can, to a certain extent, offer a more satisfactory solution to the hardship issue. Based on this principle, parties are under a duty to renegotiate in response to intervening hardship, unless there is compelling reason not to do so, such as due to the complete breakdown of the relationship between the parties. This principle not only encourages the parties to act in good faith, but also innovatively sets boundaries around the duty to renegotiate a contract and the power to adapt it.

Section 6.2 of this chapter will outline the ongoing conflict between the needs of certainty and of flexibility in international contract practice. Section 6.3 of this chapter will highlight the necessity to find a relational and good faith solution to hardship in the context of *Lex Mercatoria*. Section 6.4 will propose that '*pacta sunt servanda bona fide*' is the most appropriate approach to deal with hardship issues from a good faith and relational perspective because it strikes a satisfactory and feasible balance between certainty and flexibility. Section 6.5 concludes the book.

P. Guo, *Good Faith in Long-Term Relational Supply Contracts in the Context of Hardship from A Comparative Perspective*,
https://doi.org/10.1007/978-981-16-5513-5_6

6.2 Old but Continuing Issue: Certainty Versus Flexibility

The necessity of legal certainty that requires maintaining stable contractual relations reflects a sharp distinction between the common law and the civil law jurisdictions in international trade.[1] In international contract practice, the current and predominant means of dealing with hardship is the winner-take-all approach on the basis of the principle of *pacta sunt servanda*. The most significant advantage of this approach is that it can provide certainty and predictability.

The existence of various approaches adopted by different domestic legal systems in this regard has not significantly changed the dominant position of the principle of *pacta sunt servanda*. It does invite reconsideration of whether the all-or-nothing approach produces satisfactory solutions for both the parties and the international business community. Despite the uncertainty that may be caused, in order to provide flexible, satisfactory and fair solutions to hardship issues, it is necessary to recognise a legal mechanism for judicial intervention that takes into account the requirements of equity and fairness.[2] The principle of *clausula rebus sic stantibus*, enabling flexibility to the performance of a contract, is considered as such a legal mechanism that softens the harsh consequences resulting from the principle of *pacta sunt servanda* at least relating to long-term contracts.[3] Also, although the lack of reliable precedents is another source of uncertainty, it may be possible to overcome this and to improve certainty and flexibility through the harmonisation of international commercial contracts based on relevant studies of comparative law.[4] The rules contained in the UNIDROIT Principles as discussed in Chap. 5 is a good start and a wonderful example for such harmonisation.

6.3 A Relational and Good Faith Solution to Hardship in the Context of the Lex Mercatoria

The *Lex Mercatoria* was formed and developed by merchants predominantly in the late eleventh and twelfth centuries to meet the needs arising in mercantile transactions. That *Lex Mercatoria* evolved thereafter into an integrated, autonomous and developed body of mercantile law operating trans-regionally, and after the development of the Sixteenth Century Nation State, transnationally.[5] Embodying qualities

[1] Fauvarque-Cosson, above n 32 (Chap. 3), 205.

[2] Hondius and Grigoleit, 'General Comparative Remarks', above n 94 (Chap. 3), 653–4.

[3] Mustill, above n 58 (Chap. 1), 111.

[4] Ibid, 654.

[5] For the definition of Lex Mercatoria, see Mustill, above n 58 (Chap. 1). There are two main ideas about the sources of Lex Mercatoria. Goldman and De ly argue that the sources of Lex Mercatoria are customary rules of ancient Rome; however, Berman believes that the sources of Lex Mercatoria are medieval urban civilization and commercial civilization. The theory of Modern Law Merchant

of objectivity, university, reciprocity, participatory adjudication, integration and growth, it governed international contract practice and was often adopted to govern transnational commercial contracts, notably through international commercial arbitration. The empirical evidence demonstrates that parties to such contracts tend to adopt domestic over transnational law to govern their contracts. However, the *Lex Mercatoria* continues to operate as a framework used to construe such contracts, including in light of the usages of the transnational trade and the practices of the parties.

The ideas and wisdom that evolved in merchant practice over the centuries are consolidated and incorporated into a modern *Lex Mercatoria.* It is a continually developing source of solutions to long-term supply relationships in the context of hardship. The *Lex Mercatoria* also advises rules shared by domestic legal systems and adapted to international long-term contracts.[6] So conceived, the *Lex Mercatoria* allows for greater flexibility and respect for business practices operating beyond domestic law and for international long-term contracts in particular.[7] Applied to issues of hardship it also provides some fertile ways to reconcile the principles of

or (New Law Merchant) was created by Schmitthoff. Trakman, in his book, did a comprehensive study on Lex Mercatoria as a whole. As to the legal connotation of Modern Lex Mercatoria, different scholars have different views. For example, Schmitthoff argues that Modern Lex Mercatoria is the uniform law which adjusts the relationship between businessmen. It develops from different national legal systems and in principle has no interests with nations. Goldman believes that Modern Lex Mercatoria is the unique law in international economic relations which includes transnational entity rules, customs, usages, general principles of law and so on. Trakman argues the Twenty First Century Lex Mercatoria is a quasi-private and quasi-public legal order. In addition, he tries to bring the emerging and evolving Investment Lex Mercatoria to the academic discussion. For more details on Lex Mercatoria, see Peng Guo, 'What can International Arbitration learn from Medieval Merchant Courts?' (2017) 9 *HUFS Global Law Review* 69, 69–81; Leon E Trakman, 'The Evolution of the Law Merchant: Our Commercial Heritage Part I Ancient and Medieval Law Merchant' (1980) 12 *Journal of Maritime Law and Commerce* 1; Leon E Trakman, 'The Evolution of the Law Merchant: Our Commercial Heritage Part II The Modern Law Merchant' (1981) 12 *Journal of Maritime Law and Commerce* 153; Leon E Trakman, 'The Twenty-First-Century Law Merchant' (2011) 48 *American Business Law Journal* 775; Wyndham A Bewes, *The Romance of the Law Merchant* (Sweet & Maxwell, 1923); Leon E Trakman, *The Law Merchant: The Evolution of Commercial Law* (Fred B Rothman & Co., 1983); W Mitchell, *Essay on the Early History of the Law Merchant* (Burt Franklin, 1904, reprinted 1969) Clive M Schmitthoff, 'International Business Law: A New Law Merchant' in Chia-Jui Cheng (ed), *Clive. M. Schmitthoff's Select Essays on International Trade Law* (Martinus Nijhoff Publishers and Graham & Trotman, 1988) 20–37; Aleksandar Goldštajn, 'The New Law Merchant Reconsidered' in Fritz Fabricius (ed), *Law and International Trade, Festschrift für Clive M. Schmitthoff zum 70. Geburtstag* (Atbenäum Verlag, 1973) 171–185. Berthold Goldman, *Lex Mercatoria* (Forum Internationale, 1983); Klaus Peter Berger, *The Creeping Codification of the New Lex Mercatoria* (Kluwer Law International, 2nd, 2010) Filip De Ly, *International Business Law and Lex Mercatoria* (North Holland, 1992); Harold J Berman, *Law and Revolution: The Formation of the Western Legal Tradition* (Harvard University Press, 1983) vol II, 333–356. Orsolya Toth, The Lex Mercatoria in Theory and Practice (Oxford University Press, 2017).

[6] Emmanuel Gaillard, 'Use of General Principles of International Law in International Long-Term Contracts' (1999) 27 *International Business Lawyer* 214, 222.

[7] Nystén-Haarala, above n 31 (Chap. 1), 29.

pacta sunt servanda and *clausula rebus sic stantibus*, despite a certain degree of contradiction between them.[8] This includes providing a basis for the adaptation of contracts and their renegotiation in the context of hardship.[9]

The UNIDROIT Principles are 'a non-legislative codification of the general part of the law of international commercial contracts'.[10] To a certain degree, the UNIDROIT Principles can be regarded as a restatement of the *Lex Mercatoria.*[11] The UNIDROIT Principles resolve the myths and enigmas of the *Lex Mercatoria.*[12]

Although there are not many among the large numbers of arbitral cases that have directly applied the hardship rules in the UNIDROIT Principles, the UNIDROIT Principles are often used to interpret rules relating to hardship in other international instruments, such as Article 79 of the CISG.[13] Also, given most disputes are resolved by arbitration which is usually confidential, it is hard to determine how often the UNIDROIT Principles are actually used and how.[14] However, it should be noted that international trade is different from domestic trade, and the UNIDROIT Principles deserve certain respect in relation to the role that they do and will play in dealing with hardship issues in long-term relational supply contracts. Twenty years ago, scholars argued that the solutions provided by the UNIDROIT Principles may indicate the developmental direction of the law in this regard for the twenty-first century.[15] The trend at that time was not strong enough to guarantee that the UNIDROIT Principles' approach would evolve into a general doctrine for international contract practices.[16] Now, twenty years later, the law is still slowly moving in that direction, although not as optimistically as envisaged. However, the change in the business model may accelerate this process. The relational factor is more obvious in business engaging in long-term contracts, and in long-term relational supply contracts in

[8] Gaillard, above n 6, 221.

[9] Ole Lando, 'Renegotiation and Revision of International Contracts' (1980) 23 *Germany Yearbook of International Law* 37, 56–8.

[10] Bonell, 'Towards a Legislative Codification of the UNIDROIT Principles?', above n 38 (Chap. 1).

[11] Federica Rongeat-Oudin and Martin Oudin, 'La Reception des Principles UNIDROIT par La Lex Mercatoria: L'Exemple de La Bonne Foi/The Reception of the UNIDROIT Principles by the Lex Mercatoria: The Example of Good Faith' (2009) 6 *Revue de Droit des Affaires Internationales/ International Business Law Journal* 697, 717–8.

[12] Richard E Speidel, 'The Revision of UCC Article 2, Sales in Light of the United Nations Convention on Contracts for the International Sale of Goods' (1995) 16 *Northwestern Journal of International Law and Business* 165, 167.

[13] See, eg, 2009 Belgian case *Scafom International BV v Lorraine Tubes S.A.S.* See also, Chap. 5, Sections "Case Law on the Duty to Renegotiate" and "Case Law on Adaptation and Termination". See also, Luke R. Nottage, 'Practical and Theoretical Implications of the Lex Mercatoria for Japan: Central's Empirical Study on the Use of Transnational Law' (2000) 4 *Vnidobona Journal of International Commercial Law and Arbitration* 132, 136–146.

[14] Ibid.

[15] Perillo, above n 11 (Chap. 1), 26–8.

[16] Nassar, above n 25 (Chap. 1), 230.

particular.[17] Co-operation between merchants is valued as it takes a relational, rather than an adversarial approach, based on arm's length transactions between parties. There is a need for a change in how hardship issues are addressed and resolved in international commercial law, at least relating to long-term relational contracts.

The UNIDROIT Principles in particular, reflect the shifting direction of international contract law and the practice of adapting a contract on the grounds of hardship. Parties to long-term relational supply contracts are embracing this shift as it promotes a more flexible and suitable solution to disputes than strict adherence to the principle of *pacta sunt servanda.*

Rules that embrace co-operation and renegotiations can also realign the duties and interests of the parties in the case of hardship. They can ease the tension between the need to specify the responsibilities of each party at the outset and the need to adapt them over the duration of the long-term relational contractual relationship.[18] The hardship rules provided for by the UNIDROIT Principles do promote co-operation and renegotiation on the basis of the principle of good faith and the relational nature of long-term contracts. Hence, they can assist in striking a better balance between the two tensions faced by parties to a long-term relational supply contract. The result is likely to be the resolution of hardship issues in a more satisfactory and equitable way. It is worth noting that, although the application of good faith and judicial intervention in international long-term supply contracts may achieve a more satisfactory resolution of disputes, they should be limited to certain circumstances.[19] Also, the duty to renegotiate should be subject to a compelling reason or reasons that cause the ongoing relationship between the parties to break down and thereby affect the performance of their long-term relational supply contract.

The final consequences of the development of the hardship rules are still uncertain. Moreover, we may never be able to identify the best judicial approach to long-term contracts because a solution depends on too many variables and unknown factors.[20] However, in the era of relational contracts, the hardship rules in the UNIDROIT Principles will undoubtedly have an increasingly important role to play on the basis of its wide acceptance in international contract practices. The Principles' soft law nature offers flexibility to the performance of a contract and the maintenance of an ongoing contractual relationship.

[17] See Chap. 2, Sect. 2.2.2.3. See Donald Robertson, 'Investment Treaty Arbitration and Market Governance: A Principled Approach to Assessing Regulatory Action' Sydney Law School, Legal Studies Research Paper No. 17/19, March 2017, available at https://papers.ssrn.com/sol3/papers.cfm?abstract_id=2928381.

[18] Baird, above n 72 (Chap. 5), 586.

[19] Arthur Hartkamp, 'The Concept of Good Faith in the UNIDROIT Principles for International Commercial Contracts' (1995) 3 *Tulane Journal of International and Comparative Law* 65, 71. On the limitation on the judicial intervention, See Chap. 5, Sect. 5.3.2.

[20] Hillman, 'Maybe Dick Speidel Was Right about Court Adjustment', above n 179 (Chap. 5), 596.

6.4 A New Wine, Not a Simple Mixture of Two Old Ones

In ICC Award No. 5953 it was stated that:

> [A]nother principle, albeit with a reduced degree of generality because it only concerns the execution of contracts, is formulated by the maxim 'pacta sunt servanda'. The respect for this rule requires parties to execute their contractual undertakings. However, the modalities of this execution are not indicated [by this general rule]. It is the preceding principle [of good faith] which provides this precision in a way that one can merge both principles into one when it comes to the performance of a contractual obligation: '*pacta sunt servanda bona fide*'.[21]

It is argued that '[i]n spite of 200 years of legal nationalization, contract law is still more international in substance and character than tort law, property law, or family law'.[22] Fundamental concepts and ideas relating to contract law have not been tremendously influenced by developments in the course of legal nationalism. Therefore, it is still possible to identify common issues and to strive for reasonable solutions on the basis of a common understanding and of a series of common arguments.[23] Research may aid the development of a common legal understanding within the international business community and such understanding is needed for avoiding or settling contractual disputes.[24]

The research of this book shows that a principle of *pacta sunt servanda bona fide* is emerging as the doctrinal basis for a shared legal understanding of the nature and application of hardship relating, inter alia, to long term relational contracts. Both the principle of *pacta sunt servanda* and the principle of good faith are conceived separately as old wine, both being considered as part of the *Lex Mercatoria*.[25] However, when mixed together, they potentially evolve into a new, fuller bodied and delicious wine.

To some extent, the principle of *pacta sunt servanda bona fide* respects the principle of *pacta sunt servanda*. It recognises not only the sanctity of contracts, but also the significance, necessity and utility of the need for certainty in international trade and in international commercial law. Conversely, it also emphasises the functions of good faith. Good faith should not be regarded as inimical to the freedom of contract or to the sanctity of contract. It should offer strong guidance on the general

---

[21] Available at https://www.trans-lex.org/205953/_/icc-award-no-5953-clunet-1990-at-1056-et-seq/.

[22] Zimmermann, 'European Contract Law', above n 36 (Chap. 1).

[23] Ibid.

[24] Horn, 'Standard Clauses on Contract Adaptation in International Commerce', above n 16 (Chap. 3), 121.

[25] Mustill, above n 58 (Chap. 1), 110–1. Both these principles are incorporated into the Trans-Lex Principles. For pacta sunt servanda, see IV.1.1 (Sanctity of contracts), available at https://www.trans-lex.org/919000/highlight_pacta_sunt_servanda/sanctity-of-contracts/ and for good faith, see I.1.1 (Good faith and fair dealing in international trade), available at https://www.trans-lex.org/901000/highlight_good_faith/good-faith-and-fair-dealing-in-international-trade/.

application of law and provides values which may be reified into concrete rules.[26] From a relational point of view, good faith should be invoked to temper opportunistic behaviour allowed by unfettered freedom of contract.[27] It should redress difficulties arising from parties' complete freedom to agree on terms and the absolute discretion to allocate the risks of all potential contingencies, regardless of any potential unfairness, unreasonableness or unconscionable result that might eventuate.[28] Giving unlimited freedom to the parties could well result in bad faith behaviours or give rein to contractual opportunism.[29] In contrast, good faith can be used to regulate bad faith or opportunistic behaviours, and as a tool to adapt contracts to achieve a just and equitable result. When *pacta sunt servanda* and good faith are combined into new wine, they become more robust than either was previously conceived of separately.

From a practical point of view, by entering into a long-term relational supply contract, the parties consent to their ongoing relationship being continuously subject to adaptation upon the occurrence of hardship. This consent is implied from the long-term and relational nature of the supply contract, and from the mutual trust and confidence between the parties when entering into the contract. Moreover, viewed functionally, the solution to hardship issues should necessarily and unavoidably reflect the changing nature of their relationship. Taking into account the hardship context and the relational nature of a long-term supply contract, and based on the principle of *pacta sunt servanda bona fide*, parties to such contracts are under a duty to renegotiate, unless there is compelling reason not to do so. Judges or arbitrators in turn should have the power to adapt such a contract to sustain the ongoing relationship between the parties, unless there is a complete breakdown of the relationship or the adaptation will cause one. The application of this doctrine not only encourages parties to act in good faith, but innovatively sets boundaries around the duty to renegotiate a contract and the power of courts and arbitrators to adapt it. Also, if the parties fail to renegotiate in good faith, the court or arbitral tribunal can conceivably direct them to engage in supervised negotiations, or even in mediation.[30] In addition, if the disadvantaged party fails to provide grounds for

---

[26] Sornarajah, 'Introduction', above n 235 (Chap. 5), 2.

[27] Burton and Anderson, above n 74 (Chap. 4), 414–6.

[28] Ibid.

[29] Ibid, 416–8.

[30] See Chap. 5, Sect. 5.3.2. It should be, however, borne in mind that whether judges or arbitrators can direct the parties to engage in mediation is a controversial issue. A series of problems can arise relating to the court or the tribunal's power to refer the parties to mediation, such as the source of the power, the risk of disqualification, the enforceability of the award. As discussed in Chap. 5, Sect. 5.3.2, if a case is before a court, it is likely that the court can refer the parties to mediation during litigation, as the courts do in Australia. However, if a case is before an arbitral tribunal, the tribunal will face the aforementioned series of problems. 'Arbitration-Mediation' meaning that arbitrators can possibly and actively encourage settlement during arbitration is complicated, controversial and not commonly practice, such as in Australia. Due to the fact that the dominant theory in international commercial contract law is still 'neo-classical' and that the practice in international commercial arbitration, which is closely connected to the dominant theory, is formalised and con-

renegotiations, judges or arbitrators can affirm the contract and order the parties to continue to perform on the grounds that there is no, or insufficient, hardship to modify or terminate the contract.[31] By combining these mechanisms, courts and arbitral tribunals can regulate different aspects of the ongoing relationship. They can also promote co-operation between the parties and keep the long-term supply contract alive 'in much the same way as the super powers rely on both conventional and nuclear weapons as deterrents against acts of aggression and non-cooperation by the other'.[32]

To sum up, the argument presented in this book for the development of the principle of *pacta sunt servanda bona fide* is not only intended to serve as part of transnational law. It is also intended to accommodate domestic legal solutions and to provide common ground upon which to reconcile differences in how domestic legal systems treat hardship in long term supply relationships.

6.5 Conclusion

Hardship is a heated and controversial issue in international commercial transactions.[33] Many issues may arise from hardship. These issues cause problems not only in terms of how the parties can perform contracts and deal with hardship arising in

centrates on formal reasoning and the agreement between parties, 'Arbitration-Mediation' is not widely accepted. However, from a relational contract theory's perspective, international commercial arbitration is over-formalised, which may reduce the flexibility that is needed in international contract practice. This book intends to argue that, the underlying contract theory for international commercial contract law governing international long-term relational contracts in general, and international long-term relational supply contracts in particular, should be the relational contract theory, and the formalised international commercial arbitration correspondingly should become more flexible, by lowering its formality. Given the diversity of domestic legal systems and legal traditions, the potential role and scope of the relational contract theory should be limited to the international level at the first stage and may expand if the theory could be widely accepted by the international contract and commercial arbitration practice. To achieve, arbitral institutions, such as the ICC, may publish a practice note encouraging 'Arbitration-Mediation'. If parties agree to use ICC arbitration, then they agree that arbitrators can refer them to mediation by applying the practice note. See Luke R Nottage, 'A Weathermap for International Arbitration: Mainly Sunny, Some Cloud, Possible Thunderstorms' Sydney Law School, Legal Studies Research Paper No. 15/62, July 2015, available at https://papers.ssrn.com/sol3/papers.cfm?abstract_id=2630401; James Morrison and Luke R Nottage, 'Country Report on Australia for: International Commercial Arbitration – An Asia-Pacific Perspective' Sydney Law School, Legal Studies Research Paper No. 14/95, October 2014, available at https://papers.ssrn.com/sol3/papers.cfm?abstract_id=2514124; Luke R Nottage, 'The Procedural Lex Mercatoria: The Past, Present and Future of International Commercial Arbitration' Sydney Law School, Legal Studies Research Paper No. 06/51, December 2006, available at https://papers.ssrn.com/sol3/papers.cfm?abstract_id=838028.

[31] Ibid.

[32] Scott, 'Risk Distribution and Adjustment in Long-Term Contracts', above n 135 (Chap. 5), 93.

[33] In the Tokyo Intercollegiate Negotiation Competition on moot arbitration and negotiation over more than a decade, the change of circumstances topic often appeared. The 2017 competition

their contractual relationship, but also in determining how judges or arbitrators can resolve the issues. Therefore, it is necessary and ideal to have a set of rules, such as the UNIDROIT Principles, that could be referred to in cases where the long-term relational supply contracts are affected by hardship.

The selected domestic laws that have been examined in this book show that there is no consensus on how to deal with the issue of hardship. Different jurisdictions have their own solutions. At the international level, the CISG and the UNIDROIT Principles deal with hardship differently. However, similarities can still be discerned, despite the differences among domestic legal systems and the international instruments. Apart from English law, most domestic and international rules variously refer to good faith.

Good faith is not a concept that can be accurately defined. The vagueness of good faith attracts both praise and criticism. The vagueness results in difficulty and unpredictability in its recognition and application. However, this vagueness also leads to a flexibility that can bring justice and fairness, which may be significantly valuable to the parties. Its charm lies in its vagueness; its weakness also lies in its vagueness.

Due to its vagueness, different domestic laws treat the concept of good faith in contracting differently. For example, English law rejects the concept of good faith, while German law and French law recognise it as a general principle. However, the differences between English contract law and German and French contract laws in respect to good faith are less pivotal from a functional perspective, than from a structural or conceptual perspective.[34] In the CISG, the status of good faith is unclear, while in the UNIDROIT Principles, good faith is a general principle as in German and French law. But good faith is reflected in many other articles, and in many ways, in both the CISG and the UNIDROIT Principles. Therefore, it is reasonable to infer that good faith has various levels and many facets which can be applied when dealing with hardship issues.

Good faith can be visualised as analogous to a Swiss army knife that can solve many difficult problems.[35] Hardship is one of the many problems. For long-term relational supply contracts facing hardship issues, the manifestations of good faith encompass the parties' duties to renegotiate the contract and the judges or the arbitrators' power to adapt or terminate the contract, taking into account the mutual trust and confidence and the ongoing relationship between the parties.

Considering the unpredictability and the flexibility arising from the vagueness of good faith, it is necessary to set certain legal boundaries around the manifestations of good faith. As to the legal duty to renegotiate, the parties can be discharged from this duty if either of them can provide and prove the existence of a compelling reason. Arbitrators and courts ordinarily cannot adapt a contract if such adaptation involves essentially rewriting the contract or producing a total breakdown of the

---

problem was again involving hardship in a quite realistic scenario. See http://www.negocom.jp/eng/.

[34] Vogenauer, *Commentary on the UNIDROIT Principles of International Commercial Contracts (PICC)*, above n 130 (Chap. 3), 209.

[35] Ziegler and Baumgartner, above n 295 (Chap. 4), 9.

ongoing relationship between the parties. In addition, to determine whether the parties have acted in good faith, the courts or arbitral tribunals should take a double construction approach to interpret the parties' behaviour and have regard to the list of factors outlined below.[36]

On the basis of its various levels and many facets, good faith can be regarded as a 'universal travel adaptor'. Once it is plugged in, good faith can connect basic and fundamental understandings and views on law and is capable of tackling the intractable and tricky legal issues. In the development of rules relating to hardship in long-term relational contracts, particularly supply contracts, the *pacta sunt servanda bona fide* principle can affirm the trend in recognising and applying the hardship rules in the context of the *Lex Mercatoria.*

An explicit legal mechanism, regulating hardship issues is necessary and desirable in international contract practice, particularly in long-term relational supply contracts. In the gradual formation of such a legal mechanism based on the results of international harmonisation of contract law and on international case law, good faith plays a significant role, and will continue to contribute to the development of such a mechanism. We will await to see what the future brings us.

[36] The list of factors has been discussed in Chap. 5, Sect. 5.4.2.

General Conclusions

Hardship is an important issue to businesses engaging in international trade and frequently occurs in long-term contracts. Therefore, it would be of great value and use to have a set of rules that could assist international businesses in achieving a satisfactory and equitable result when dealing with hardship.

This book proposed a key solution to deal with hardship. In the context of hardship, the parties to a long-term relational supply contract are under a duty to renegotiate the contract unless there is a compelling reason not to do so. Additionally, the judges or arbitrators have the power to adapt the contract unless there is a complete breakdown of the contractual relationship or the adaptation will cause one or rewrite the contract. Alternatively, they may choose to terminate the contract on the basis of good faith, the relational nature and characteristics of such a contract and the mutual trust and confidence between the parties. This book argued that the parties' duty to renegotiate the contract and the power of courts or arbitral tribunals to adapt or terminate the contract should be limited to international long-term relational contracts, and in particular, international long-term relational supply contracts. By analysing this solution in international contract practice, this book demonstrated that a principle of *pacta sunt servanda bona fide* is emerging in international commercial contract law.

Chapter Two identified the relational nature of a long-term contract. The relational characteristics of a long-term contract formed one of the foundations for the solution. Chapter Three outlined how different domestic legal systems and international instruments deal with hardship. Most of the solutions adopted by domestic laws and international instruments relate to good faith. Chapter Four analysed the role of good faith in finding a solution to hardship at both national and international levels and proposed a new understanding of good faith with many facets and various levels. Chapter Five examined in detail the concrete facets of good faith from both a UNIDROIT Principles' perspective and a normative perspective. The aforementioned key solution was also proposed in this chapter. In addition, a double

P. Guo, *Good Faith in Long-Term Relational Supply Contracts in the Context of Hardship from A Comparative Perspective*,
https://doi.org/10.1007/978-981-16-5513-5

construction approach was suggested in determining whether the parties should perform their duty to renegotiate in good faith and whether judges or arbitrators should adapt or terminate a contract. This approach proposes that both the contract itself and the relationships relating to the contract, viewed horizontally or vertically, determine the rights and duties of the parties to a long-term relational supply contract on the basis of good faith. More specifically, the terms of the contract, the intention, and the expectations of the parties should be considered and balanced against not only the ongoing relationship between the parties, but also other economic or social relationships that the parties have and that may be affecting the long-term relational supply contract. Chapter Six argued that hardship issues relating to long-term contracts, and in particular long-term relational supply contracts, should be considered and tackled from both a good faith perspective and a relational one. It also predicted that a principle of *pacta sunt servanda bona fide* is emerging and will be the trend in international contract law and contract practice, particularly relating to long-term relational supply contracts.

This book provides three rectifications or amendments to the existing rules. Firstly, this book proposes a 'compelling reason' boundary around the parties' duty to renegotiate. It also proposes a boundary around the 'complete breakdown of the ongoing contract relationship between the parties'. This includes providing courts and arbitrators with a test for circumstances in which it is manifestly unreasonable for the parties to be willing to maintain the contractual relationship. The book also argues for the 'compelling reason' doctrine to be developed in the future, not only as a boundary on the duty to renegotiate, but also on the duty to co-operate and even on the scope of the principle of good faith.

Secondly, the book proposes a double construction approach in determining whether the parties should perform their duty to renegotiate, subject to whether they have behaved in good faith and whether judges or arbitrators should adapt or terminate a contract. This approach proposes that both the contract itself and the relationships relating to the contract, viewed horizontally or vertically, determine the rights and duties of the parties. The relationship between the parties are viewed as horizontal, while the relationship between parties and industries or even governments are considered as vertical.

Finally, this book outlines a new understanding of good faith with many facets and various levels. It also provides a list of behavioural factors to be taken into account by judges or arbitrators when determining whether or not the parties have acted in good faith.

Bibliography

A Articles/Books/Reports

Andrews, Neil, 'Good Faith Beneath the Surface: The Ethical Sensitivity of English Contract Law' in the UNIDROIT (ed), *Eppur si muove: The age of Uniform Law, Essays in honour of Michael Joachim Bonell to celebrate his 70th birthday* (the UNIDROIT, 2016) vol 2, 953

Arden, Lady Justice, 'Coming to Terms with Good Faith' (2013) 30 *Journal of Contract Law* 199

Arowolo, Oluseye, 'Abolition of Long-Term Contracts: The Implications and Options for Bankability in Energy Project Financing' (2006) 24 *Journal of Energy and Natural Resources Law* 16

Asante, Samuel B, 'Stability of Contractual Relations in the Transnational Investment Process' (1979) 28 *International and Comparative Law Quarterly* 401

Baird, Douglas G, 'Self-Interest and Cooperation in Long-Term Contracts' (1900) 19 *The Journal of Legal Studies* 583

Barnett, David, 'Commentary on Long-Term Contracts' [1991] *Australian Mining and Petroleum Law Association (AMPLA) Yearbook* 351

Basedow, Jürgen, 'General Principles of European Private Law and Interest Analysis: Some Reflections in the Light of *Mangold* and *Audiolux*' (2016) 3-4 *European Review of Private Law* 331

Beale, Hugh and Tony Dugdale, 'Contracts between Businessmen: Planning and the Use of Contractual Remedies' (1975) 2 *British Journal of Law and Society* 45

Beale, Hugh, 'Relational Values in English Contract Law' in David Campbell, Linda Mulcahy and Sally Wheeler (eds), *Changing Concepts of Contract: Essays in Honour of Ian Macneil* (Palgrave Macmillan, 2013) 116

Bell, Gary F., 'New Challenges for the Unification of laws: How the CISG is Challenged by "Asian Values" and Islamic Law' in Ingeborg Schwenzer and Lisa Spagnolo (eds), Towards Uniformity the 2nd Annual MAA Schlechtriem CISG Conference (ELEVEN International Publishing, 2011) 11, 18-9

Bell, John, 'The Effect of Changes in Circumstances on Long-Term Contracts: English Report' in Donald Harris and Denis Tallon (eds), *Contract Law Today: Anglo-French Comparisons* (Clarendon Press, 1989) 195

Berger, Klaus Peter, 'Renegotiation and Adaptation of International Investment Contracts: The Role of Contract Drafters and Arbitrators' (2003) 36 *Vanderbilt Journal of Transnational Law* 1347

P. Guo, *Good Faith in Long-Term Relational Supply Contracts in the Context of Hardship from A Comparative Perspective*,
https://doi.org/10.1007/978-981-16-5513-5

Berger, Klaus Peter, 'The Relationship between the UNIDROIT Principles of International Commercial Contracts and the New Lex Mercatoria' (2010) 1 *Uniform Law Review* 157

Berger, Klaus Peter and Olivia Johanna Erdelyi,'Force Majeure in International Contract Law: A Comment on National Oil Corporation v Sun Oil' in Patrick Wautelet, Thalia Kruger and Govern Coppens (eds), *The Practice of Arbitration: Essays in Honour of Hans van Houtte* (Hart Publishing, 2012) 61

Berger, Klaus Peter and Thomas Arntz, 'Good Faith as a 'General Organising Principles' of the Common Law' (2016) 32 *Arbitration International* 167

Bergsten, Eric, 'Methodological Problems in the Drafting of the CISG' in André Janssen and Olaf Meyer (eds), CISG Methodology (Sellier European Law Publishers, 2009) 5

Bermingham, John P, 'Extending Good Faith: Does the U.C.C. Impose a Duty of Good Faith Negotiation under Changed Circumstances' (1987) 61 *St. John's Law Review* 217

Bernini, Giorgio, 'Report: Adaptation of Contracts' in Pieter Sanders (ed), *New Trends in the Development of International Commercial Arbitration and the Role of Arbitral and Other Institutions, ICCA Congress Series* (Kluwer Law International, 1983) vol 1, 193

Bianca, C M and M J Bonell (eds), *Commentary on the International Sales Law: the 1980 Vienna Sales Convention* (Giuffrè, 1987)

Block, Guy, 'Arbitration and Changes in Energy Prices: A Review of ICC Awards with respect to Force Majeure, Indexation, Adaptation, Hardship and Take-or-Pay Clauses' (2009) 20 *ICC International Court of Arbitration Bulletin* 51.

Bobeff, Peter, 'Long-Term Contracts for the Sale of Mineral Commodities' [1991] *Australian Mining and Petroleum Law Association (AMPLA) Yearbook* 335

Bonell, Michael Joachim, 'Policing the International Commercial Contract against Unfairness under the UNIDROIT Principles' (1995) 3 *Tulane Journal of International and Comparative Law* 73

Bonell, Michael Joachim, 'The UNIDROIT Principles of International Commercial Contracts and CISG – Alternatives or Complementary Instruments?' (1996) 1 *Uniform Law Review* 26

Bonell, Michael Joachim, 'A "Global" Arbitration Decided on the Basis of the UNIDROIT Principles: *In re Andersen Consulting Business Unit Member Firms v Arthur Andersen Business Unit Member Firms and Andersen Worldwide Société Coopérative*' (2001) 17 *Arbitration International* 249

Bonell, Michael Joachim, 'Towards a legislative Codification of the UNIDROIT Principles?' (2007) 12 *Uniform Law Review* 233

Bonell, Michael Joachim, 'The CISG, European Contract Law and the Development of a World Contract Law' (2008) 56 *American Journal of Comparative Law* 1

Bonell, Michael Joachim, *An International Restatement of Contract Law: The UNIDROIT Principles of International Commercial Contracts* (Martinus Nijhoff Publishers, 3rd ed, 2010)

Bonell, Michael Joachim, 'International Investment Contracts and General Contract Law: A Place for the UNIDROIT Principles of International Commercial Contracts?' (2012) 17 *Uniform Law Review* 141

Bonell, Michael Joachim, 'The UNIDROIT Principles of International Commercial Contract and Long-Term Contracts', Principles of International Commercial Contracts Working Group on Long-Term Contracts, First Session, UNIDROIT 2014, Study L – Doc. 126

Bortolotti, Fabio, 'The UNIDROIT Principles and the Arbitral Tribunals' (2000) 1 *Uniform Law Review* 141

Bortolotti, Fabio, 'Reference to the UNIDROIT Principles in Contract Practice and Model Contracts' in the International Chamber of Commerce (ed), *UNIDROIT Principles: New Developments and Applications, ICC International Court of Arbitration Bulletin, 2005 Special Supplement* (ICC Publishing, 2005) 57

Böckstiegel, Karl-Heinz, 'Hardship, *Force* Majeure and Special Risks Clauses in International Contracts' in Norbert Horn (ed), *Adaptation and Renegotiation of Contracts in International Trade and Finance* (Kluwer Law International, 1985) 159, 159-160.

Bridge, Michael, '*Does Anglo-Canadian Contract Law need a Doctrine of Good Faith*' (1984) 9 *The Canadian Business Law Journal* 385

Bridge, Michael, 'Good Faith in Commercial Contracts' in Roger Brownsword, Norma J Hird and Geraint Howells (eds), *Good Faith in Contract: Concept and Context* (Ashgate and Dartmouth, 1999) 139

Bridge, Michael, 'The UK Sale of Goods Act, the CISG and the UNIDROIT Principles' in Petar Sarcevic and Paul Volken (eds), *International Sale of Goods Revisited* (Kluwer Law International, 2001) 115

Bridge, Michael, 'The CISG and the UNIDROIT Principles of International Commercial Contracts' (2014) 19 *Uniform Law Review* 623

Bridge, Michael, 'Good Faith, the Common Law and the CISG' (2017) 22 *Uniform Law Review* 98.

Brownsword, Roger, *Contract Law: Themes for the Twenty-First Century* (Oxford University Press, 2nd ed, 2006)

Brunner, Christoph, *Force Majeure and Hardship under General Contract Principles: Exemption for Non-performance in International Arbitration* (Kluwer Law International, 2008)

Burrows, Andrew, *A Restatement of the English Law of Contract* (Oxford University Press, 2016)

Burton, Steven J, 'Breach of Contract and the Common Law Duty to Perform in Good Faith' (1981a) 94 *Harvard Law Review* 369

Burton, Steven J, 'Good Faith Performance of a Contract Within Article 2 of the Uniform Commercial Code' (1981b) 67 *Iowa Law Review* 1

Burton, Steven J, 'More on Good Faith Performance of a Contract: A Reply to Professor Summers' (1984) 69 *Iowa Law Review* 497

Burton, Steven J, 'Good Faith in Articles 1 and 2 of the U.C.C.: The Practice View' (1994) 35 *William and Mary Law Review* 1533

Burton, Steven J, and Eric G Anderson, *Contractual Good Faith, Formation, Performance, Breach, Enforcement* (Little, Brown and Company, 1995)

Burton, Steven J, 'History and Theory of Good Faith Performance in the United States' in Larry Dimatteo and Martin Hogg (eds), *Comparative Contract Law: British and American Perspectives* (Oxford University Press, 2015) 211

Campbell, David and Donald Harris, 'Flexibility in Long-Term Contractual Relationships: The Role of Cooperation' (1993) 20 *Journal of Law and Society* 166

Campbell, David, 'The Relational Constitution of the Discrete Contract' in David Campbell and Peter Vincent-Jones (eds), *Contract and Economic Organization: Social-Legal Initiatives* (Dartmouth, 1996) 40

Campbell, David, 'Relational Contract and the Nature of Private Ordering: A Comment on Vincent-Jones' (2007) 14 *Indiana Journal of Global Legal Studies* 279

Campbell, David, 'Good Faith and the Ubiquity of the 'Relational' Contract' (2014) 77 *Modern Law Review* 475

Carlin, Tyrone M, 'The Rise (and Fall?) of Implied Duty of Good Faith in Contractual Performance in Australia' (2002) 25 *University of New South Wales Law Journal* 99

Carter, J W and Andrew Stewart, 'Interpretation, Good Faith and the 'True Meaning' of Contracts: The Royal Botanic Decision' (2002) 18 *Journal of Contract Law* 182

Carter, John W, *Contract Law in Australia* (LexisNexis Butterworths, 6th ed, 2013)

Carter, J W and Wayne Countney, 'Good Faith in Contracts: Is There an Implied Promise to Act Honestly?' (2016) 75 *Cambridge Law Journal* 608

Cartwright, John and Simon Whittaker (eds), *The Code Napoléon Rewritten: French Contract Law after the 2016 Reforms* (Hart Publishing, 2017)

Circo, Carl J, 'The Evolving Role of Relational Contract in Construction Law' (2012) 32 *The Construction Lawyer* 16

Collins, Hugh, *The Law of Contract* (Weidenfeld and Nicolson, 1986)

Collins, Hugh, 'Competing Norms of Contractual Behaviour' in David Campbell and Peter Vincent-Jones (eds), *Contract and Economic Organization: Social-Legal Initiatives* (Dartmouth, 1996) 67

Collins, Hugh, 'Implied Terms: The Foundation in Good Faith and Fair Dealing' (2014) 67 *Current Legal Problems* 297

Comment, 'Relief from Burdensome Long-Term Contracts: Commercial Impracticability, Frustration of Purpose, Mutual Mistake of Fact, and Equitable Adjustment' (1982a) 47 *Missouri Law Review* 79

Comment, 'Equitable Reformation of Long-Term Contracts – The "New Spirit" of ALCOA' (1982b) *Utah Law Review* 985

Crocker, Keith J and Scott E Masten, 'Pretia Ex Machina? Prices and Process in Long-Term Contracts' (1991) 34 *The Journal of Law and Economics* 69

Daintith, Terence, 'The Design and Performance of Long-Term Contracts' in Terence Daintith and Gunther Teubner (ed), *Contract and Organisation: Legal Analysis in the Light of Economic and Social Theory* (Walter de Gruyter, 1986) 164

Daintith, Terence C, 'Contract Design and Practice in the Natural Resources Sector' in Fritz Nicklisch (ed), *The Complex Long-Term Contract: Structures and International Arbitration* (C F Müller Juristisch Verlag, 1987) 151

Dannemann, Gerhard, 'Comparative Law: Study of Similarities or Differences?' in Mathias Reimann and Reinhard Zimmermann (eds), The Oxford Handbook of Comparative Law (Oxford University Press, 2006) 383

Davis, Paul, 'Renegotiating Long-Term Energy Supply Contracts with Japanese Buyers' (2014) 38 *Journal of Japanese Law* 29.

Dewez, Julie et al, 'The Duty to Renegotiate an International Sales Contract under CISG in Case of Hardship and the Use of the UNIDROIT Principles' (2011) 1 *European Review of Private Law* 101

Dharmananda, Kanaga SC and Leon Firios, 'Introduction' in Kanaga Dharmananda SC and Leon Firios (eds), *Long Term Contracts* (Federation Press, 2013) 4

Diamond, Aubrey, 'Force Majeure and Frustration under International Sales Contracts' in Ewan Mckendrick (ed), *Force Majeure and Frustration Contract* (Lloyd's of London, 2nd ed, 1995) 257

Diederichsen, Uwe and Karl-Heinz Gursky, 'Principles of Equity in German Civil Law' in Ralph A Newman (ed), *Equity in the World's Legal Systems: A Comparative Study dedicated to René Cassin* (Établissements Émile Bruylant, 1973) 277

Digwa-Singh, Sukhnam, 'The Application of Commercial Impracticability under Article 2-615 of the Uniform Commercial Code' in Ewan Mckendrick (ed) *Force Majeure and Frustration Contract* (Lloyd's of London, 2nd ed, 1995) 305

Dixon, Bill, 'Common Law Obligations of Good Faith in Australian Commercial Contracts-A Relational Recipe' (2005) 33 *Australian Business Law Review* 87

Draetta, Ugo, 'Les Clauses de Force Majeure et de Hardship dans les Contrats Internationaux/ Hardship and Force Majeure Clauses in International Contracts' (2002) 3-4 *Revue de Droit des Affaires Internationales/International Business Law Journal* 347

D'Souza, Selwyn, 'Commercial Perspectives on Long Term Contracting' in Kanaga Dharmananda SC and Leon Firios (eds), *Long Term Contracts* (Federation Press, 2013) 9

Ebke, Werner F and Bettina M Steinhauer, 'The Doctrine of Good Faith in German Contract Law' in Jack Beatson and Daniel Friedmann (eds), *Good Faith and Fault in Contract Law* (Clarendon Press, 1995) 171

Edlund, Hans Henrik, 'Imbalance in Long-Term Commercial Contracts' (2009) 4 *European Review of Contract Law* 427

Eisenberg, Melvin A, 'Relational Contracts' in Jack Beatson and Daniel Friedmann (eds), *Good Faith and Fault in Contract Law* (Clarendon Press, 1995) 291

Eisenberg, Melvin A, 'Why There is no Law of Relational Contracts' (2000) 94 *Northwestern University Law Review* 805

Ellinghaus, M P, 'An Australian Contract Law?' (1989) 2 *Journal of Contract Law* 13

Enderlein, Fritz and Dietrich Maskow, *International Sales Law, United Nations Convention on Contracts for the International Sale of Goods, Convention on the Limitation Period in the International Sale of Goods* (Oceana Publications, 1992)

Eörsi, Gyula, 'A Propos the 1980 Vienna Convention on Contracts for the International Sale of Goods' (1983) 31 *The American Journal of Comparative Law* 333

Estrella Faria, José Angelo, 'The Influence of the UNIDROIT Principles of International Commercial Contracts on National Laws' (2016) 21 *Uniform Law Review* 238

Farnsworth, E Allan, 'Good Faith Performance and Commercial Reasonableness under the Uniform Commercial Code' (1963) 30 *University of Chicago Law Review* 666

Farnsworth, E Allan, 'Precontractual Liability and Preliminary agreements: Fair Dealing and Failed Negotiations' (1987) 87 *Columbia Law Review* 217

Farnsworth, E Allan, *The Concept of Good Faith in American Law* (Centro di Studi e Ricerche di Diritto Comparato e Straniero, 1993)

Farnsworth, E Allan, 'An American View of the Principles as a Guide to Drafting Contract in ICC institute of International Business Law and Practice' in Jean-Paul Béraudo (ed), *The UNIDROIT Principles for International Commercial Contracts: a new lex mercatoria? ICC/ Dossier of the Institute of International Business Law and Practice ICC publication no. 490/1* (ICC Publishing, 1995a) 88

Farnsworth, E Allan, 'Duties of Good Faith and Fair Dealing under the UNIDROIT Principles, Relevant International Conventions, and National Laws' (1995b) 3 *Tulane Journal of International and Comparative Law* 47

Farnsworth, E Allan, 'Ten Questions About Good Faith and Fair Dealing in United States Contract Law' [2002] *Australian Mining and Petroleum Law Association (AMPLA) Yearbook* 1

Fauvarque-Cosson, Bénédicte, 'Does Review on the Ground of *Imprévision* Breach the Principle of the Binding Force of Contracts' in John Cartwright and Simon Whittaker (eds), *The Code Napoléon Rewritten: French Contract Law after the 2016 Reforms* (Hart Publishing, 2017) 187

Feinman, Jay M, 'Relational Contract and Default Rules' (1994) 3 *Southern California Interdisciplinary Law Journal* 43

Feinman, Jay M, 'Relational Contract Theory in Context' (2000) 94 *Northwestern University Law Review* 737

Feinman, Jay M, 'The Duty of Good Faith: A Perspective on Contemporary Contract Law' (2015) 66 *Hasting Law Journal* 937

Felemegas, John, 'Comparative Editorial Remarks on the Concept of Good Faith in the CISG and the PECL' (2001) 13 *Pace International Law Review* 399

Ferrari, Franco, 'CISG Case Law: A New Challenge for Interpreters?' (1998) 17 *Journal of Law and Commerce* 245

Flechtner, Harry M (ed), 'Transcript of a Workshop on the Sales Convention: Leading CISG Scholars discuss Contract Formation, Validity, Excuse for Hardship, Avoidance, Nachfrist, Contract Interpretation, Parol Evidence, Analogical Application, and Much More' (1999) 18 *Journal of Law and Commerce* 191

Flechtner, Harry M, 'Uniformity and Politics: Interpreting and Filling Gaps in the CISG' in Peter Mankowski and Wolfgang Wurmnest (eds), *Festschrift für Ulrich Magnus zum 70. Geburtstag* (Sellier European Law Publishers, 2014) 193

Foerstl, Uli, *The general Principle of Good Faith under the CISG: A functional Approach to Theory and Practice of the United Nations Convention on Contracts for the International Sale of Goods* (VDM Verlag Dr. Müller, 2011)

Fontaine, Marcel, 'The UNIDROIT Principles: An Expression of Current Contract Practice' in the International Chamber of Commerce and the UNIDROIT (eds), *UNIDROIT Principles of International Commercial Contracts: Reflections on their Use in International Arbitration, ICC International Court of Arbitration Bulletin, 2002 Special Supplement* (ICC Publishing, 2002) 95

Fontaine, Marcel, 'The International 'Rayonnement' of the UNIDROIT Principles' (2017) 22 *Uniform Law Review* 202

Fontaine, Marcel and Filip De Ly, *Drafting International Contracts: An Analysis of Contract Clauses* (Martinus Nijhoff Publishers, 2009)

Frick, Joachim G, *Arbitration and Complex International Contracts* (Kluwer Law International, 2001)

Furmston, Michael and J W Carter, 'Good Faith in Contract Law: A Commonwealth Survey' in the UNIDROIT (ed), *Eppur si muove: The age of Uniform Law, Essays in honour of Michael Joachim Bonell to celebrate his 70th birthday* (the UNIDROIT, 2016) vol 2, 988

Gaillard, Emmanuel, 'Use of General Principles of International Law in International Long-Term Contracts' (1999) 27 *International Business Lawyer* 214

Garro, Alejandro M, 'CISG Advisory Council Opinion No 7 – Exemple of Liability for Damages under Article 79 of the CISG' in Ingeborg Schwenzer (ed), The CISG Advisory Council Opinions (Eleven International Publishing, 2017) 167

Garvey, John, 'Commentary on Long-Term Contracts' [1991] *Australian Mining and Petroleum Law Association (AMPLA) Yearbook* 362

Gergen, Mark P, 'Liability for Mistake in Contract Formation' (1990) 64 *Southern California Law Review* 1

Gillette, Clayton P, 'Commercial Rationality and the Duty to Adjust Long-Term Contracts' (1985) 69 *Minnesota Law Review* 521

Gillette, Clayton P and Steven D Walt, *The UN Convention on Contracts for the International Sale of Goods: Theory and Practice* (Cambridge University Press, 2nd ed, 2016)

Girard, Philip, '"Good Faith" in Contract Performance: Principle or Placebo?' (1983) 5 *The Supreme Court Law Review* 309

Glossner, Ottoarndt, 'Contract Adaptation through Third Party Intervener; the Referee Arbitral' in Norbert Horn (ed), *Adaptation and Renegotiation of Contracts in International Trade and Finance* (Kluwer Law International, 1985) 191

Goddard, David, 'Long-Term Contracts: A Law and Economics Perspective' [1997] *New Zealand Law Review* 423

Goetz, Charles J and Robert E Scott, 'Principles of Relational Contracts' (1981) 67 *Virginia Law Review* 1089

Goetz, Charles J and Robert E Scott, 'The Mitigation Principle: Toward a General Theory of Contractual Obligation' (1983) 69 *Virginia Law Review* 967

Goldberg, Victor P, 'Price Adjustment in Long-Term Contracts' 1985 *Wisconsin Law Review* 527

Goldberg, Victor P and John R Erickson, 'Quantity and Price Adjustment in Long-Term Contracts: A Case Study of Petroleum Coke' (1987) 30 *The Journal of Law and Economics* 369

Goldberg, Victor P, 'Discretion in Long-Term Open Quantity Contracts: Reining in Good Faith' (2002) 35 *University of California Davis Law Review* 319

Goode, Roy, *The Concept of 'Good Faith' in English Law* (Centro di Studi e Ricerche di Diritto Comparato e Straniero, 1992)

Goodin, Robert E, *Protecting the Vulnerable: A Reanalysis of Our Social Responsibilities* (University of Chicago Press, 1985)

Gooley, John, Peter Radan and Ilija Vickcvich, *Principles of Australian Contract Law* (LexisNexis Butterworths, 3rd ed, 2014)

Gordon, Robert W, 'Macaulay, Macneil, and the Discovery of Solidarity and Power in Contract Law' (1985) *Wisconsin Law Review* 565

Gotanda, John Y, 'Renegotiation and Adaptation Clauses in Investment Contracts, Revisited' (2003) 36 *Vanderbilt Journal of Transnational Law* 1461

Gottlieb, Gidon, 'Relationism: Legal Theory for a Relational Society' (1983) 50 *University of Chicago Law Review* 567

Gudel, Paul J, 'Relational Contract Theory and the Concept of Exchange' (1998) 46 *Buffalo Law Review* 763

Guo, Peng, 'What can International Arbitration learn from Medieval Merchant Courts?' (2017) 9 *HUFS Global Law Review* 69

Guo, Peng, 'Termination for a Compelling Reason under the UNIDROIT Principles: Status Quo and the Way Forward' (2018) 21 International Trade and Business Law Review 1

Hadfield, Gillian K, 'Problematic Relations: Franchising and the Law of Incomplete Contracts' (1990) 42 *Stanford Law Review* 927

Haley, John Owen, *The Spirit of Japanese Law* (University of Georgia Press, 1998)

Hamilton, John P et al (eds), *NSW Civil Procedure Handbok 2017* (Thomson Reuters, 2017)

Hardingham, I J, 'Problems with Long-Term Contracts: Change of Circumstance' [1986] *Australian Mining and Petroleum Law Association Yearbook (AMPLA Yearbook)* 474

Hartkamp, Arthur, 'The Concept of Good Faith in the UNIDROIT Principles for International Commercial Contracts' (1995) 3 *Tulane Journal of International and Comparative Law* 65

Hauteclocque, Adrien de and Jean-Michel Glachant, 'Long-Term Energy Supply Contracts in Europe Competition Policy: Fuzzy not Crazy' (2009) 37 *Energy Policy* 5399

Hayne, K M, 'Problems with Long-Term Contracts: Conflict of Laws' [1986] *Australian Mining and Petroleum Law Association Yearbook (AMPLA Yearbook)* 467

Herrmann, Gerold, 'The UNCITRAL Conciliation Rules: An Aid also in Contract Adaptation (and Performance Facilitation)' in Norbert Horn (ed), *Adaptation and Renegotiation of Contracts in International Trade and Finance* (Kluwer Law International, 1985) 217

Hesselink, Martijn, 'The Concept of Good Faith' in Arthur S Hartkamp et al (eds), *Towards a European Civil Code* (Kluwer Law International and Ars Aequi Libri, 4th ed, 2010) 619

Hillman, Robert A, 'Court Adjustment of Long-Term Contracts: An Analysis under Modern Contract Law' (1987) *Duke Law Journal* 1

Hillman, Robert A, 'Maybe Dick Speidel Was Right about Court Adjustment' (2009) 46 *San Diego Law Review* 595

Hoellering, Michael F, 'Emerging Techniques of Private Dispute Resolution in Long-Term Contracts' in Fritz Nicklisch (ed), *The Complex Long-Term Contract: Structures and International Arbitration* (C F Müller Juristisch Verlag, 1987) 523

Hofmann, Nathalie, 'Interpretation Rules and Good Faith as Obstacles to the UK's Ratification of the CISG and to the Harmonization of Contract Law in Europe' (2010) 22 *Pace International Law Review* 145

Hondius, Ewoud and Hans Christoph Grigoleit, 'Introduction: An Approach to the Issues and Doctrines Relating to Unexpected Circumstances' in Ewoud Hondius and Hans Christoph Grigoleit (eds), *Unexpected Circumstances in European Contract Law* (Cambridge University Press, 2011a) 3

Hondius, Ewoud and Hans Christoph Grigoleit, 'Overview: Concepts Dealing with Unexpected Circumstances' in Ewoud Hondius and Hans Christoph Grigoleit (eds), *Unexpected Circumstances in European Contract Law* (Cambridge University Press, 2011b) 55

Hondius, Ewoud and Hans Christoph Grigoleit, 'General Comparative Remarks: Converging Tendencies, Remaining Differences and the Unsolved Mystery of Adjustment' in Ewoud Hondius and Hans Christoph Grigoleit (eds), *Unexpected Circumstances in European Contract Law* (Cambridge University Press, 2011c) 641

Honnold, John O, *Documentary History of the Uniform Law for International Sales* (Kluwer Law and Taxation Publishers, 1989)

Honnold, John O, *Uniform Law for International Sales* (Kluwer Law International, 3rd ed, 1999)

Honnold, John O, 'The Sales Convention in Action-Uniform International Words: Uniform Application?' (2008) 8 *Journal of Law and Commerce* 207

Honnold, John O and Harry M Flechtner, *Uniform Law for International Sales under the 1980 United Nations Convention* (Kluwer Law International, 4th ed, 2009)

Norbert Horn, 'The Concepts of Adaptation and Renegotiation in the Law of Transnational Commercial Contracts' in Norbert Horn (ed), *Adaptation and Renegotiation of Contracts in International Trade and Finance* (Kluwer Law International, 1985a) 3

Norbert Horn, 'Changes in Circumstances and The Revision of Contracts in some European Laws and in International Law' in Norbert Horn (ed), *Adaptation and Renegotiation of Contracts in International Trade and Finance* (Kluwer Law International, 1985b) 15

Norbert Horn, 'Standard Clauses on Contract Adaptation in International Commerce' in Norbert Horn (ed), *Adaptation and Renegotiation of Contracts in International Trade and Finance* (Kluwer Law International, 1985c) 111

Norbert Horn, 'Procedures of Contract Adaptation and Renegotiation in International Commerce' in Norbert Horn (ed), *Adaptation and Renegotiation of Contracts in International Trade and Finance* (Kluwer Law International, 1985d) 173

'Hungarian State Enterprise v Jugoslavenski Naftovod (Yugoslav Crude Oil Pipeline), Award, 6 July 1983' in Pieter Sanders (ed), *Yearbook Commercial Arbitration 1984* (Kluwer Law International, 1984) vol 9, 69

Morten Hviid, 'Long-Term Contracts and Relational Contracts' in Boudewijn Bouckaert and Gerrit De Geest (eds), *Encyclopaedia of Law and Economics: The Regulation of Contracts* (Edward Elgar, 2000) vol 3, 46

Joerges, Christian, 'Relational Contract Theory in a Comparative Perspective: Tensions between Contract and Antitrust Law Principles in the Assessment of Contract Relations between Automobile Manufacturers and Their Dealers in Germany' (1985) *Wisconsin Law Review* 581

Joskow, Paul L, 'Vertical Integration and Long-Term Contracts: The Case of Coal-Burning Electric Generating Plants' (1985) 1 *Journal of Law, Economics, and Organization* 33

Joskow, Paul L, 'Price Adjustment in Long-Term Contracts: The Case of Coal' (1998) 31 *The Journal of Law and Economics* 47

Kahn-Freund, Otto, Claudine Lévy and Bernard Rudden, *A Source-book on French Law: System, Methods, Outlines of Contract* (Clarendon Press, 2nd ed, 1979)

Kastely, Amy H, 'Unification and Community: A Rhetorical Analysis of the United Nations Sales Convention' (1988) 8 *Northwestern Journal of International Law and Business* 574

Keily, Troy, 'Good Faith and the Vienna Convention on Contracts for the International Sale of Goods (CISG)' (1999) 3 *Vindobona Journal of International Commercial Law and Arbitration* 15

Klein, John, 'Good Faith in International Transactions' (1993) 15 *Liverpool Law Review* 115

Komarov, Alexander S, 'Internationality, Uniformity and Observance of Good Faith as Criteria in Interpretation of CISG: Some Remarks on Article 7(1)' (2005) 25 *Journal of Law and Commerce* 75

Koneru, Phanesh, 'The International Interpretation of the UN Convention on Contracts for the International Sale of Goods: An Apporach Based on General Principles' (1997) 6 *Minnesota Journal of Global Trade* 105

Kozolchyk, Boris, *Comparative Commercial Contracts: Law, Culture and Economic Development* (West Academic Publishing, 2014)

Kötz, Hein, 'Towards a European Civil Code: The Duty of Good Faith' in Peter Cane and Jane Stapleton (eds), *The Law of Obligations: Essays in Celebration of John Fleming* (Clarendon Press, 1998) 243

Kröll, Stefan, 'Selected Problems Concerning the CISG's Scope of Application' (2005) 25 *Journal of Law and Commerce* 39

Kröll, Stefan, Loukas Mistelis and Pilar Perales Viscasillas (eds), *UN Convention on Contracts for the International Sale of Goods (CISG)* (C H Beck, 2011)

Kumar, Miiko, Michael Legg and Ilija Vichovich (eds), *Civil Procedure in New South Wales* (Thomson Reuters, 3rd ed, 2016)

Ladbury, Rich, 'Implied Duty of Good Faith: A Comment' [2002] *Australian Mining and Petroleum Law Association (AMPLA) Yearbook* 22

Lando, Ole, 'Renegotiation and Revision of International Contracts' (1980) 23 *Germany Yearbook of International Law* 37

Lando, Ole, 'The CISG and the UNIDROIT Principles in a Global Commercial Code' in Mélanges offerts Marcel Fontaine (2003)

Lando, Ole, 'Out on a Limb-Four English Peculiarities in Contract Law' in Andrea Büchler and Markus Müller-Chen (eds), *Private Law national – global – comparative, Festschrift für Ingeborg Schwenzer zum 60 Geburtstag* (Stämpfli Verlag AG Bern and Intersentia, 2011) vol 2, 1001

Lando, Ole and Hugh Beale (eds), *Principles of European Contract Law, Part I and II, Combined and Revised* (Kluwer Law International, 2000)

Lapiashvili, Natia, *Modern Law of Contracts and Sales in Eastern Europe and Central Asia* (ELEVEN International Publishing, 2011)

Leggatt, George, 'Making Sense of Contracts: the Rational Choice Theory' (2015) 131 *Law Quarterly Review* 454.

Lorfing, Pascale Accaoui, 'La Regegociation Contractuellement Imprevue/The Contractually Unforeseen Renegotiation' (2010) 1 *Revue de Droit des Affaires Internationales/International Business Law Journal* 35

Lücke, H K, 'Good Faith and Contractual Performance' in Paul Finn (ed), *Essays on Contract* (The Law Book, 1987) 155

Macaulay, Stewart, 'Non-Contractual Relations in Business: A Preliminary Study' (1963) 28 *American Sociological Review* 55

Macaulay, Stewart, 'An Empirical View of Contract' (1985) *Wisconsin Law Review* 465

Macaulay, Stewart, 'Relational Contracts Floating on A Sea of Custom? Thoughts about the Ideas of Ian Macneil and Lisa Bernstein' (2000) 94 *Northwestern University Law Review* 775

Macaulay, Stewart, 'The Real and the Paper Deal: Empirical Pictures of Relationships, Complexity and the Urge for Transparent Simple Rules' (2003) 66 *Modern Law Review* 44

Macaulay, Stewart et al, *Contracts: Law in Action, the Introductory Course* (Carolina Academic Press, 4th ed, 2016) vol 1

Macaulay, Stewart et al, *Contracts: Law in Action: The Advanced Course* (Carolina Academic Press, 4th ed, 2017) vol 2

Macneil, Ian R, *Contracts: exchange, transactions and relations cases and materials* (Foundation Press, 2nd ed, 1978)

Macneil, Ian R, *The New Social Contract: An Inquiry into Modern Contractual Relations* (Yale University Press, 1980)

Macneil, Ian R, 'Economic Analysis of Contractual Relations: Its Shortfalls and the Need for a "Rich Classificatory Apparatus"' (1981) 75 *Northwestern University Law Review* 1018

Macneil, Ian R, 'Values in Contract: Internal and External' (1984) 78 *Northwestern University Law Review* 340

Macneil, Ian R, 'Reflections on Relational Contract' (1985a) 141 *Zeitschrift für die gesamte Stattswissenschaft/Journal of Institutional and Theoretical Economics* 541

Macneil, Ian R, 'Relational Contract: What We Do and Do Not Know' (1985b) *Wisconsin Law Review* 483

Macneil, Ian R, 'Barriers to the Idea of Relational Contracts' in Fritz Nicklisch (ed), *The Complex Long-Term Contract: Structures and International Arbitration* (C F Müller Juristisch Verlag, 1987a) 31

Macneil, Ian R, 'Relational Contract Theory as Sociology: A Reply to Professors Lindenberg and de Vos' (1987b) 143 *Journal of Institutional and Theoretical Economics (JITE)/Zeitschrift für die gesamte Staatswissenschaft* 272

Macneil, Ian R, 'Contracting Worlds and Essential Contract Theory' (2000a) 9 *Social and Legal Studies* 431

Macneil, Ian R, 'Relational Contract Theory: Challenges and Queries' (2000b) 94 *Northwestern University Law Review* 877

Magnus, Ulrich, 'Remarks on Good Faith: The United Nations Convention on Contracts for the International Sale of Goods and the International Institute for the Unification of Private Law, Principles of International Commercial Contracts' (1998) 10 *Pace International Law Review* 89

Magnus, Ulrich, 'Comparative editorial remarks on the provisions regarding good faith in CISG Article 7(1) and the UNIDROIT Principles Article 1.7' in John Felemegas (ed), *An International Approach to the Interpretation of the United Nations Convention on Contracts for the International Sale of Goods (1980) as Uniform Sales Law* (Cambridge University Press, 2007) 45

Magnus, Ulrich, 'Harmonization and Unification of Law by the Means of General Principles' in Morten M Fogt (ed), *Unification and Harmonization of International Commercial Law: Interaction or Deharmonization?* (Kluwer Law International, 2012) 161

Maltese, Demetrio and Marco Farina, 'Theory of the Firm and Organisational Contracts: The Remedial Aspects of Good Faith' (2016) 27 *European Business Law Review* 51

Markesinis, B S, W Lorenz and G Dannemann, *the German Law of Obligations, the Law of Contracts and Restitution: A Comparative Introduction* (Clarendon Press, 1997) vol 1

Markesinis, Basil S, Hannes Unberath and Angus Johnston, *The German Law of Contract: A Comparative Treatise* (Hart Publishing, 2nd ed, 2006)

Maskow, Dietrich, 'Hardship and Force Majeure' (1992) 40 *American Journal of Comparative Law* 657

Mason, Anthony, 'Contract, Good Faith and Equitable Standards in Fair Dealing' 2000 (116) *The Law Quarterly Review* 66

McCamus, John D, 'The New General "Principle" of Good Faith Performance and the New 'Rule' of Honesty in Performance in Canadian Contract Law' (2015) *32 Journal of Contract Law* 103

McCarthy, Shane B, 'Change and Stability in LNG Sales Contract Terms' [1985] *Australian Mining and Petroleum Law Association Yearbook (AMPLA Yearbook)* 210

Mcinnis, J Arthur, 'Frustration and Force Majeure in Building Contracts' in Ewan Mckendrick (ed), *Force Majeure and Frustration Contract* (Lloyd's of London, 2nd ed, 1995) 195

McKendrick, Ewan, 'The Regulation of Long-term Contracts in English Law' in Jack Beatson and Daniel Friedmann (eds), *Good Faith and Fault in Contract Law* (Clarendon Press, 1995a) 305

McKendrick, Ewan, 'The Consequence of Frustration-The Law Reform (Frustrated Contracts) Act 1943' in Ewan Mckendrick (ed), *Force Majeure and Frustration Contract* (Lloyd's of London, 2nd ed, 1995b) 223

McKendrick, Ewan, 'Good Faith: A Matter of Principle?' in A D M Forte (ed), *Good Faith in Contract and Property* (Hart Publishing, 1999) 39

McKendrick, Ewan, 'Good Faith in the Performance of a Contract in English Law' in Larry Dimatteo and Martin Hogg (eds), *Comparative Contract Law: British and American Perpectives* (Oxford University Press, 2015) 197

McKendrick, Ewan, *Contract Law: Texts, Cases and Materials* (Oxford University Press, 7th ed, 2016a)

McKendrick, Ewan, *Goode on Commercial Law* (Penguin Books, 5th ed, 2016b)

McKendrick, Ewan and Qiao Liu, 'Good Faith in Contract Performance in the Chinese and Common Laws' in Larry A DiMatteo and Lei Chen (eds), *Chinese Contract Law: Civil and Common Law Perspectives* (Cambridge University Press, 2017) 72

McKillop, C J R, 'Commentary on Effect of Changed Circumstances on Mineral and Petroleum Sales Contracts' [1984] *Australian Mining and Petroleum Law Association (AMPLA) Yearbook* 361

McLure, Carmel, 'Long Term Contracts: Principles for Determining Content' in Kanaga Dharmananda SC and Leon Firios (eds), *Long Term Contracts* (Federation Press, 2013) 115

Mezger, Ernst, 'The ICC Rules for The Adaptation of Contracts' in Norbert Horn (ed), *Adaptation and Renegotiation of Contracts in International Trade and Finance* (Kluwer Law International, 1985) 205

Michaels, Ralf, 'The Functional Method of Comparative Law' in in Mathias Reimann and Reinhard Zimmermann (eds), The Oxford Handbook of Comparative Law (Oxford University Press, 2006) 339

Micklitz, Hans-W and Leticia Diez Sanchez, 'The Politics of Fairness in CISG' in Ingeborg Schwenzer (ed), *35 Years CISG and Beyond* (Eleven International Publishing, 2016) 269

Mitchell, Catherine, *Contract Law and Contract Practice: Bridging the Gap between Legal Reasoning and Commercial Expectation* (Hart Publishing, 2013)

Morgan, Jonathan, *Contract Law Minimalism: A Formalist Restatement of Commercial Contract Law* (Cambridge University Press, 2013)

Morrison, James and Nottage, Luke R, 'Country Report on Australia for: International Commercial Arbitration – An Asia-Pacific Perspective' Sydney Law School, Legal Studies Research Paper No. 14/95, October 2014

Moss, Giuditta Cordero, 'International Contracts between Common Law and Civil Law: Is Non-State Law to Be Preferred? The Difficulty of Interpreting Legal Standards Such as Good Faith' (2007) 7 *Global Jurist* 28

Mulherin, J Harold, 'Complexity in Long-Term Contracts: An Analysis of Natural Gas Contractual Provisions' (1986) 2 *Journal of Law, Economics, and Organization* 105

Munoz, Edgardo, *Modern Law of Contracts and Sales in Latin America, Spain and Portugal* (Eleven International Publishing, 2011)

Munro, Howard, 'The "Good Faith" Controversy in Australian Commercial Law: A Survey of the Spectrum of Academic Legal Opinion' (2009) 28 *The University of Queensland Law Journal* 167

Mustill, Lord Justice, 'The New Lex Mercatoria: The First Twenty-five Years' in Maarten Bos (ed), Liber Amicorum for the Rt. Hon. Lord Wilberforce (Oxford University Press, 1987) 86

Nalin, Paulo, 'International Fair Trade (Fair Trade in International Contracts and Ethical Standard)' in Ingeborg Schwenzer (ed), *35 Years CISG and Beyond* (Eleven International Publishing, 2016) 317

Nassar, Nagla, *Sanctity of Contracts Revisited: A Study in the Theory and Practice of Long-Term International Commercial Transactions* (Martinus Nijhoff Publishers, 1995)

Neilson, William A W, 'Price Adjustments in Long-term Supply Contracts: The Saga of the Quintette Coal Arbitration' (1991) 18 *Canadian Business Law Journal* 76

Newman, L W, 'Problems with Long Term Contracts: A Practical Viewpoint' [1986] *Australian Mining and Petroleum Law Association Yearbook (AMPLA Yearbook)* 487

Newman, Ralph A, 'The General Principles of Equity' in Ralph A Newman (ed), *Equity in the World's Legal Systems: a comparative study* (Etablissements Emile Bruylant, 1973) 589

Nicholas, Barry, *The French Law of Contract* (Clarendon Press, 2nd ed, 1992)

Nicholas, Barry, *The United Kingdom and the Vienna Sales Convention: Another Case of Splendid Isolation?* (Centro di Studi e Ricerche di Diritto Comparato e Straniero, 1993)

Nicholas, Barry, 'Force Majeure in French Law' in Ewan Mckendrick (ed), *Force Majeure and Frustration Contract* (Lloyd's of London, 2nd ed, 1995) 21

Nicklisch, Fritz, 'Taking Account of Project Duration and Project Disturbances in Complex Long-Term Contracts' in Fritz Nicklisch (ed), *The Complex Long-Term Contract: Structures and International Arbitration* (C F Müller Juristisch Verlag, 1987a) 365

Nicklisch, Fritz, 'Advantages of a Doctrine of Long-Term Contracts' in Fritz Nicklisch (ed), *The Complex Long-Term Contract: Structures and International Arbitration* (C F Müller Juristisch Verlag, 1987b) 17

Nottage, Luke R, 'Form and Substance in US, English, New Zealand and Japanese Law: A Framework for Better Comparisons of Developments in the Law of Unfair Contracts' (1996) 26 *Victoria University Wellington Law Review* 247

Nottage, Luke R, 'Planning and Renegotiating Long-Term Contracts in New Zealand and Japan: An Interim Report on an Empirical Research Project' (1997a) *New Zealand Law Review* 482

Nottage, Luke R, 'Economic Dislocation and Contract Renegotiation in New Zealand and Japan: A Preliminary Empirical Study' (1997b) 27 *Victoria University Wellington Law Review* 59

Nottage, Luke R, 'Practical and Theoretical Implications of the Lex Mercatoria for Japan: Central's Empirical Study on the Use of Transnational Law' (2000) 4 *Vnidobona Journal of International Commercial Law and Arbitration* 132

Nottage, Luke R, 'The Procedural Lex Mercatoria: The Past, Present and Future of International Commercial Arbitration' Sydney Law School, Legal Studies Research Paper No. 06/51, December 2006

Nottage, Luke R, 'Changing Contract Lenses: Unexpected Supervening Events in English, New Zealand, US, Japanese, and International Sales Law and Practice' (2008) 14 *Indiana Journal of Global Legal Studies* 385

Nottage, Luke R, 'Tracing Trajectories in Contract Law Theory: Form in Anglo-New Zealand Law, Substance in Japan and the United States' (2013) 4 Yonsei Law Journal 175

Nottage, Luke R, 'A Weathermap for International Arbitration: Mainly Sunny, Some Cloud, Possible Thunderstorms' Sydney Law School, Legal Studies Research Paper No. 15/62, July 2015

Nystén-Haarala, Soili, *The Long-Term Contract: Contract Law and Contracting* (Kauppakaari OYJ, 1998)

O'Conner, J F, *Good Faith in English Law* (Dartmouth, 1990)

Oosterhuis, Janwillem (Pim), 'Commercial Impracticability and the Missed Opportunity of the French Contract Law Reform: Doctrinal, Historical and Law and Economics Arguments-Comment on Lutzi's Introducing *Imprévision* in to French Contract Law' in S Stijns and S Jansen (eds), *The French Contract Law Reform: A Source of Inspiration?* (Intersentia 2016) 113

Palay, Thomas M, 'A Contract Does Not a Contract Make' (1985) *Wisconsin Law Review* 561

Paterson, Jeannie, Andrew Robertson and Arlen Duke, *Principles of Contract Law* (Thomson Reuters, 5th ed, 2016)

Peden, Elisabeth, *Good faith in the performance of contracts* (LexisNexis Butterworths, 2003)

Peden, Elisabeth, 'Good Faith in the Performance of Contract Law' (2004) 42 *Law Society Journal* 64

Peden, Elisabeth, '"Implicit Good Faith"- or Do We Still Need an Implied Term of Good Faith?' (2009) 25 *Journal of Contract Law* 50

Perillo, Joseph M, 'Force Majeure and Hardship under the UNIDROIT Principles of International Commercial Contracts' (1997) 5 *Tulane Journal of International and Comparative law* 5

Perry, Christina, 'Good Faith in English and US Contract Law: Divergent Theories, Practical Similarities' (2016) 17 *Business Law International* 27

Peter, Wolfgang, 'International Investment Agreement-Types, Arbitration and Renegotiation' in Fritz Nicklisch (ed), *The Complex Long-Term Contract: Structures and International Arbitration* (C F Müller Juristisch Verlag, 1987) 119

Petrash, Jeffrey M, 'Long-Term Natural Gas Contracts: Dead, Dying, or Merely Resting?' (2006) 27 *Energy Law Journal* 545

Pirozzi, Roberto, 'The Effect of Changing Circumstances in International Commercial Contracts: The Scaform Case' (2012) 16 *The Vindobona Journal of International Commercial Law and Arbitration* 207

Posner, Richard A and Andrew M Rosenfield, 'Impossibility and Related Doctrines in Contract Law: An Economic Analysis' (1977) 6 *The Journal of Legal Studies* 83

Powell, Raphael, 'Good Faith in Contracts' (1956) 9 *Current Legal Problems* 16

Powers, Paul J, 'Defining the Undefinable: Good Faith and the United Nations Convention on Contracts for the International Sale of Goods' (1999) 18 *Journal of Law and Commerce* 333

Radan, Peter and Cameron Stewart, *Principles of Australian Equity and Trusts* (LexisNexis Butterworths, 3rd ed, 2016)

Rakoff, Todd D, 'Good Faith in Contract Performance: Market Street Associates Ltd. Partnership v Frey' (2007) 120 *Harvard Law Review* 1187

Reynolds, R M B, 'Problems with Long Term Contracts: Alternative Methods of Resolving Disputes' [1986] *Australian Mining and Petroleum Law Association Yearbook (AMPLA Yearbook)* 451

Rickett, Charles E F, 'Some Reflections on Open-Textured Commercial Contracting' [2001] *Australian Mining and Petroleum Law Association (AMPLA) Yearbook* 374

Ridder, Philip and Marc-Philippe Weller, 'Unforeseen Circumstances, Hardship, Impossibility and Force Majeure under German Contract Law' (2014) 3 *European Review of Private Law* 371

Rimke, Joern, 'Force Majeure and Hardship: Application in International Trade Practice with Specific Regard to the CISG and the UNIDROIT Principles of International Commercial Contracts' *Pace Review of the Convention on Contracts for the International Sale of Goods (1999-2000)* (Kluwer Law International, 2001) 197

Rivkin, David W., 'Lex Mercatoria and Force Majeure' in Emmanuel Gaillard (ed), *Transnational Rules in International Commercial Arbitration* (ICC Publishing, 1993) 161

Robin, Guy, 'Le Principe de La Bonne Foi dans Les Contrats Internationaux/The Principle of Good Faith in International Contracts' (2005) 6 *Revue de Droit des Affaires Internationales/International Business Law Journal* 695

Rodner, James Otis, 'Hardship under the UNIDROIT Principles of International Commercial Contracts' in Gerald Aksen et al (eds), *Global Reflections on International Law, Commerce and Dispute Resolution: Liber Amicorum in Honour of Robert Briner* (ICC Publishing, 2005) 677

Rongeat-Oudin, Federica and Martin Oudin, 'La Reception des Principles UNIDROIT par La Lex Mercatoria: L'Exemple de La Bonne Foi/The Reception of the UNIDROIT Principles by the Lex Mercatoria: The Example of Good Faith' (2009) 6 *Revue de Droit des Affaires Internationales/International Business Law Journal* 697

Rosher, Peter, 'French Contract Law Reform' (2016) 17 *Business Law International* 59

Rowan, Solène, 'The New French Law of Contract' (2017) 66 *International and Comparative Law Quarterly* 805

Schlechtriem, Peter, *Good Faith in German Law and in International Uniform Laws* (Centro di Studi e Ricerche di Diritto Comparato e Straniero, 1997)

Schlechtriem, Peter and Ingeborg Schwenzer (eds), *Commentary on the UN Convention on the International Sale of Goods (CISG)* (Oxford University Press, 2nd (English) ed, 2005)

Schmitthoff, Clive M, 'Hardship and Intervener Clauses' in Chia-Jui Cheng (ed), *Clive M Schmitthoff's Select Essays on International Trade Law* (Martinus Nijhoff Publishers and Graham and Trotman, 1988) 415

Schulze, Reiner (ed), *Common European Sales Law: Commentary* (Nomos Verlagsgesellschaft, Verlag C H Beck and Hart Publishing, 2012)

Schwarts, Alan, 'Relational Contracts in the Courts: An Analysis of Incomplete Agreements and Judicial Strategies' (1992) 21 *Journal of Legal Studies* 271

Schwenzer, Ingeborg, 'Force Majeure and Hardship in International Sales Contracts' (2009) 39 *Victoria University of Wellington Law Review* 709

Schwenzer, Ingeborg (ed), *Commentary on the UN Convention on the International Sale of Goods(CISG)* (Oxford University Press, 3rd ed, 2010)

Schwenzer, Ingeborg, Pascal Hachem and Christopher Kee, *Global Sales and Contract Law* (Oxford University Press, 2012)

Schwenzer, Ingeborg, 'Global Unification of Contract Law' (2016a) 21 *Uniform Law Review* 60

Schwenzer, Ingeborg (ed), *Schlechtriem and Schwenzer Commentary on the UN Convention on the International Sale of Goods (CISG)* (Oxford University Press, 4th ed, 2016b)

Scott, Robert E, 'Risk Distribution and Adjustment in Long-Term Contracts' in Fritz Nicklisch (ed), *The Complex Long-Term Contract: Structures and International Arbitration* (C F Müller Juristisch Verlag, 1987) 51

Scott, Robert E, 'The Case for Formalism in Relational Contract' (2000) 94 *Northwestern University Law Review* 847

Sharp, B M H and B Simon, 'Long-Term Natural Resource Contracts' (1992) 26 *New Zealand Economic Papers* 27

Sim, Disa, 'The Scope and Application of Good Faith in the Vienna Convention on Contracts for the International Sale of Goods' 2001

Smythe, Donald J, 'Bounded Rationality, the Doctrine of Impracticability, and the Governance of Relational Contracts' (2004) 13 *Southern California Interdisciplinary Law Journal* 227

Sornarajah, M, 'Introduction' in Andrew D Mitchell, M Sornarajah and Tania Voon (eds), *Good Faith and International Economic Law* (Oxford University Press, 2015) 1

Spagnolo, Lisa, 'Opening Pandora's Box: Good Faith and Precontractual Liability in the CISG' (2007) 21 *Temple International and Comparative Law Journal* 261

Speidel, Richard E, 'Court-imposed Price Adjustments under Long-Term Supply Contracts' (1981) 76 *Northwestern University Law Review* 369

Speidel, Richard E, 'The New Spirit of Contract' (1982) 2 *Journal of Law and Commerce* 193

Speidel, Richard E, 'Article 2 and Relational Sales Contracts' (1993) 26 *Loyola of Los Angeles Law Review* 789

Speidel, Richard E, 'The Revision of UCC Article 2, Sales in Light of the United Nations Convention on Contracts for the International Sale of Goods' (1995) 16 *Northwestern Journal of International Law and Business* 165

Speidel, Richard E, 'The Characteristics and Challenges of Relational Contracts' (2000) 94 *Northwestern University Law Review* 823

Summers, Robert S, '"Good Faith" in General Contract Law and the Sales Provisions of the Uniform Commercial Code' (1968) 54 *Virginia Law Review* 195

Summers, Robert S, 'The Conceptualisation of Good faith in American Contract Law: A General Account' in Reinhard Zimmermann and Simon Whittaker (eds), *Good Faith in European Contract Law* (Cambridge University Press, 2000) 118

Summers, Robert S, 'Good Faith Revisited: Some Brief Remarks Dedicated to the Late Richard E Speidel – Friend, Co-Author, and UCC Specialist' (2009) 46 *San Diego Law Review* 723

Stalev, Zhivko, 'Arbitration to adapt Long-Term International Economic Contracts to Changed Circumstances' in Pieter Sanders (ed), *New Trends in the Development of International Commercial Arbitration and the Role of Arbitral and Other Institutions, ICCA Congress Series* (Kluwer Law International, 1983) vol 1, 199

Stein, Ted L, 'The Approach of the Different Drummer: The Principle of the Persistent Objector in International Law' (1985) 26 *Harvard International Law Journal* 457

Steyn, Justice, 'The Role of Good Faith and Fair Dealing in Contract Law: A Hair-Shirt Philosophy?' (1991) 6 *The Denning Law Journal* 131

Story, J, *Commentaries on Equity Jurisprudence: as Administered in England and America* (Hillard, Gary and Company, 1836) §334, cited by Henry E Smith, 'Fusing the Equitable Function in Private Law' in Kit Barker, Karen Fairweather and Ross Grantham (eds), *Private Law in the 21st Century* (Hart Publishing, 2017) 173, 179.

Tallon, Denis, *Le Concept de Bonne Foi en Droit Français du Contrat* (Centro di Studi e Ricerche di Diritto Comparato e Straniero, 1994)

Tang, Chuanlong, 'Structure and Price Adjustments in Long-Term Contracts: The Case of Coking Coal Trade in the Asian-Pacific Market' (1993) *September Energy Policy* 944

Taylor, Veronica L, 'Continuing Transactions and Persistent Myths: Contracts in Contemporary Japan' (1993) 19 *Melbourne University Law Review* 352

Teubner, Gunther, 'Legal Irritants: Good Faith in British Law or How Unifying Law Ends Up in New Divergences' (1998) 61 *Modern Law Review* 11

Trakman, Leon E, 'The Evolution of the Law Merchant: Our Commercial Heritage Part I Ancient and Medieval Law Merchant' (1980) 12 *Journal of Maritime Law and Commerce* 1

Trakman, Leon E, 'The Evolution of the Law Merchant: Our Commercial Heritage Part II The Modern Law Merchant' (1981) 12 *Journal of Maritime Law and Commerce* 153

Trakman, Leon E, 'Winner Take Some: Loss Sharing and Commercial Impracticability' (1985) 69 *Minnesota Law Review* 471

Trakman, Leon E, 'Pluralism in Contract Law' (2010) 58 *Buffalo Law Review* 1031

Trakman, Leon E, 'The Twenty-First-Century Law Merchant' (2011) 48 *American Business Law Journal* 775

Trakman, Leon E and Kunal Sharma, 'The Binding Force of Agreements to Negotiate in Good Faith' (2014) 73 *The Cambridge Law Journal* 598

Tricot, Daniel, 'La bonne foi dans les Principes d'UNIDROIT' (2017) 22 *Uniform Law Review* 116

Uchida, Takashi, 'Contract Law Reform in Japan and the UNIDROIT Principles' (2011) 16 Uniform Law Review 705

Unger, Roberto, 'The Critical Legal Studies Movement' (1983) 96 *Harvard Law Review* 561

Uribe, Rodrigo Momberg, *The Effect of a Change of Circumstances on the Binding Force of Contracts: Comparative Perspectives* (Intersentia, 2011)

Vaughan, D A J and D W Shenton, 'Arbitration in Long-Term Contracts' (1977) 5 *International Business Lawyer* 41

Velloso, Adolfo Alvarado, 'Conciliation and Arbitration' in Fritz Nicklisch (ed), *The Complex Long-Term Contract: Structures and International Arbitration* (C F Müller Juristisch Verlag, 1987) 475

Veneziano, Anna, 'UNIDROIT Principles and CISG: Change of Circumstances and Duty to Renegotiate according to the Belgian Supreme Court' (2010) 15 *Uniform Law Review* 137

Vogenauer, Stefan, 'The UNIDROI Principles of International Commercial Contracts at twenty: experiences to date, the 2010 edition, and future prospects' (2014) 19 *Uniform Law Review* 481

Vogenauer, Stefan (ed), *Commentary on the UNIDROIT Principles of International Commercial Contracts (PICC)* (Oxford University Press, 2nd ed, 2015)

von Bar, Christian and Eric Clive (eds), *Principles, Definitions and Model Rules of European Private Law: Draft Common Frame of Reference (DCFR)* (Sellier European Law Publishers, 2009) vol 1

Waddams, Stephen, 'Good Faith, Good Conscience, and the Taking of Unfair Advantage' in Andrew Dyson, James Goudkamp and Frederick Wilmot-Smith (eds), *Defences in Contract* (Hart Publishing, 2017) 63

Walt, Steven D, 'The Modest Role of Good Faith in Uniform Sales Law' (2015) 33 *Boston University International Law Journal* 37

Warren, Marilyn, 'Good Faith: Where are We at?' (2010) 34 *Melbourne University Law Review* 344

Whittaker, Simon, '"General Principles" and "Underlying Principles" in the Proposed Common European Sales Law and Their Role in Its Interpretation' in Jacobien Rutgers and Pietro Sirena (eds), *Rules and Principles in European Contract Law* (Intersentia, 2015) 99

Winship, Peter, 'Commentary on Professor Kastley's *Rhetorical Analysis*' (1988) 8 *Northwestern Journal of International Law and Business* 623

Wiseman, Richard M, 'Current Problems in International Crude Oil and Petroleum Product Sales' [1985] *Australian Mining and Petroleum Law Association Yearbook (AMPLA Yearbook)* 225

Wladis, John, 'Common Law and Uncommon Events: The development of the Doctrine of Impossibility of Performance in English Contract Law' (1987) 75 *Gegoertown Law Journal* 1575

Wöss, Herfried et al, *Damages in International Arbitration under Complex Long-Term Contracts* (Oxford University Press, 1st ed, 2014)

Wright, M E, 'Effect of Changed Circumstances on Mineral and Petroleum Sales Contracts' [1984] *Australian Mining and Petroleum Law Association (AMPLA) Yearbook* 331

Yildirim, Ahmet Cemil, *Equilibrium in International Commercial Contracts: with Particular Regard to Gross Disparity and Hardship Provisions of the UNIDROIT Principles of International Commercial Contracts* (Wolf Legal Publishers, 2010)

Young, Marvin O, 'Construction and Enforcement of Long-Term Coal Supply Agreements-Coping with Conditions Arising from Foreseeable and Unforeseeable Events-Force Majeure and Gross Inequities Clauses' (1981) 27 *Annual Rocky Mountain Mineral Law Institute* 127

Zeller, Bruno, 'Good Faith - The Scarlet Pimpernel of the CISG' (2001) 6 *International Trade and Business Law Review* 227

Zeller, Bruno, 'Good Faith - Is it a Contractual Obligation? (2003) 15 *Bond Law Review: Festschrift for David Allan and Mary Hiscock* 214

Zeller, Bruno, *Damages under the Convention on Contracts for the International Sale of Goods* (Oceana Publications, 2nd ed, 2005)

Zeller, Bruno, 'The Observance of Good Faith in International Trade' in André Janssee and Olaf Meyer (eds), *CISG Methodology* (Sellier, 2009) 133

Zeller, Bruno, 'The UNIDROIT Principles of Hardship and the Application of Article 79 CISG: Are They Compatible?' in Ingeborg Schwenzer and Lisa Spagnolo (eds) State of Play the 3rd Annual MAA Schlechtriem CISG Conference (Eleven International Publishing, 2012) 113

Zeller, Bruno, and Camilla Baasch Andersen, 'Good Faith - The Gordian Knot of International Commerce' (2016) 28 *Pace International Law Review* 1

Ziegler, Andreas R and Jorun Baumgartner, 'Good Faith as a General Principle of (International) Law' in Andrew D Mitchell, M Sornarajah and Tania Voon (eds), *Good Faith and International Economic Law* (Oxford University Press, 2015) 9

Zimmermann, Reinhard, *The Law of Obligations: Roman Foundations of the Civilian Tradition* (Oxford University Press, 1996)

Zimmermann, Reinhard et al, 'Long-term business relationships I' and 'Long-term business relationships II' in Reinhard Zimmermann and Simon Whittaker (eds), *Good Faith in European Contract Law* (Cambridge University Press, 2000) 532

Zimmermann, Reinhard, *Breach of Contract and Remidies under the New German Law of Obligations* (Centro di Studi e Ricerche di Diritto Comparato e Straniero, 2002)

Zimmermann, Reinhard, 'The UNIDROIT Principles of International Commercial Contracts 2004 in Comparative Perspective' (2006) 21 *Tulane European and Civil Law Forum* 1

Zimmermann, Reinhard, 'European Contract Law: General Report' (2007) 15 *Europäische Zeitschrift für Wirtschaftsrecht* 455

Zweigert, Konrad and Hein Kötz, *Introduction to Comparative Law* (Tony Weir trans, Clarendon Press, 3rd ed, 1998) [trans of: *Einführung in die Rechtsvergleichung* (3rd ed, 1996)].

B Cases

Aluminium Co. of America v Essex Group, Inc. 499 F. Supp. 53 (W.D. Pa. 1980)

Braganza v BP Shipping Ltd [2015] UKSC 17

Bristol Groundschool v Intelligent Data Capture [2014] EWHC 2145 (Ch)

Burger King Corp v Hungry Jack's Pty Ltd (2001) 69 NSWLR 558 *Vodafone Pacific Limited v Mobile Innovations Limited* [2004] NSWCA 15

Carr v J A Berriman Pty Ltd (1953) 89 CLR 327

Carter v Boehm (1766) 97 ER 1162

Central Exchange Ltd v Anaconda Nickel Ltd [2002] WASCA 94

Codelfa Construction Pty Ltd v State Rail Authority of New South Wales (1982) 149 CLR 337

Commonwealth Bank of Australia v Barker (2014) 253 CLR 169

Compagnie d'éclairage de Bordeaux C.E. 30.3.1916, S.1916.3.17, D.1916.3.25

Compass Group UK *and Ireland Ltd v Mid-Essen Hospital Services NHS Trust Ltd* [2012] EWCA Civ 781

Davis Contractors Ltd v Fareham UDC [1956] AC 696

De Gallifet v Commune de Pélissanne D. 1876. 1. 193

De Pasquale v The Australian Chess Federation Incorporated [2000] ACTSC 94

D&G Cars Ltd v Essex Police Authority [2015] EWHC 226 (QB)

Esso Australia Resources Pty Ltd v Southern Pacific Petroleum NL [2005] VSCA 228

Far Horizons Pty Ltd v McDonalds Australia Ltd [2000] VSC 310

Florida Power and Light Company v Westinghouse Electric Corporation 517 F. Supp. 440 (E.D. Va. 1981)

GSA Group v Siebe PLC (1993) 30 NSWLR 573

Hughes Aircraft Services International v Airservices Australia [1997] 76 FCR 151

Hunter Valley Skydiving Centre Pty Ltd v Central Coast Aero Club Ltd [2008] NSWSC 539

Interfoto Picture Library Ltd v Stiletto Visual Programmes Ltd [1988] 1 All. E.R. 348

J Lauritzen AS v Wijsmuller BV (The Super Servant Two) [1990] 1 Lloyd's Rep. 1

Kable v Director of Public Prosecutions (NSW) (1996) 189 CLR 51

Knatchbull-Huguessen v SISU Captial Ltd [2014] EWHC 1194 (QB)

Krell v Henry [1903] 2 K.B. 740

Lange v Australian Broadcasting Corporation (1997) 189 CLR 520

Lipohar v The Queen (1999) 200 CLR 485

Maitland Main Collieries Pty Limited v Xstrata Mt Owen Pty Limited [2006] NSWSC 1235

Mcginnis v Cayton 312 S.E.2d 765 (W. Va. 1984)

MSC Mediterranean Shipping Co v Cottonex Anstalt [2015] EWHC 283 (Comm)

MSC Mediterranean Shipping Co SA v Cottonex Anstalt [2016] EWCA Civ 789
oOh! Media Roadside Pty Ltd v Diamond Wheels Pty Ltd [2011] VSCA 116
Overlook Management BV v Foxtel Management Pty Ltd [2002] NSWSC 17
Paradine v Jane 82 Eng. Rep. 897 (K.B. 1647)
Petromec v Petroleo Brasileiro SA Petrobas [2005] EWCA Civ 891
Portsmouth City Council v Ensign Highways Ltd [2015] EWHC 1969 (TCC)
Renard Constructions (ME) Pty Ltd v Minister for Public Works (1992) 26 NSWLR 234
Royal Botanic Gardens and Domain Trust v South Sydney City Council (2002) 186 ALR 289
Scafom International BV v Lorraine Tubes S.A.S. Hof van Cassatie, 19 June 2009, No. C.07.0289.N.
South Sydney District Rugby League Football Club v News Ltd [2000] FCA 1541
Superior Overseas Development Corporation v British Gas Corporation [1982] 1 Lloyd's Rep 262
Taylor v Caldwell 122 Eng. Rep. 309
Tone Tasmania Pty Ltd v Garrott [2008] TASSC 86
Tsakiroglou v Noblee Thori [1962] A.C. 93
Unihealth v U.S. Healthcare Inc. 14 F. Supp. 2d 623 (D. N. J. 1998)
Veremu Pty Ltd v Ezishhop.Net Ltd [2003] NSWCA 317
Walford v Miles [1992] 2 AC 128
Yam Seng Pte v International Trade Corporation Ltd [2013] EWHC 111 (QB)

C Arbitral Awards

ad hoc arbitration case *Hungarian State Enterprise v Jugoslavenski Naftovod (Yugoslav Crude Oil Pipeline)*, Award, 6 July 1983
ICC arbitral award No 1512
ICC arbitral award No 2291
ICC arbitral award No 2292
ICC arbitral award No 4761
ICC arbitral award No 5953
ICC arbitral award No 6219
ICC arbitral award No 7365
ICC arbitral award No 8365
ICC arbitral award No 8873
ICC arbitral award No 9029
ICCarbitral award No 9479
ICC arbitral award No 9797
ICC arbitral award No 9994
ICC arbitral award No 10021

D Legislation

Australian Consumer Law and Fair Trading Act *2012* (Vic)
French Civil Code
Frustrated Contracts Act 1978 (NSW)
Frustrated Contracts Act 1988 (SA)
German Civil Code
New South Wales Civil Procedure Act (2005)
Uniform Commercial Code

E Treaties

United Nations Convention on Contracts for the International Sale of Goods, opened for signature 11 April 1980, 1489 UNTS 3 (entered into force 1 January 1988)

Vienna Convention on the Law of Treaties, opened for signature 23 May 1969, 1155 UNTS 331 (entered into force 27 January 1980)

F Other

Common European Sales Law

Draft Common Frame of Reference

ICC Hardship Clause 1985

ICC Hardship Clause 2003

Principles of European Contract Law

Report of the United Nations Commission on International Trade Law, (UNCITRAL 40th sess.) UN GAOR, 62nd sess, Supp No 17, UN Doc A/62/17(Part I) (25 June-12 July 2007)

Report of the United Nations Commission on International Trade Law (UNCITRAL 45th sess.) UN GAOR, 67th sess, Supp No 17, UN Doc A/67/17 (25 June-6 July 2012)

Restatement (Second) of Contracts

TransLex-Principles of Transnational Commercial Law

UNIDROIT Governing Council, Item No. 4 on the Agenda: International Commercial Contracts: Adoption of Additional Rules and Comments to the UNIDROIT Principles of International Commercial Contracts Concerning Long-term Contracts, 95th session, C.D. (95)3 (18-20 May 2016)

UNIDROIT/FAO/IFAD, *Legal Guide on Contract Farming* (the International Institute for the Unification of Private law (UNIDROIT), the Food and Agriculture Organization of the United Nations (FAO) and the International Fund for Agricultural Development (IFAD), 2015)

UNIDROIT Principles of International Commercial Contracts

UNIDROIT Secretariat, 'Report on the 95th session of the Governing Council' (Report C.D. (95) 15, UNIDROIT, 2016a)

UNIDROIT Secretariat, 'Report on Second Session of Principles of International Commercial Contracts Working Group on Long-Term Contracts' UNIDROIT 2016b, Study L-Misc. 32

UNIDROIT Secretariat, 'The UNIDROIT Principles of International Commercial Contracts and Long-Term Contracts' UNIDROIT 2014, Study L-Doc. 126

CPSIA information can be obtained
at www.ICGtesting.com
Printed in the USA
LVHW082034180422
716472LV00006B/452

9 789811 655128